Designing Web Pages with Cascading Style Sheets

by Joel Sklar

**COURSE
TECHNOLOGY**

™

THOMSON LEARNING

Australia • Canada • Mexico • Singapore • Spain • United Kingdom • United States

Designing Web Pages with Cascading Style Sheets

by Joel Sklar

Product Manager:
Christine Guivernau

Managing Editor:
Jennifer Locke

Senior Acquisitions Editor:
Christine Guivernau

Development Editor:
Lisa Ruffolo, The Software Resource

Associate Product Marketing Manager:
Angie Laughlin

Product Manager:
Tricia Coia

Editorial Assistant:
Janet Aras

Production Editor:
Karen Jacot

Cover Designer:
Christy A. Amlicke, Black Fish Design

Compositor:
GEX Publishing Services

Manufacturing Coordinator:
Denise Sandler

BRIEF
Contents

TABLE OF
Contents

CHAPTER THREE
Using the Font and Type Properties   **61**

Preface

Cascading Style Sheets (CSS) is a style language that lets you design appealing, innovative Web pages. If you know HTML or XML, you can use CSS to bring desktop publishing capabilities to the Web, allowing you to create more visually exciting Web page designs. Using style sheets, you can control the display properties of markup elements in a single Web page or across an entire Web site. Powerful selection techniques let you apply style rules in a variety of ways to the elements of a Web page. Enhanced support for CSS in the new generation of browsers means you can start working with this easy-to-use style language today.

CSS separates content and style, an approach that is integral to the open nature of data on the Web. Currently, Web page code mixes both document structure information and browser-based display properties, limiting the cross-platform compatibility of the content. With style sheets, the display properties are separate from the content. This means that whether you come to a Web site using a desktop PC, handheld computer, or cellular phone, the Web server can supply a style sheet that matches your display device. The latest version of CSS, CSS2, supports a variety of media devices, including print, that allows content providers to single-source their data.

CSS expresses style information in statements called rules. Style rules are contained in text files called style sheets. Using style sheets, you can control the display properties of markup elements in a single Web page or across an entire Web site. You also can employ powerful selection techniques to apply style rules in a variety of ways to the elements of a Web page. You can create their own logical names for styles, and then apply the style using those names.

Designing Web Pages with Cascading Style Sheets is intended for students and Web professionals who have a working knowledge of HTML and want to use style sheets to control display properties on a Web site or any other application that uses HTML or XML. As you progress through the book, you practice CSS techniques by studying the supplied code, examining the sample Web pages, and then applying the principles to your own work. Each chapter concludes with a summary, project ideas, and review section that highlights and reinforces the major concepts of each chapter.

OVERVIEW OF THIS BOOK

The examples, steps, projects, and cases in this book will help you achieve the following objectives:

- Use different methods of selecting elements, allowing you to apply style rules in a variety of ways
- Use CSS properties to control typography, colors, and backgrounds
- Use the CSS box model to control margin, padding, and borders
- Use CSS properties with tables and lists
- Use the CSS positioning properties to build page layouts without tables
- Use the power and flexibility of CSS to design attractive Web pages

Chapter 1 introduces you to the history and basic concepts of Cascading Style Sheets. You will learn basic CSS syntax and how to control style information in a single file or across an entire Web site. In **Chapter 2**, you will learn about the CSS selection techniques, which allow you to select and apply style rules in a variety of ways to your HTML documents. **Chapter 3** explains the font and text properties, which let you control a wide range of typographic effects. **Chapter 4** covers the CSS box model, which controls the margin, padding, and border characteristics of block-level elements. You will also learn about the special box properties that allow you to create floating text boxes and images. **Chapter 5** explains the CSS color and background properties. These properties let you control the text color and backgrounds of any element on a Web page. In **Chapter 6** you will learn how to apply CSS properties to tables and lists. **Chapter 7** explains the CSS positioning properties, which let you build Web pages without using cumbersome tables to control page layout. With positioning you can choose the exact placement of elements within the browser window. Finally, in **Chapter 8** you will apply the skills you learned throughout this book by building three different types of complete Web pages using Cascading Style Sheets.

Each chapter in *Designing Web Pages with Cascading Style Sheets* includes the following elements to enhance the learning experience:

- **Chapter Objectives:** Each chapter in this book begins with a list of the important concepts to be mastered within the chapter. This list provides you with a quick reference to the contents of the chapter as well as a useful study aid.
- **Step-By-Step Methodology:** As new concepts are presented in each chapter, exercises provide step-by-step instructions that allow you to actively apply the concepts you are learning.
- **Tips:** Chapters contain Tips designed to provide you with practical advice and proven strategies related to the concept being discussed. Tips also provide suggestions for resolving problems you might encounter while proceeding through the chapter tutorials.

- **Chapter Summaries:** Each chapter's text is followed by a summary of chapter concepts. These summaries provide a helpful way to recap and revisit the ideas covered in each chapter.

- **Review Questions:** End-of-chapter assessment begins with a set of approximately 20 review questions that reinforce the main ideas introduced in each chapter. These questions ensure that you have mastered the concepts and understand the information you have learned.

 Hands-on Projects: Along with conceptual explanations and step-by-step tutorials, each chapter provides Hands-on Projects related to each major topic aimed at providing you with practical experience. Some of the Hands-on Projects provide detailed instructions, while others provide less detailed instructions that require you to apply the materials presented in the current chapter with less guidance. As a result, the Hands-on Projects provide you with practice developing CSS projects in real-world situations.

 Case Project: The case project builds from one chapter to the next, providing you with a finished Web site you designed using the CSS techniques covered in this book. The case is designed to help you apply what you have learned in each chapter to real-world situations. It gives you the opportunity to independently synthesize and evaluate information, examine potential solutions, and make recommendations, much as you would in a professional situation.

TEACHING TOOLS

The following supplemental materials are available when this book is used in a classroom setting. All of the teaching tools available with this book are provided to the instructor on a single CD-ROM.

Electronic Instructor's Manual. The Instructor's Manual included with this textbook includes:

- Additional instructional material to assist in class preparation, including suggestions for lecture topics.

■ Solutions to all end-of-chapter materials, including the Review Questions and Hands-on Projects.

ExamView®. This book is accompanied by ExamView, a powerful testing software package that allows instructors to create and administer printed, computer (LAN-based), and Internet exams. ExamView includes hundreds of questions that correspond to the topics covered in this text, enabling students to generate detailed study guides that include page references for further review. The computer-based and Internet testing components allow students to take exams at their computers, and also save the instructor time by grading each exam automatically.

PowerPoint Presentations. This book comes with Microsoft PowerPoint slides for each chapter. These are included as a teaching aid for classroom presentation, to make available to students on the network for chapter review, or to be printed for classroom distribution. Instructors can add their own slides for additional topics they introduce to the class.

Data Files. Data Files, containing all of the data necessary for steps within the chapters and the Hands-on Projects, are provided through the Course Technology Web site at *www.course.com*, and are also available on the Teaching Tools CD-ROM.

Solution Files. Solutions to end-of chapter review questions, exercises, and Hands-on Projects are provided on the Teaching Tools CD-ROM and may also be found on the Course Technology Web site at *www.course.com*. The solutions are password protected.

Distance Learning. Course Technology is proud to present online courses in WebCT and Blackboard, as well as at MyCourse.com, Course Technology's own course enhancement tool, to provide the most complete and dynamic learning experience possible. When you add online content to one of your courses, you're adding a lot: self tests, links, glossaries, and, most of all, a gateway to the twenty-first century's most important information resource. We hope you will make the most of your course, both online and offline. For more information on how to bring distance learning to your course, contact your local Course Technology sales representative.

ACKNOWLEDGMENTS

This book is dedicated to Diana, my perennial in a world of annuals. Thanks for your endless patience and love. Also to my daughter Samantha, whose joy for life always inspires me. The world is your stage, honey.

Thanks to the team at Course Technology for their support and encouragement during the writing of this book. A special thanks to Lisa Ruffolo for her insight and subtle encouragement.

The author wishes to acknowledge the Corel Corporation for the use of clip art from the Corel Gallery Clipart Collection.

The information source for this book is the World Wide Web Consortium's Cascading Style Sheet CSS2 Specification, available at *http://www.w3.org/TR/REC-CSS2/*.

Thanks to Lynn Braender, The College of New Jersey, Ric Heishman, Northern Virginia Community College, Alan Rea, Western Michigan University, and Carol Schwab for their thorough reviews and helpful suggestions for this book.

READ THIS BEFORE YOU BEGIN

Computer Requirements

You can use your own computer to complete the tutorials, Hands-on Projects, and Case Projects in this book. To use your own computer, you will need the following:

- **A Web browser,** such as Microsoft Internet Explorer version 5.0 or later, Netscape Navigator version 6, or Opera version 5.0. Older versions of the browsers do not offer enough CSS support to complete the projects in this book.

- **A code-based HTML editor,** such as Allaire HomeSite, or a text editor such as Notepad.

Visit Our World Wide Web Site

Additional materials designed especially for you might be available for your course on the World Wide Web. Go to *http://www.course.com*. Periodically search this site for more details.

INTRODUCING CASCADING STYLE SHEETS

When you complete this chapter, you will be able to:

♦ Understand the history of HTML and CSS, and how CSS is supported in the major browsers

♦ Explain why the separation of HTML structure from style information is so important to the future of the Web

♦ Identify what enhancements are included in CSS Release 2 (CSS2)

♦ Use basic CSS syntax and combine style rules with your HTML code

♦ Understand the concepts of the cascading mechanism and inheritance

In this chapter, you will learn about the history and implementation of Cascading Style Sheets (CSS). By examining the ongoing evolution of **Hypertext Markup Language (HTML)**, you will see how the popularity of the Web quickly overcame the capabilities of HTML and why the need for an easy-to-use, expressive style language became apparent. You will also learn how the support for CSS in the popular browsers dictated whether HTML authors could successfully implement this new style language and why it has taken so long for CSS to be accepted. You will see why HTML structure information must be separate from style information and why the current methods of styling Web pages is hindering the accessibility of Web documents. You will also examine the basic syntax of CSS and learn how to combine CSS rules with your HTML code.

Section 1: A Brief History of HTML and CSS

When Tim Berners-Lee first proposed HTML in 1989, he was looking for a simple way to manage and share large amounts of information among colleagues. Berners-Lee created HTML from the **Standard Generalized Markup Language (SGML)**, a standard system for specifying document structure. When Berners-Lee created HTML, he adopted only the necessary elements of SGML for representing basic office documents such as memos and reports. The first working draft of HTML included elements such as titles, headings, paragraphs, and lists.

Berners-Lee wanted to make documents as portable as possible, so he decided to let the user's browser determine how the HTML pages were displayed. The first browser, Mosaic, had little support for any style characteristics, and most Web pages were simple, left-justified documents. Figure 1-1 shows a basic Web page displayed in the Mosaic 1.0 browser.

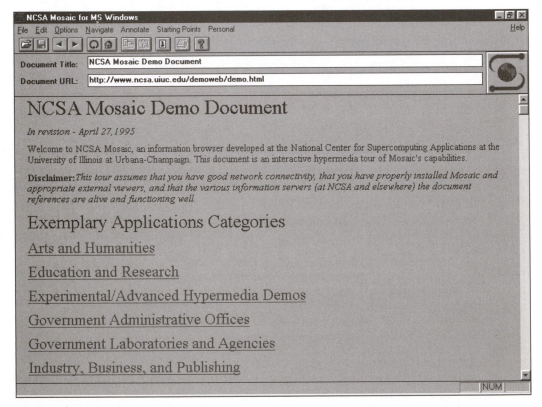

Figure 1-1 The Mosaic 1.0 browser

As the Web evolved, its potential to be an ideal publishing medium became obvious. What Web developers needed was a way to have more control over the visual display of content.

Users and publishers who were familiar with the visual display power of modern page layout and word-processing tools found HTML sorely lacking in its ability to handle even the most basic display characteristics, such as changing the color or typeface of text. Berners-Lee and his colleagues realized early in the development of HTML that a style and display language, expressed separately from the structural HTML code, would give authors more control over the visual display of their content.

In 1994, Häkon Lie of Conseil Européen pour la Recherche Nucléaire (CERN), the European Laboratory for Particle Physics, released a proposal for the Cascading Style Sheet Language. This style language contained a number of common design characteristics and included the ability to apply a number of different style sheets—a "cascade" of styles—to the same document. The ability to cascade multiple style sheets, and to determine which sheets and styles take precedence, is a fundamental feature of CSS. Applying multiple style sheets to a document means that users can supply their own style sheets that override the author's style sheet. The novel idea of allowing the users to supply their own style sheets lets users adapt content to their own preferences. For example, users with sight disabilities could add a style sheet that increases the size of text to make it more legible. You will read more about applying multiple style sheets to a document later in this chapter.

A few days after the release of Lie's proposal, the first beta version of Netscape Navigator, nick-named Mozilla, was released. Among other enhancements, the Netscape browser supported the <CENTER> tag, a new element that was not contained in the HTML specification. Elements like <CENTER> change HTML from a simple document structure language into a language that displays both style and structure. As you see later in the chapter, this mixing of style and structure can cause significant compatibility problems for the future of the Web.

Netscape continued to add more elements, including <FONT>, to the HTML mix, hoping to garner a larger market share for their browser. Netscape reasoned that if they gave HTML authors the display control they wanted, the authors would build Web pages that favored the Netscape browser. These new elements quickly became so popular and pervasive that competing products such as Internet Explorer had to support them or cease being viable as a browser.

As the Web continued to evolve, more factors contributed to the loosening of the structural nature of HTML. The browser war between Netscape and Microsoft started to heat up, and each company introduced proprietary elements. These elements, such as <MARQUEE> (Internet Explorer only) and <BLINK> (Netscape only), work only within the browser for which they were designed. Using proprietary elements like these defeat the open, portable nature of HTML. Also, the advent of HTML table elements brought a new level of complexity to HTML code. Although originally intended for tabular data, Web designers quickly realized that they could build print-like design structures that allowed them to break away from the left-alignment constraints of basic HTML. Unfortunately, this method of coding (still the predominate method of coding on the Web today) meant that HTML code had evolved into a mixture of display and structure information. Web pages had become hard-coded for a specific destination media, the computer screen. Display information that is designed for only one medium severely limits the future portability of Web-based content, which now needs to be viewed on a variety of different devices, as you will see later in this section.

Battling against this increasing fracturing of HTML was the newly founded World Wide Web Consortium (W3C). Founded in 1994, the W3C sets standards for HTML and provides an open, nonproprietary forum for industry leaders and academics to add to the evolution of this new medium. In 1996, the W3C released the first completed specification for Cascading Style Sheets—CSS1. CSS1 consisted of an easy-to-use, declarative syntax that used familiar typesetting and design terminology and allowed HTML authors much more expressive control over the appearance of their Web pages. The only problem was that there was not a single browser that supported CSS.

BROWSER SUPPORT FOR CSS

Microsoft Internet Explorer 3.0 was the first browser to offer rudimentary support for CSS1. As Internet Explorer evolved, it continued to provide increasing support for CSS, although it did not fully support style sheets until release 5.0 for the Macintosh in 1999. Netscape has resisted CSS, supporting only the most basic features through release 4.75. Figures 1-2 through 1-5 illustrate the difference in support between browsers. Figure 1-2 shows an HTML file styled with CSS style rules in Microsoft Internet Explorer 5.5. This page includes a number of CSS properties, including specifying font characteristics, alignment, margins, and backgrounds. You will learn how to write the style rules for this page in a later chapter.

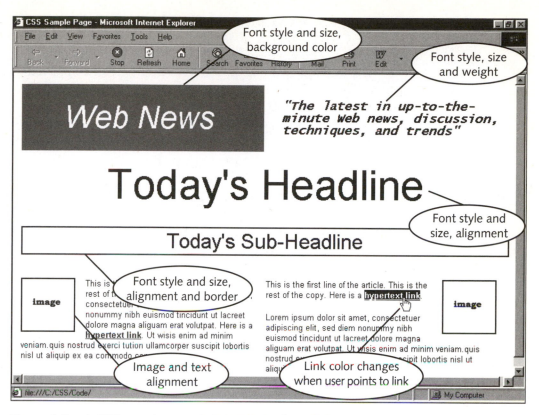

Figure 1-2   A CSS sample page in Internet Explorer 5.5

In contrast, Figure 1-3 illustrates the poor support for CSS in Netscape Navigator 4.75. The reluctance of Netscape to support the CSS standard has been the single most important limiting factor in the acceptance of CSS among HTML authors, who were reluctant to address the complexity of cross-browser compatibility issues.

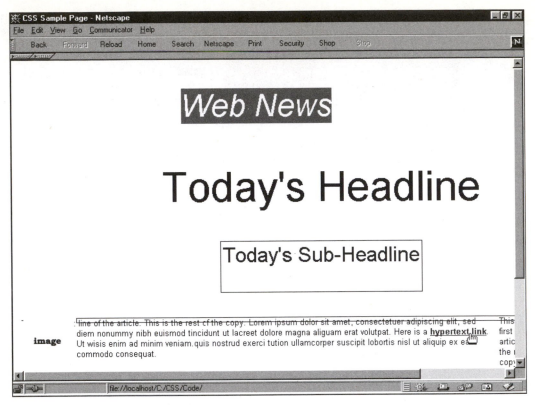

Figure 1-3   Netscape Navigator 4.75 cannot correctly display the CSS sample page

Netscape finally gave in to the CSS trend, and, as a result, Netscape 6 offers excellent support for CSS. Figure 1-4 shows the same page in Netscape Navigator 6 and the great strides Netscape has made in supporting CSS.

Figure 1-5 shows the sample page in Opera, the popular browser from Norway. This browser, now in release 5.0, also contains good support for CSS properties.

Four years after its initial release (a long time at the current pace of Web development), CSS is ready for prime time. HTML authors who have been clamoring for page layout control since the inception of the Web now have a powerful style language at their disposal. The W3C has continued the development of CSS, and in 1998 CSS2 was released. CSS2 incorporates many new features while retaining most of the original CSS specification. You will read more about CSS2's enhancements later in this chapter.

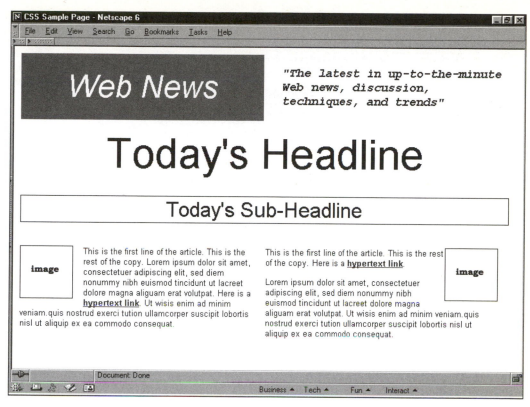

Figure 1-4　　A CSS sample page in Netscape Navigator 6.0

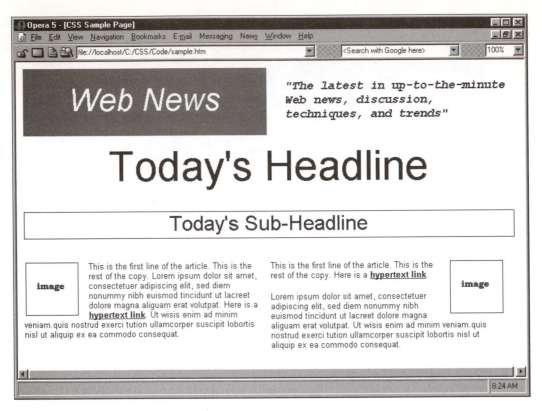

Figure 1-5   A CSS sample page in Opera 5.0

SEPARATING STYLE FROM STRUCTURE

View the source code for any page on the Web, and you see a jumbled hodgepodge of structural HTML elements, such as <H1>, <P>, and <DIV>, mixed with visual elements, such as <FONT>, <TABLE>, and <CENTER>. Adding to the general confusion are a number of HTML attributes whose sole purpose is to provide visual display information to the browser, such as BGCOLOR, FACE, and ALIGN. Although this may not seem to be a problem, consider how much code on the average Web page is devoted to structural information and how much to display instructions. In many cases, the display information is more than double the amount of code. Not only does the additional code add to the complexity of the HTML, display instructions are a very inefficient way to handle the display characteristics of multipage Web sites. For example, assume that you want all of your <H1> headings to appear green and centered everywhere on your Web site. For every instance of an <H1> element, you would have to include the following code in each HTML document:

```
<H1 ALIGN="CENTER"><FONT COLOR="GREEN">Some Heading
Text</FONT></H1>
```

Using a single CSS rule, you can express the same style this way:

```
H1 {color: green; text-align: center;}
```

If you place this rule in a single document, every <H1> element in that document will be green and centered. If you place this rule in an external file called a style sheet, and then connect every page on your Web site to that style sheet (explained in detail later in this chapter), then every <H1> element in your Web site will be green and centered. With a minimum of code, you've expressed the same result. Later, if you want to change the <H1> color to red, you simply change the style sheet rule to change every page on your site, resulting in easier code maintenance.

Another equally important reason to separate the style information from the structure of the document is that the mixture of this information limits the cross-platform compatibility of the content. The display information embedded in Web pages is tailored toward one type of display medium, the computer screen. With style sheets, the display properties are separate from the content. This accommodates the diversity of devices that are becoming available to browse the Web. Whether you come to the Web with a Personal Digital Assistant (PDA), a Personal Communication Services (PCS) telephone, or Windows CE device, the Web server can determine the type of requesting device and supply a style sheet that matches the device. Additionally, CSS2 supports a variety of media types, including print, handheld devices, and Braille, that allows content providers to use a single source for their data regardless of the number of destination formats, as illustrated in Figure 1-6.

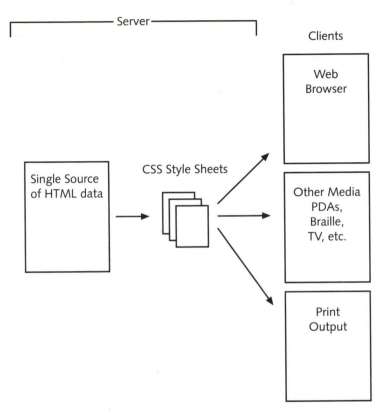

Figure 1-6 Formatting data for multiple destinations

SECTION 2: CSS BASICS

CSS is based on a syntax that is designed to be easy to write and read. With CSS, you write style rules that select an HTML element and declare style characteristics for the element. The W3C (*http://www.w3.org*) maintains the specifications that define CSS. Currently, there are two versions of CSS, Release 1 (CSS1) and Release 2 (CSS2). These are also called CSS Level 1 and CSS Level 2, respectively.

CSS1 and CSS2

CSS1 was released in December 1996. Internet Explorer 5.5, Netscape 6, and Opera 5 offer good to excellent support for CSS1. CSS2 was released in May 1998. At the time of this writing, no browsers fully support CSS2, but some of the new properties are variously supported by the browsers listed earlier. As always, you must test your work in multiple browsers to ensure the compatibility of your code.

Webreview.com maintains a CSS1 compatibility chart at *www.webreview.com/ style/css1/charts/mastergrid.shtml*. Richinstyle.com has a CSS2 "bug" chart at *www.richinstyle.com/bugs/table.html*. Use these charts as a guide, but remember to always test your code in multiple browsers.

Some of the more important new features in CSS2 include the following:

- **Media types** – Allows one document to contain style rules for different types of destination media, described in Appendix B

- **Paged media support** – Allows formatting of page breaks and margins when the destination media is printed rather than viewed on the Web, described in Appendix B

- **Aural style sheets** – Provides capabilities for text-to-speech devices, speech synthesis, and audio texts, described in Appendix B

- **Table properties** – Presents table information visually for display devices or aurally for speech synthesis, described in the "Working with Tables and Lists" chapter

- **New selection techniques** – Includes new ways to classify and apply rules to elements in an HTML document. Chapter 2 examines selectors and selection techniques in detail.

- **Display enhancements** – Includes new color, font, and border properties

- **Generated content** – Allows generation of content that is not supplied in the HTML source document, such as automatic numbering of chapters and lists, described in Appendix B

- **Enhanced positioning schemes** – Allows exact positioning of objects on the page without tables or transparent images. Chapter 7 examines the positioning properties in detail.

This book focuses on the CSS2 properties that are supported by the browsers and can be used today. CSS2 features that are not widely supported by the browsers are described in the appendices.

Understanding Style Rules

In CSS, **style rules** express the style characteristics for an HTML element. A set of style rules is called a **style sheet**. Style rules are easy to write and interpret. The following code shows a simple style rule for the <P> element. Note that the style rules are contained in the <STYLE> element in the document's <HEAD> section. This rule sets all <P> elements in the document to blue 24-point text:

```
<HEAD>
<STYLE type="text/css">
P {color: blue; font-size: 24pt;}
</STYLE>
</HEAD>
```

A **style rule** is composed of two parts: a selector and a declaration. The style rule expresses the style information for an element. The **selector** determines the element to which the rule is applied. As you will see in the next chapter, CSS contains a variety of powerful selection techniques. The **declaration** details the exact property values. Figure 1-7 shows an example of a simple style rule that sets all <H1> headings to red.

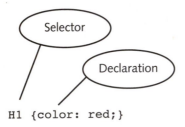

`H1 {color: red;}`

Figure 1-7   Style rule syntax

As illustrated in Figure 1-8, the declaration contains a property and a value. The **property** is a quality or characteristic, such as color, font-size, or margin, followed by a colon (:). The **value** is the precise specification of the property, such as blue for color, 12pt (point) for font-size, or 30px (pixels) for margin, followed by a semicolon (;). CSS contains a wide variety of properties, each with a specific list of values.

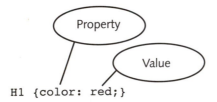

`H1 {color: red;}`

Figure 1-8   Property declaration syntax

The style rule in Figure 1-8 is a basic example of a style rule. As you will see in Chapter 2, you can combine selectors and property declarations in a variety of ways.

Combining CSS Rules with HTML

You can combine CSS rules with HTML code in the following three ways. Each method is discussed in detail in the following sections.

- The STYLE attribute
- The <STYLE> element
- An external style sheet

Using the STYLE Attribute

You can define the style for a single element using the STYLE attribute.

```
<H1 STYLE="color: blue">Some Text</H1>
```

You generally use the STYLE attribute to override a style that was set at a higher level in the document, as when you want a particular heading to be a different color from the rest of the headings on the page. The STYLE attribute is also useful for testing styles during development. You will probably use this method of styling an element the least because it only affects one instance of an element in a document.

Using the <STYLE> Element

The <STYLE> element is always contained in the <HEAD> section of the document. Style rules contained in the <STYLE> element only affect the document in which they reside. The following code shows a <STYLE> element that contains a single style rule:

```
<HEAD>
<TITLE>Sample Document</TITLE>
<STYLE TYPE="text/css">
H1 {color: red;}
</STYLE>
</HEAD>
```

In the previous code, note the TYPE attribute to the <STYLE> element. The value "text/css" defines the style language as Cascading Style Sheets. Although not required, the TYPE attribute should always be included in all of your <STYLE> elements for future compatibility as more style languages become available.

Using External Style Sheets

Placing style sheets in an external document lets you specify rules for different HTML documents. This is an easy and powerful way to use style sheets. An external style sheet is simply a text document that contains the style rules. External style sheets have a .css extension. Here's an example of a simple external style sheet named styles.css:

```
H1 {color: white; background-color: green;}
H2 {color: red;}
```

The style sheet file does not contain any HTML code, just CSS style rules, because the style sheet is not an HTML document. It is not necessary to use the <STYLE> element in an external style sheet.

Linking to an External Style Sheet

The <LINK> element lets you establish document relationships. It can only be used within the <HEAD> section of a document. To link to an external style sheet, add the <LINK> element as shown in the following code:

```
<HEAD>
```

```
<TITLE>Sample Document</TITLE>
<STYLE TYPE="text/css">
<LINK HREF="styles.css" REL="stylesheet">
</STYLE>
</HEAD>
```

The <LINK> element in this code tells the browser to find the specified style sheet. The HREF attribute states the relative URL of the style sheet. The REL attribute specifies the relationship between the linked and current documents. The browser displays the HTML file based on the CSS display information. The advantage of the external style sheet is that you can state the style rules in one document and affect all the pages on a Web site. When you want to update a style, you only have to change the style rule once in the external style sheet.

Adding Comments

CSS allows comments within the <STYLE> element or in an external style sheet. CSS comments begin with the slash and asterisk characters (/*) and end with the asterisk and slash characters (*/). You can use comments in a variety of ways, as shown in the following code:

```
<STYLE TYPE="text/css">
/* This is the basic style sheet */
H1 {color: grey;} /* The headline color */
H2 {color: red;} /* The sub-head color */
</STYLE>
```

Comments provide documentation for your style rules. Because they are embedded directly in the style sheet, they provide immediate information to anyone who needs to understand how the style rules work. Comments are always useful, and you should consider using them in all of your code, whether as a simple reminder to yourself or as an aid to others with whom you work.

Combining Multiple Style Sheets

The **@import** keyword lets you import style rules from other style sheets. Multiple @import statements are allowed, letting you combine multiple style sheets for one document. Any @import rules must precede all rules in a style sheet or they will be ignored by the browser. The @import keyword must be followed by the URL of the style sheet you want to include, as shown in the following code:

```
<STYLE TYPE="text/css">
@import "basic.css";
@import "enhanced.css";
H1 {color: white; background: green;}
H2 {color: red;}
</STYLE>
```

The CSS cascading mechanism (described later in this chapter) resolves conflicts between style sheets imported with the @import keyword. The style rules contained within the document always take precedence over imported style rules. Additionally, the weight of the imported style sheets is based on its import order. In the previous example, the internal style rules for the <H1> and <H2> elements take precedence over competing rules from the imported style sheets. Any rules stated in the basic.css style sheet take precedence over competing rules in enhanced.css because of the import order.

BUILDING A BASIC STYLE SHEET

In the following set of steps, you will build and test a basic style sheet. Save your file and test your work in the browser as you complete each step. Refer to Figure 1-10 as you progress through the steps to see the results you will achieve.

To build a basic style sheet:

1. Open the file **basic.htm** in your HTML editor and save it in your work folder as **basic1.htm.**

2. In your browser, open the file **basic1.htm.** When you open the file, it looks like Figure 1-9.

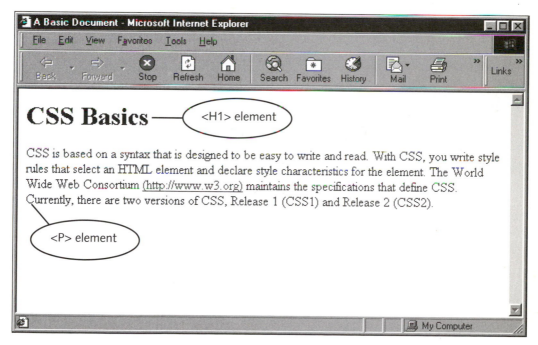

Figure 1-9   The original HTML document

3. Examine the code. Notice that the file contains basic HTML code with no style information. The complete code for the page follows:

```
<HTML>
<HEAD>
<TITLE>A Basic Document</TITLE>
</HEAD>
<BODY>
<H1>CSS Basics</H1>
<P>CSS is based on a syntax that is designed to be easy
to write and read. With CSS, you write style rules that
select an HTML element and declare style characteristics
for the element. The World Wide Web Consortium <A
HREF="http://www.w3.org">(http://www.w3.org)</A> main-
tains the specifications that define CSS. Currently,
there are two versions of CSS, Release 1 (CSS1) and
Release 2 (CSS2).</P>
</BODY>
</HTML>
```

4. Add a <STYLE> element in the <HEAD> section to contain your style rules as shown in the following code. Leave a few lines of white space between the <STYLE> tags to contain the style rules.

```
<HEAD>
<TITLE>A Basic Document</TITLE>
<STYLE type="text/css">


</STYLE>
</HEAD>
```

5. Add a style rule for the <H1> element as shown in the following code fragment. This style rule uses the text-align property to center the heading.

```
<HEAD>
<TITLE>A Basic Document</TITLE>
<STYLE type="text/css">
H1 {text-align: center;}
</STYLE>
</HEAD>
```

6. Save the file **basic1.htm**, and then reload it in the browser. The <H1> element is now centered, as shown in Figure 1-10.

7. Add a style rule for the <P> element, as shown in the following code fragment. This style rule uses the font-family property to specify sans-serif font for the paragraph text.

```
<HEAD>
<TITLE>A Basic Document</TITLE>
<STYLE type="text/css">
H1 {text-align: center;}
P {font-family: sans-serif;}
</STYLE>
</HEAD>
```

8. Save the file **basic1.htm**, and then reload it in the browser. Figure 1-10 shows the finished Web page. Notice that <P> element is now displayed in a sans-serif typeface.

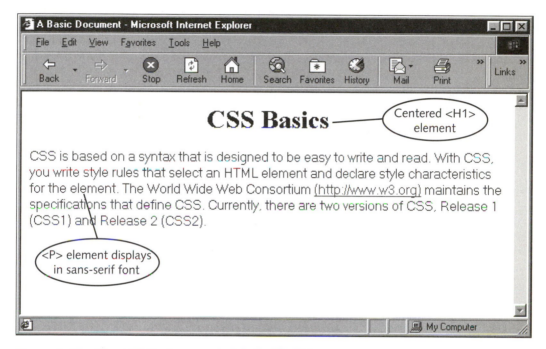

Figure 1-10   The HTML document styled with CSS

Linking to an External Style Sheet

In this set of steps, you will link an HTML file to an external style sheet that contains style rules. You can just as easily link multiple files to the same style sheet using the syntax you will learn here.

 Make sure that both basic2.htm and basic2.css are located in the same directory folder for this procedure to work properly.

1. Open the file **basic2.htm** in your browser. When you open the file it looks like Figure 1-11.

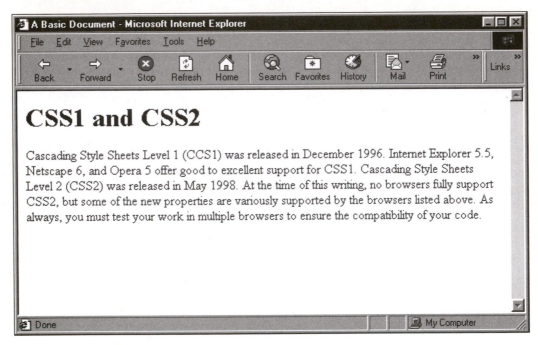

Figure 1-11   The original HTML document

2. Open the **basic2.htm** file in your HTML editor, and examine the code. Notice that the file contains basic HTML code with no style information. The complete code for the page follows:

```
<HTML>
<HEAD>
<TITLE>A Basic Document</TITLE>
</HEAD>
<BODY>
<H1>CSS1 and CSS2</H1>
<P>Cascading Style Sheets Level 1 (CCS1) was released in
December 1996. Internet Explorer 5.5, Netscape 6, and
Opera 5 offer good to excellent support for CSS1.
Cascading Style Sheets Level 2 (CSS2) was released in
May 1998. At the time of this writing, no browsers fully
support CSS2, but some of the new properties are vari-
ously supported by the browsers listed above. As always,
you must test your work in multiple browsers to ensure
the compatibility of your code.</P>
</BODY>
</HTML>
```

3. Add the <LINK> element within the <HEAD> element, as shown in the following code fragment. The HREF attribute specifies the location of the style sheet file. The REL attribute specifies the resource as a style sheet.

```
<HEAD>
<TITLE>A Basic Document</TITLE>
<LINK HREF="basic2.css" REL="stylesheet">
</HEAD>
```

4. Save the file as **basic2.htm** in your work folder, and then view it in the browser. The Web page now displays the style characteristics specified in the external style sheet, as shown in Figure 1-12.

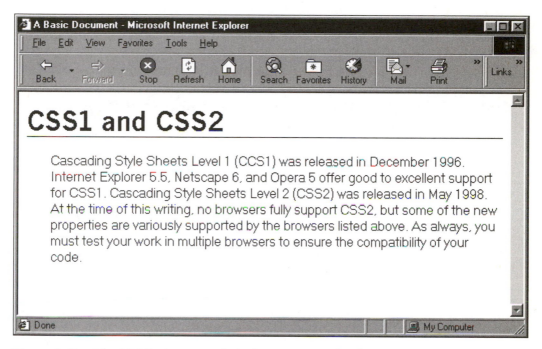

Figure 1-12   The HTML document linked to an external style sheet

5. Open the style sheet file **basic2.css** in your HTML editor and examine the style rules. The complete style sheet code follows:

```
/* This is the style sheet for the basic2.htm file */
H1 {font-family: sans-serif; border-bottom: solid 1px;}
P {font-family: sans-serif; margin-left: 30px;}
```

No code other than the style rules are necessary in an external style sheet. As you can see, the style rules are easy to interpret, even for someone who is not familiar with CSS.

UNDERSTANDING THE CASCADE

One of the fundamental features of CSS is that style sheets **cascade**. This means that multiple style sheets and style rules can apply to the same document. HTML authors can attach a preferred style sheet, while the reader might have a personal style sheet to adjust for preferences such as human or technological handicaps. However, only one rule can apply to an element. The CSS cascading mechanism determines which rules are applied to document elements by assigning a weight to each rule based on the following four variables, listed in the order in which they are applied:

- Use of the !important keyword
- Origin of the rule
- Specificity of the selector
- Order of the rule in the style sheet

Determining Rule Weight with the !important Keyword

A conflict can arise when both the author's and user's style sheets contain a rule for the same element. By default, rules in an author's style sheet override those in a user's style sheet. To balance the bias towards the author's style sheet, CSS has an !important keyword. **!important** lets the user override the author's style setting for a particular element. The following user's style sheet states a rule for <P> elements that sets the font size to 18 points, regardless of the rule supplied by the author of the HTML document:

```
<STYLE TYPE="text/css">
P {font-size: 18pt !important}
</STYLE>
```

This CSS feature improves accessibility of documents by giving users with special requirements control over document presentation, such as increasing font size or changing color contrast.

 In CSS1, !important in an author's style sheet took precedence over !important in a user's style sheet. In CSS2, the reverse is true, giving the user more control over display properties.

Determining Rule Weight by Origin

A style rule's weight can be determined by the style sheet in which it resides. CSS allows style sheets to be applied by the HTML author, the user, and the browser. Figure 1-13 shows the style sheet order of precedence.

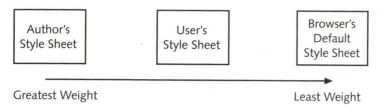

Greatest Weight   Least Weight

Figure 1-13 The cascading order of precedence

In the cascading order, rules from the author's style sheet have the greatest weight. This is the page display that most users want to see—the author's intended page design.

The user's style sheet is next in order of importance. Although the designer's rules have more weight, users have the option of turning off the author's styles in the browser or using the !important keyword to give their rules more weight. If the browser allows, the user can attach his or her own style sheet to the document. This allows the user to adjust, for example, the font size or link color to make a page more legible.

The browser's style sheet has the least weight. This is the style sheet that contains the default display information, such as displaying an <H1> heading in Times Bold with a hard return before and after. The browser's style sheet controls the display of elements that do not have an associated style rule.

Determining Rule Weight by Specificity

Another method of determining style rule weight is the specificity of the rule's element selector. Rules with more specific selectors take precedence over rules with less specific selectors. Examine the following style rules:

```
BODY {color: black;}
H1 {color: red;}
```

The first rule uses a nonspecific selector, the <BODY> element. This rule sets the text color for all elements within <BODY> to black. The second rule has a much more specific selector that sets a rule only for <H1> elements. Because the second rule has a more specific selector, it takes precedence for all <H1> elements within the document.

Determining Rule Weight by Order

CSS applies weight to a rule based on its order within a style sheet. Rules that are included later in the style sheet order take precedence over earlier rules. Examine the following style rules for an example:

```
BODY {color: black;}
H1 {color: red;}
H1 {color: green;}
```

In this example, <H1> elements in the document will appear green because of the last style rule which specifies green as the color.

Understanding Inheritance

The elements in an HTML document are structured in a hierarchy of parent and child elements. Figure 1-14 represents the structure of a simple HTML document.

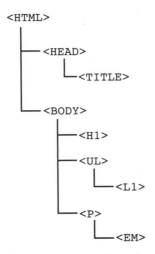

```
<HTML>
    ├── <HEAD>
    │       └── <TITLE>
    └── <BODY>
            ├── <H1>
            ├── <UL>
            │       └── <L1>
            └── <P>
                    └── <EM>
```

Figure 1-14   HTML document structure

Note the hierarchical structure of the elements. <HTML> is the parent element of the document. **Parent elements** contain nested elements called **child elements**. Both <HEAD> and <BODY> are immediate child elements of <HTML>. <HEAD> and <BODY> are parent elements as well, because they contain other nested elements. As you travel further down the document hierarchy, you find other elements that are both parent and child elements, such as <P> and <UL>.

By default, CSS rules inherit from parent elements to child elements. Therefore, if you set a style rule for <UL> elements in the document shown in Figure 1-14, the style rules inherit to the <LI> elements, unless you have specifically set a rule for <LI>.

You can style multiple document elements with just a few style rules if you let inheritance work for you. For example, consider the following set of style rules for the original document shown in Figure 1-9:

```
<STYLE TYPE="text/css">
H1 {color: red;}
P {color: red;}
UL {color: red;}
EM {color: red;}
LI {color: red;}
</STYLE>
```

This style sheet sets the color to red for five different elements in the document. Inheritance lets you write a far simpler rule to accomplish the same results:

```
<STYLE TYPE="text/css">
BODY {color: red;}
</STYLE>
```

This rule works because all of the elements are children of <BODY> and because all the rules are the same. It is much more efficient to write a single rule for the parent element and let the child elements inherit the style. <BODY> is the parent element of the content area of the HTML file; therefore, it is the selector to use whenever you want to apply a style across the entire document.

CHAPTER SUMMARY

This chapter presents the history of CSS development, the need to separate HTML structure from CSS style information, and the basic syntax of the CSS language. CSS has traveled a long road, but it is finally ready for widespread use on the Web. As you will see in the upcoming chapters, CSS is an easy-to-use style language that lets you gain visual control over the display of your Web content.

❑ CSS evolved from the popularity of the Web as a publishing medium and the demand from HTML authors who wanted common desktop publishing controls over the display of their Web content.

❑ CSS was poorly supported by browsers at first but now is becoming widely supported.

❑ CSS supports the separation of style from structure, allowing repurposing of a single source of data to multiple destination media.

❑ CSS rules can be combined with your HTML in a number of ways. CSS rules are easy to write and read.

❑ You can combine multiple style sheets using the @import keyword.

❑ CSS uses cascading and inheritance to determine which style rules take precedence. The !important declaration lets users override the author's style rules.

REVIEW QUESTIONS

1. Who is recognized as the creator of HTML?
2. HTML is a subset of which markup language?
3. How did Berners-Lee attempt to make HTML as portable as possible?
4. What are the benefits of allowing the same document to have multiple style sheets?
5. What are two of the style elements introduced by Netscape?

6. What is a proprietary element?

7. What are two examples of proprietary elements?

8. What is the purpose of the World Wide Web Consortium?

9. What was the first browser to support CSS?

10. What was the single most important limiting factor in the acceptance of CSS?

11. What are two benefits of separating style from structure?

12. List and describe three enhancements in CSS2.

13. What are the two parts of a style rule?

14. What are the three ways to combine CSS rules with your HTML code?

15. List two reasons to state a style using the STYLE attribute.

16. What are the advantages of using an external style sheet?

17. What keyword would you use to import style rules from other style sheets?

18. What is the inheritance default for CSS rules?

19. What is the benefit of the !important declaration?

HANDS-ON PROJECTS

1. Visit the World Wide Web Consortium Web site (*http://www.w3.org*). Find the Cascading Style Sheets Release 2 specification. List and describe ten style properties that you can affect with a style rule.

2. By yourself or with a partner, choose a mainstream publishing Web site, such as a newspaper or periodical site. Examine the style characteristics of the site. What common styles can be applied across the site, such as headings, paragraphs, and bylines? Write an analysis of the site's style requirements, and list the styles you would include in the site's style sheet.

3. Jakob Nielsen is a well-known expert on interface design. Read his article on CSS at *http://www.useit.com/alertbox/9707a.html*, and write a short paper describing his views and what you learned that you can implement in your own CSS design efforts.

4. View and copy the source code from a Web page of your choice into your HTML editor. Examine the code for existing display elements (such as <FONT>) and attributes (such as BGCOLOR, ALIGN). Write a paper describing how CSS properties could replace the existing display information, detailing the benefits of CSS. Refer to Appendix A for a listing of CSS properties. Include the HTML code from the Web page with your report.

5. In this project, you will have a chance to test a few simple style rules on a standard HTML document and to view the results in your browser.

   a. Using your HTML editor, create a simple HTML file (or open an existing file) that contains <BODY>, <H1>, and <P> elements. Add some text and an <H1> heading. Save the file as csstest1.htm in your work folder.

   b. Add a <STYLE> element to the <HEAD> section, as shown in the following code:

```
<HEAD>
<TITLE>CSS Test Document</TITLE>
<STYLE TYPE="text/css">
</STYLE>
</HEAD>
```

   c. Add a style rule that uses BODY as a selector and sets the color property to green, as shown in the following code:

```
<STYLE TYPE="text/css">
BODY {color: green;}
</STYLE>
```

   d. Save the file, and view it in the browser. All of the document text should now be green.

   e. Now add a style rule that sets <H1> elements to display in black:

```
<STYLE TYPE="text/css">
BODY {color: green;}
H1 {color: black;}
</STYLE>
```

   f. Save the file as csstest1.htm, and view the results in the browser.

   g. Finally, add a style rule that sets a margin for <P> elements to 30 pixels:

```
<STYLE TYPE="text/css">
BODY {color: green;}
H1 {color: black;}
P {margin: 30px;}
</STYLE>
```

   h. Save the file, and view the results in the browser.

CASE STUDY

To complete the ongoing case study for this book, you must create a complete stand-alone Web site that uses CSS properties to control all design characteristics of the site. Your instructor may choose to make this either an individual or team project. You can choose your own content for the Web site. For example, you can build a personal interest site, a site for your favorite nonprofit organization, or a work-related topic. At the end of each chapter you will complete a different facet of the project, each contributing to the finished Web site. For this chapter, you will get started by creating a project proposal, as outlined below.

Project Proposal

Create a one-or-two page basic HTML document that states the basic considerations for your project Web site. This is a preliminary draft that you will hand in to your instructor and possibly review with other members of the class. You will have a chance to modify the draft and resubmit a more finished effort at the end of the next chapter.

Include the following items, if applicable.

- **Site title** – The working title of the site

- **Developer** – You and anyone else who will work on the site

- **Content and goals** – What type of content will the site contain? What are the broad goals of the site? Provide an outline of the content topics.

- **Target audience** – Describe the typical audience for the site

- **Style considerations** – Describe the style requirements for the site and how you hope to fill these needs with CSS. What will be your font and color choices, and why? How will your design aid the user? Remember that this is a proposal and you will get to modify these choices as you work through the case study.

- **Site map** – Sketch out a preliminary map of the Web site, indicating individual file names and how the files will be linked together.

- **Limiting factors** – List the technical, audience, or development factors that could limit the design goals of the site.

2

UNDERSTANDING CSS SELECTION TECHNIQUES

In this chapter you will learn:

♦ How to use basic CSS selectors that match element names to apply style rules

♦ How to use the CLASS and ID attributes

♦ How to apply style rules to <DIV> and <SPAN> elements

♦ About the pseudo-classes and elements that allow you to apply style rules to abstract characteristics of a document

♦ About the newest CSS2 selector characteristics and capabilities

The power in CSS comes from the various methods of selecting elements, allowing an HTML author to apply style rules in a variety of ways. In this chapter, you will learn about basic selection techniques, some of which you saw in the previous chapter, and how you can combine these to create simple but powerful style rules. You will also explore the advanced selection techniques, which allow a wide range of expression and many ways to hone in on the exact element you want to affect. You will see how CSS provides methods of selecting abstract document characteristics, such as the first letter of a paragraph, that are not expressed with standard HTML elements. You also will see these techniques in action as you step through the creation of style sheets using both basic and advanced selection. Finally, you will explore the newest CSS2 selectors and see the power they will provide for the future of publishing on the Web.

BASIC SELECTION TECHNIQUES

In this section, you will review style rule syntax and learn about the following basic selection techniques:

- Using type selectors
- Grouping selectors
- Combining declarations
- Using descendant selectors

Using Type Selectors

As you learned in the "Introducing Cascading Style Sheets" chapter, the selector determines the element to which a style declaration is applied. To review, examine the syntax of the style rule shown in Figure 2-1. This rule selects the H1 element in the document and sets the text color to red.

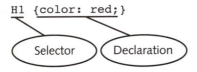

```
H1 {color: red;}
```

Figure 2-1   Style rule syntax

This rule uses a **type selector** to apply the rule to every instance of the element in the document. This is the simplest type of selector, and many style sheets are composed primarily of type selector style rules, as shown in the following code:

```
BODY {color: gray;}
H2 {color: red;}
P {font-size: 10pt;}
```

The style rules in this chapter use a variety of CSS style rules as examples. Although you have not yet learned about these properties in detail, you will see that the CSS property names express common desktop publishing characteristics, such as font-family, margin, text-indent, and so on. The property values sometimes use abbreviations such as px for pixel and pt for point, percentages such as 200%, or keywords such as bold. You will learn about these properties and values in detail as you progress through this book.

Grouping Selectors

To make your style rules more concise, you can group selectors to which the same rules apply. For example, the following style rules set the same declaration for two different elements—they set the color of <H1> and <H2> elements to red:

```
H1 {color: red;}
H2 {color: red;}
```

These two style rules can be expressed in a simpler way by separating the selectors with commas:

```
H1, H2 {color: red;}
```

Combining Declarations

In many instances, you will want to state multiple property declarations for the same selector. The following style rules set the <P> element to 12-point blue text:

```
P {color: blue;}
P {font-size: 12pt;}
```

These two style rules can be expressed in a simpler fashion by combining the declarations in one rule. The declarations are separated by semicolons:

```
P {color: blue; font-size: 12pt;}
```

Using Descendant Selectors

A descendant selector (sometimes known as a contextual selector) is based on the hierarchical structure of the elements in the document tree. This selector lets you select elements that are the descendants of other elements. For example, the following rule selects only <B> elements that are contained within <P> elements. All other <B> elements in the document will not be affected.

```
P B {color: blue;}
```

Notice that the selector contains multiple elements, separated only by white space. You can use more than two elements if you prefer to choose more specific selection characteristics. For example, the following rule selects <B> elements within <LI> elements within <UL> elements only:

```
UL LI B {color: blue;}
```

Using the Basic Selection Techniques

In the following set of steps, you will build a style sheet that uses basic selection techniques. Save your file and test your work in the browser as you complete each step. Refer to Figure 2-3 as you progress through the steps to see the results you will achieve.

To build the style sheet:

1. Open the file **oz.htm** in your HTML editor, and save it in your work folder as **oz1.htm**.

2. In your browser, open the file **oz1.htm**. When you open the file, it looks like Figure 2-2.

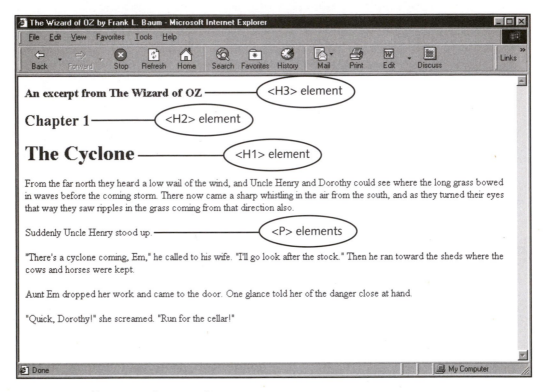

Figure 2-2 The original HTML document

3. Examine the code. Notice that the file contains basic HTML code with no style information. The complete code for the page follows:

```
<HTML>
<HEAD>
<TITLE>The Wizard of OZ by Frank L. Baum</TITLE>
</HEAD>
<BODY>
<H3>An excerpt from The Wizard of OZ</H3>
<H2>Chapter 1</H2>
<H1>The Cyclone</H1>
```

```
<P>From the far north they heard a low wail of the wind,
and Uncle Henry and Dorothy could see where the long
grass bowed in waves before the coming storm. There now
came a sharp whistling in the air from the south, and as
they turned their eyes that way they saw ripples in the
grass coming from that direction also.</P>
<P>Suddenly Uncle Henry stood up.</P>
<P>"There's a cyclone coming, Em," he called to his wife.
"I'll go look after the stock."  Then he ran toward the
sheds where the cows and horses were kept.</P>
<P>Aunt Em dropped her work and came to the door.  One
glance told her of the danger close at hand.</P>
<P>"Quick, Dorothy!" she screamed.  "Run for the
cellar!"</P>
</BODY>
</HTML>
```

4. Add a <STYLE> element in the <HEAD> section to contain your style rules as shown in the following code. Leave a few lines of white space between the <STYLE> tags to contain the style rules.

```
<HEAD>
<TITLE>The Wizard of OZ by Frank L. Baum</TITLE>
<STYLE type="text/css">


</STYLE>
</HEAD>
```

5. Write the style rule for the <H3> element. The requirements for this element are right-aligned gray text. The style rule looks like this:

```
<HEAD>
<TITLE>The Wizard of OZ by Frank L. Baum</TITLE>
<STYLE type="text/css">
H3 {text-align: right; color: gray;}
</STYLE>
</HEAD>
```

6. Write the style rules for the <H1> and <H2> elements, which share some common property values. Both elements have a left margin of 20 pixels (abbreviated as px) and a sans-serif font style. Because they share these properties, group the two elements to share the same style rule as shown in the following code:

```
<HEAD>
<TITLE>The Wizard of OZ by Frank L. Baum</TITLE>
<STYLE type="text/css">
H3 {text-align: right; color: gray;}
H1, H2 {margin-left: 20px; font-family: sans-serif;}
</STYLE>
</HEAD>
```

7. Write an additional rule for the <H1> element. The <H1> element has two style properties that it does not share with <H2>, so a separate style rule is necessary to express the border and padding white space within the border. This rule uses the border shortcut property to specify multiple border characteristics—a 1 pixel border-weight and solid border-style.

```
<HEAD>
<TITLE>The Wizard of OZ by Frank L. Baum</TITLE>
<STYLE type="text/css">
H3 {text-align: right; color: gray;}
H1, H2 {margin-left: 20px; font-family: sans-serif;}
H1 {border: 1px solid; padding: 5px;}
</STYLE>
</HEAD>
```

8. Write a style rule for the <P> elements so they have a 20-pixel left margin (to line up with the other elements on the page), a serif font style, and a 14-point font size.

```
<HEAD>
<STYLE type="text/css">
H3 {text-align: right; color: gray;}
H1, H2 {margin-left: 20px; font-family: sans-serif;}
H1 {border: 1px solid; padding: 5px;}
P {margin-left: 20px; font-family: serif;
font-size: 14pt;}
</STYLE>
</HEAD>
```

Figure 2-3 shows the finished document with the style properties.

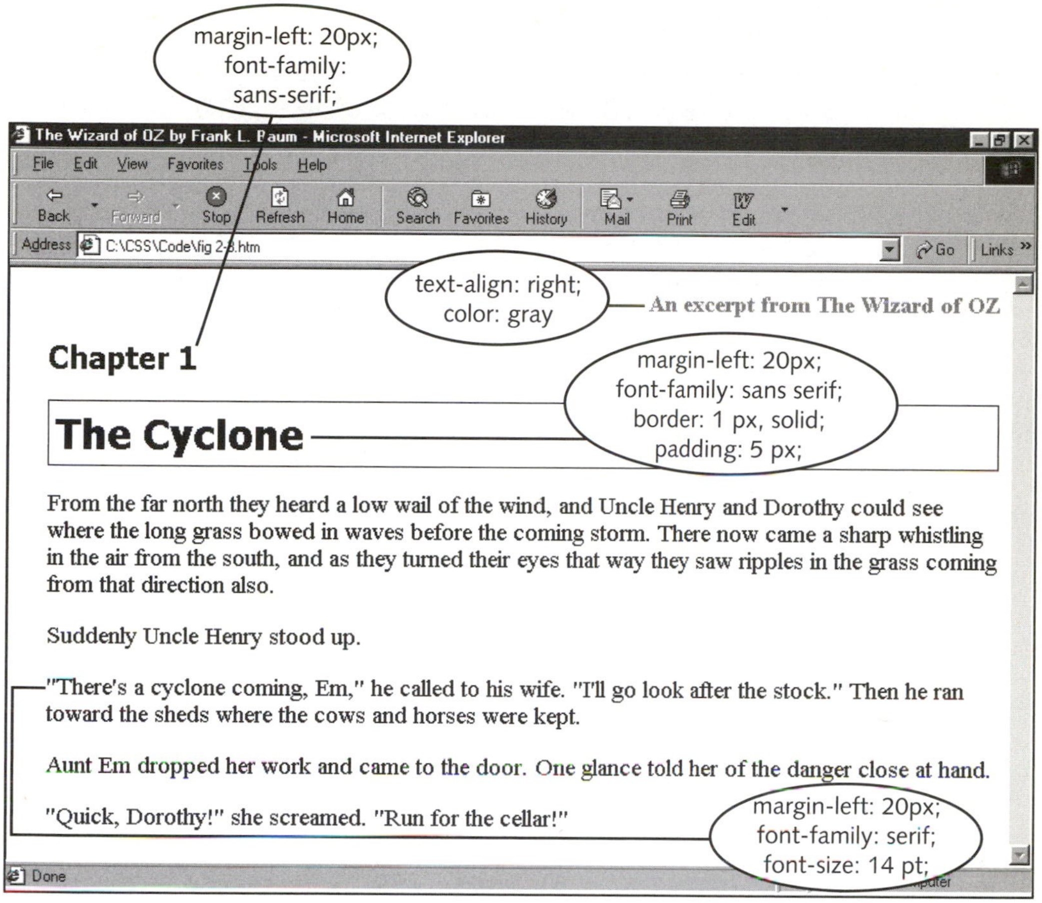

margin-left: 20px;
font-family:
sans-serif;

2

The Wizard of OZ by Frank L. Paum - Microsoft Internet Explorer

File   Edit   View   Favorites   Tools   Help

Back   Forward   Stop   Refresh   Home   Search   Favorites   History   Mail   Print   Edit

Address   C:\CSS\Code\fig 2-8.htm   Go   Links »

text-align: right;
color: gray

An excerpt from The Wizard of OZ

Chapter 1

margin-left: 20px;
font-family: sans serif;
border: 1 px, solid;
padding: 5 px;

The Cyclone

From the far north they heard a low wail of the wind, and Uncle Henry and Dorothy could see where the long grass bowed in waves before the coming storm. There now came a sharp whistling in the air from the south, and as they turned their eyes that way they saw ripples in the grass coming from that direction also.

Suddenly Uncle Henry stood up.

"There's a cyclone coming, Em," he called to his wife. "I'll go look after the stock." Then he ran toward the sheds where the cows and horses were kept.

Aunt Em dropped her work and came to the door. One glance told her of the danger close at hand.

"Quick, Dorothy!" she screamed. "Run for the cellar!"

margin-left: 20px;
font-family: serif;
font-size: 14 pt;

Done   puter

Figure 2-3   The document styled with CSS rules

ADVANCED SELECTION TECHNIQUES

This section describes the CSS advanced selection techniques that are supported in Internet Explorer 5.0, Netscape 6.0, and Opera 5.0. These techniques allow more than the basic element-based selection described in the previous section. You will learn to select elements of an HTML document using the following methods:

- The CLASS attribute
- The ID attribute
- The <DIV> and <SPAN> elements
- The pseudo-class and pseudo-element selectors
- The universal selector

Using the Class Attribute Selector

The CLASS attribute selector lets you write rules, give them a name, and then apply that name to any elements you choose. You can use CLASS with any HTML element because it is a core attribute. The **core attributes** are ID, CLASS, STYLE, and TITLE, which apply to all HTML elements. To apply the style rule to an element, you can add the CLASS attribute to the element and set it to the name you have specified.

To create a class, declare a style rule. The period (.) flag character indicates that the selector is a class selector. Figure 2-4 shows an example of a rule with a class selector.

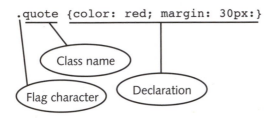

Figure 2-4   Class syntax

After writing the style rule, add it to the document by using the CLASS attribute, as shown in the following code fragment:

```
<P CLASS="quote">This text will appear red with a 30 pixel margin.</P>
```

The CLASS attribute lets you select elements with greater precision. For example, read the following style rule:

```
P {font-size: 10pt;}
```

This rule sets all <P> elements in the document to a font size of 10 points. Now suppose that you want one <P> element in your document to have a different style characteristic, such as bold text. You need a way to specifically select that one paragraph. To do this, use a CLASS selector. The following style rule sets the style for the class named "special."

```
.special {font-size: 10pt; font-weight: bold;}
```

The class selector can be any name you choose. In this instance, the class name "special" denotes a special paragraph of the document. Now apply the rule to the <P> element in the document using the CLASS attribute:

```
<P CLASS="special">This is the first paragraph of the
document. It has a different style based on the "special"
CLASS selector.</P>
<P>This is the second paragraph of text in the document. It
is a standard paragraph without a CLASS attribute.</P>
```

Figure 2-5 shows the result of the style rule.

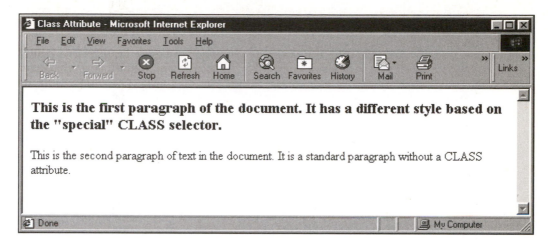

Figure 2-5   Styling with a class attribute

Making CLASS Selectors More Specific

Using the CLASS attribute is a powerful selection technique, because it allows you to write style rules with names that are meaningful to your organization or information type. The more specific your class names become, the greater control you need over the way they are applied. In the preceding example, you saw a style rule named "special" that was applied to a <P> element. However, the special style can be applied to any element in the document, not just <P>. To solve this problem, you can restrict the use of the CLASS attribute to a single element type.

For example, your organization might use a special style for a procedure heading. The style is based on an <H1> element, with a sans-serif font and left margin of 20 pixels. Everyone in your organization knows this style is named "procedure." You can use this same style name in your style sheet as shown in the following style rule:

```
.procedure {font-family: sans-serif; margin-left: 20px;}
```

To use these rules in the document, you apply the CLASS attribute as shown in the following code fragment:

```
<H1 CLASS="procedure">Procedure Heading</H1>
```

This works well, but what happens if someone on your staff neglects to apply the classes properly? For the style rule to work, it must be applied to an <H1> element. To restrict the use of the class to <H1> elements, include a prefix for the CLASS selector with the element to which you want it applied:

```
H1.procedure {font-family: sans-serif; margin-left: 20px;}
```

These style rules restrict the use of the procedure style to <H1>.

Using the ID Attribute Selector

The ID attribute, like the CLASS attribute, is an HTML core attribute. The difference between ID and CLASS is that ID refers to only one instance of the ID attribute value within a document. This allows you to specify an ID value and apply it to one unique element in a document. For example, you might want to specify that only one <P> element can have the ID preface and its associated style rule. Figure 2-6 shows a style rule that uses the ID preface as a selector.

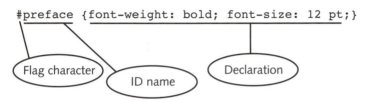

Figure 2-6   Using the ID selector

Notice that the ID selector uses a pound sign (#) flag character instead of the period you used with the CLASS selector. You can apply the ID name to the appropriate element in the document, in this example a <P> element:

```
<P ID="preface">This is a unique paragraph that is the pref
ace of the document.</P>
```

The ID value uniquely identifies this one <P> element as the preface. No other elements in the document can share this exact ID value.

Using the <DIV> and <SPAN> Elements

The <DIV> (division) and <SPAN> (span of words) elements are designed to be used with CSS. They let you specify logical divisions within a document that have their own name and style properties. The difference between <DIV> and <SPAN> is their element display type, which is described in more detail in the "Box Properties" chapter. <DIV> is a block-level element, whereas <SPAN> is its inline equivalent. Used with the CLASS and ID attributes, <DIV> and <SPAN> let you effectively create your own element names for your HTML documents.

Working with <DIV>

You can use <DIV> with the CLASS attribute to create customized block-level elements. Like other block-level elements, <DIV> contains a leading and trailing line break. However, unlike other block-level elements, <DIV> contains no additional white space around the element. You can set the margin or padding to any value that you wish. You will learn more about these properties in the "Box Properties" chapter.

To create a customized division, declare it with a CLASS or ID selector in the style rule. The following example specifies a division with a class named "introduction" as the selector for the rule:

```
DIV.introduction {font-size: 14pt; margin: 24pt; text-
indent: 28pt;}
```

To apply this rule, specify the <DIV> element in the document. Then use the CLASS attribute to specify the exact type of division. In the following example, the code defines the <DIV> element as the class named "introduction."

```
<DIV class="introduction">This is the introduction to the
document.</DIV>
```

Working with <SPAN>

The <SPAN> element lets you specify inline elements within a document that have their own name and style properties. Inline elements reside within a line of text, like the <B> or <EM> element. You can use <SPAN> with the CLASS or ID attribute to create customized inline elements.

To create a span, declare it within the <STYLE> element first. The following example specifies a span named "logo" as the selector for the rule:

```
SPAN.logo {color: white; background-color: black;}
```

Next, specify the <SPAN> element in the document. Then use the CLASS attribute to specify the exact type of span. In the following example, the code defines the <SPAN> element as the class named "logo."

```
<P>Welcome to the <SPAN CLASS="logo">Wonder Software</SPAN>
Web site.</P>
```

Figure 2-7 shows the result of the style rule.

Welcome to the Wonder Software Web site.

Figure 2-7   Using the <SPAN> element

Using Pseudo-Class and Pseudo-Element Selectors

Pseudo-classes and pseudo-element selectors let you express style declarations for characteristics of a document that are not signified with the standard HTML elements. **Pseudo-classes** select elements based on characteristics other than their element name. For example, assume that you want to change the color of a new or visited hypertext link. There is no HTML element that directly lets you express these characteristics of the <A> element. With CSS, you can use the link pseudo-class selector to change the link color. CSS2 includes a number of other pseudo-class selectors that are not consistently supported at this time. You will learn about these newer pseudo-classes in the "CSS2 Selectors" section later in this chapter.

Pseudo-elements let you change other aspects of a document that are not classified by elements, such as applying style rules to the first letter or first line of a paragraph. For example, you might want to create an initial capital or drop capital that extends below the line of type, or make the first line of a paragraph all uppercase text. These are common publishing design techniques that are not possible with standard HTML code. With CSS you can use the :first-letter and :first-line pseudo-elements to add these two style characteristics to your documents.

Using the Link Pseudo-Classes

The :link and :visited pseudo-classes let you change the style characteristics for new, unvisited links (:link) and visited links (:visited). These pseudo-classes only apply to the <A> element with an HREF attribute, because <A> is the only element in HTML that can be a hypertext link. In future applications, such as Extensible Markup Language (XML), any element could be defined as a hypertext link and could have these pseudo-classes apply. In most instances you only want to change the colors of the link from the default blue for new and purple for visited.

The following rules change the colors of the hypertext links:

```
:link {color: red;}
:visited {color: green;}
```

Because these pseudo-classes only affect the <A> element, the following style rules are the same as the ones above:

```
A:link {color: red;}
A:visited {color: green;}
```

Some Web sites choose to remove the underlining of their links. You can achieve this effect with the text-decoration property, which is described in more detail in the "Using the Font and Text Properties" chapter. The following rule removes the default link underline:

```
A:link {text-decoration: none;}
A:visited {text-decoration: none;}
```

These style rules create <A> elements that have the standard blue and purple colors, but no underlining. Whether you choose to use this style for your links depends on the design of your site and the needs of your users. Remember that many Web users are comfortable with the default underlining and that color alone may not be enough to differentiate links from the rest of your text.

Using the :first-letter Pseudo-Element

Use the :first-letter pseudo-element to apply style rules to the first letter of any element. This lets you create interesting text effects, such as initial capitals and drop capitals, which are usually set in a bolder and larger font. Initial capitals share the same baseline as the rest of the text, whereas drop capitals extend down two or more lines below the text baseline. To apply :first-letter to build an initial capital, specify a style rule like the following:

```
P:first-letter {font-weight: bold; font-size: 200%;}
```

This creates a first letter that is bold and twice the size of the <P> font. For example, if the <P> element has a font size of 12 points, the initial cap will be 24 points. This style rule applies to the first letter of every <P> element in the document without any further additions to the HTML code. However, the problem with this selector is that every <P> element gets the initial capital, even though you probably want only the first paragraph in the document to have one. To solve this problem, add a class name, such as "initial," to the rule, as shown in Figure 2-8.

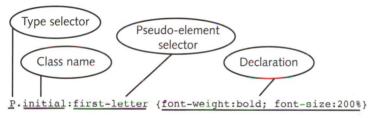

Figure 2-8   Using a class selector with a :first-letter pseudo-element

This style rule affects only <P> elements with the CLASS value of "initial," as shown in the following code:

```
<P CLASS="initial">From the far north they heard a low wail
of the wind, and Uncle Henry and Dorothy could see where
the long grass bowed in waves before the coming storm.
There now came a sharp whistling in the air from the south,
and as they turned their eyes that way they saw ripples in
the grass coming from that direction also.</P>
```

Figure 2-9 shows the result of the style rule.

You can make the initial capital a drop capital by adding the float property to the rule, which allows the letter to extend downwards. The float property is described in the "Using the Box Properties" chapter. Here is a :first-letter style rule with the float property added:

```
P.dropcap:first-letter {font-weight: bold; font-
size: 200%; float: left;}
```

From the far north they heard a low wail of the wind, and Uncle Henry and Dorothy could see where the long grass bowed in waves before the coming storm. There now came a sharp whistling in the air from the south, and as they turned their eyes that way they saw ripples in the grass coming from that direction also.

Figure 2-9 An initial capital styled with the :first-letter pseudo-class

Notice that the CLASS has been changed to signify that this first letter is a drop capital. Remember, you can set the CLASS attribute to any naming value that makes sense to you.

This style rule affects only <P> elements with the CLASS value of "dropcap" as shown in the following code:

```
<P CLASS="dropcap">From the far north they heard a low wail
of the wind, and Uncle Henry and Dorothy could see where
the long grass bowed in waves before the coming storm.
There now came a sharp whistling in the air from the south,
and as they turned their eyes that way they saw ripples in
the grass coming from that direction also.</P>
```

Figure 2-10 shows the result of the new style rule.

Drop capital

From the far north they heard a low wail of the wind, and Uncle Henry and Dorothy could see where the long grass bowed in waves before the coming storm. There now came a sharp whistling in the air from the south, and as they turned their eyes that way they saw ripples in the grass coming from that direction also.

Figure 2-10 A drop capital using the :first-letter pseudo-class

The :first-letter pseudo-element can only be applied to a block-level element. Additionally, only the following properties can be applied to the :first-letter selector:

- Font properties
- Color properties
- Background properties
- Margin properties

- Padding properties
- Word-spacing
- Letter-spacing
- Text-decoration
- Vertical-align
- Text-transform
- Line-height
- Text-shadow
- Clear

Using the :first-line Pseudo-Element

The :first-line pseudo-element works in much the same way as :first-letter, except for the obvious difference that it affects the first line of text in an element. For example, the following rule sets the first line of every <P> element to uppercase letters:

```
P:first-line {text-transform: uppercase;}
```

The problem with this code is that it affects every <P> element in the document. As you saw in the :first-letter selector above, you can add a CLASS attribute to more narrowly define the application of the :first-line style:

```
P.introduction:first-line {text-transform: uppercase;}
```

This rule transforms to uppercase the first line of the <P> element when it contains the following code:

```
<P CLASS="introduction">From the far north they heard a low
wail of the wind, and Uncle Henry and Dorothy could see
where the long grass bowed in waves before the coming
storm. There now came a sharp whistling in the air from the
south, and as they turned their eyes that way they saw
ripples in the grass coming from that direction also.</P>
```

Figure 2-11 shows the results of the style rule.

FROM THE FAR NORTH THEY HEARD A LOW WAIL OF THE WIND, AND UNCLE Henry and Dorothy could see where the long grass bowed in waves before the coming storm. There now came a sharp whistling in the air from the south, and as they turned their eyes that way they saw ripples in the grass coming from that direction also.

Figure 2-11   First line transformation using the :first-line pseudo-element

The :first-line pseudo-element can only be applied to a block-level element. Additionally, only the following properties can be applied to :first-line. Notice that :first-line does not support padding, margin, or border properties.

- Font properties
- Color properties
- Background properties
- Word-spacing
- Letter-spacing
- Text-decoration
- Text-transform
- Line-height
- Text-shadow
- Clear

Using the Universal Selector

The universal selector lets you quickly select groups of elements and apply a style rule. The symbol for the universal selector is the asterisk (*). For example, to set a default color for all elements within a document, use the following rule:

```
* {color: purple;}
```

You can also use the universal selector to select all children of an element. For example, the following rule sets all elements within a <DIV> element to a sans-serif typeface:

```
DIV * {font-family: sans-serif;}
```

The universal selector is always overridden by more specific selectors. The following style rules show a universal selector along with two other rules that have more specific selectors. In this example, the <H1> and <H2> rules override the universal selector for the <H1> and <H2> elements.

```
* {color: purple;}
H1 {color: red;}
H2 {color: black;}
```

Using the Advanced Selection Techniques

In this set of steps, you have a chance to apply some advanced selection techniques you learned about in this chapter. For this set of steps, assume that you have a collection of documents that require style rules. To enforce style consistency across the collection, you will create class names that can be applied to document elements throughout the collection. Your test document is a chapter fragment from Lewis Carroll's *Alice's Adventures in Wonderland*. As you work through the steps, refer to Figure 2-13 to see the results you will achieve. Save your file and test your work in the browser as you complete each step.

1. Open the file **alice.htm** in your HTML editor, and save it in your work folder as **alice1.htm**

2. In your browser, open the file **alice1.htm**. When you open the file, it looks like Figure 2-12.

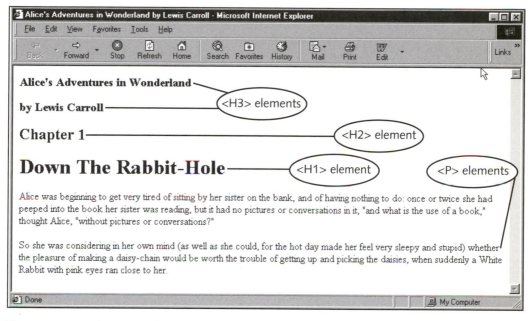

Figure 2-12   The original HTML document

3. Examine the code. Notice that the file contains basic HTML code with no style information. The complete code for the page follows:

```
<HTML>
<HEAD>
<TITLE>Alice's Adventures in Wonderland by Lewis
Carroll</TITLE>
</HEAD>
<BODY>
<H3>Alice's Adventures in Wonderland</H3>
<H3>by Lewis Carroll</H3>
<H2>Chapter 1</H2>
<H1>Down The Rabbit-Hole</H1>
<P>Alice was beginning to get very tired of sitting by
her sister on the bank, and of having nothing to do: once
or twice she had peeped into the book her sister was
```

```
reading, but it had no pictures or conversations in it,
"and what is the use of a book," thought Alice,
"without pictures or conversations?"</P>
<P>So she was considering in her own mind (as well as she
could, for the hot day made her feel very sleepy and
stupid) whether the pleasure of making a daisy-chain
would be worth the trouble of getting up and picking the
daisies, when suddenly a White Rabbit with pink eyes ran
close to her.</P>
</BODY>
</HTML>
```

4. Add a <STYLE> element in the <HEAD> section to contain your style rules, as shown in the following code. Leave a few lines of white space between the <STYLE> tags to contain the style rules.

```
<HEAD>
<TITLE>Alice's Adventures in Wonderland by Lewis Carroll
</TITLE>
<STYLE type="text/css">

</STYLE>
</HEAD>
```

5. Write a style rule for the <H3> element that contains the title of the book. The logical class name for this element is ".title." The text will be center-aligned and 125% larger than the browser default font size, as shown in the following style rule:

```
.title {text-align: center; font-size: 125%;}
```

6. Apply the style to the element that is the document title, currently an <H3> element. Change the <H3> element to a <DIV> element. This removes the default style characteristics that are built into the <H3> element. Add the CLASS attribute set to "title," as shown in the following code fragment:

```
<DIV CLASS="title">Alice's Adventures in Wonderland</DIV>
```

7. Write the style rule for the author information, which is also contained in an <H3> element. This rule uses a class selector called ".author." This more complex style rule sets a variety of properties including element's border, padding, and margins as shown below. You can set the properties on separate lines to make the rule easier to read:

```
.author    {font-size: 125%;
           text-align: center;
           border-bottom: 1px solid black;
           padding-bottom: 12pt;
           margin-left: 30pt;
           margin-right: 30pt;

}
```

8. Apply the style to the element that contains the author information, currently an <H3> element. Change the <H3> element to a <DIV> element, and add the class attribute as shown in the following code fragment:

```
<DIV CLASS="author">by Lewis Carroll</DIV>
```

9. Write style rules for the chapter number and title. The chapter number and chapter title are simple styles, with just the left margins set to 30 points. You can use the existing <H2> and <H1> elements that contain the content, but write a class name for each: ".chapternumber" and ".chaptertitle." To make sure these are used correctly, restrict their use to their respective elements, as shown in the following style rule:

```
H2.chapternumber {margin-left: 30pt;}
H1.chaptertitle {margin-left: 30pt;}
```

10. Apply the style rules with the CLASS attribute:

```
<H2 CLASS="chapternumber">Chapter 1</H2>
<H1 CLASS="chaptertitle">Down The Rabbit-Hole</H1>
```

11. Write a style rule to add a drop capital to the first paragraph of the document. This style uses the :first-letter pseudo-class, applied to a <P> element with the CLASS attribute set to "firstparagraph," as shown in the following rule:

```
P.firstparagraph:first-letter
    {font-size: 200%;
    font-weight: bold;
    border: solid thin black;
    padding: 4pt;
    margin: 2pt;
}
```

For this more complex rule, the selector and properties are on separate lines. Notice that the drop capital can have padding, margin, and border properties because it is treated like a block-level element.

12. Apply the style rules with the CLASS attribute to the first paragraph of the document:

```
<P CLASS="firstparagraph">Alice was beginning to get very
tired of sitting by her sister on the bank, and of
having nothing to do: once or twice she had peeped into
the book her sister was reading, but it had no pictures
or conversations in it, "and what is the use of a book,"
thought Alice, "without pictures or conversations?"</P>
```

13. Finally, write a style rule for the <P> elements that aligns the margins and sets the font-size:

```
P       {margin-left: 30pt;
         margin-right: 30pt;
         font-size: 125%;
}
```

Because this rule selects standard paragraph elements, you do not need to add any additional code to the <P> elements within the file.

Figure 2-13 shows the different class names used with the style rules in Internet Explorer 5.5.

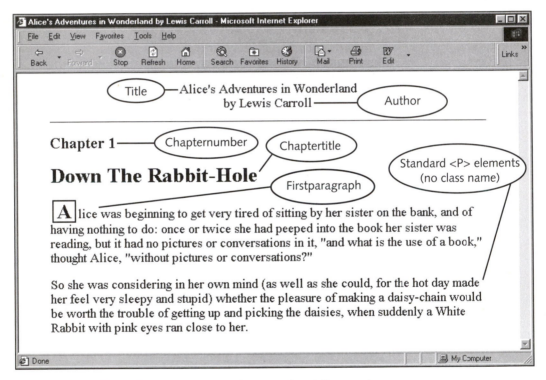

Figure 2-13   The finished document showing the different class names

The complete code for the finished document follows:

```
<HTML>
<HEAD>
<TITLE>Alice's Adventures in Wonderland by Lewis
Carroll</TITLE>
<STYLE type="text/css">
```

```
.title     {text-align: center;     font-size: 125%}
.author    {font-size: 125%;
    text-align: center;
    border-bottom: 1px solid black;
    padding-bottom: 12pt;
    margin-left: 30pt;
    margin-right: 30pt;
}
H2.chapternumber {margin-left: 30pt;}
H1.chaptertitle {margin-left: 30pt;}
P.firstparagraph:first-letter
    {font-size: 200%;
    font-weight: bold;
    border: solid thin black;
    padding: 4pt;
    margin: 2pt;
}
P     {margin-left: 30pt;
    margin-right: 30pt;
    font-size: 125%;
}
</STYLE>
</HEAD>
<BODY>
<DIV class="title">Alice's Adventures in Wonderland</DIV>
<DIV class="author">by Lewis Carroll</DIV>
<H2 class="chapternumber">Chapter 1</H2>
<H1 class="chaptertitle">Down The Rabbit-Hole</H1>
<P CLASS="firstparagraph">Alice was beginning to get very
tired of sitting by her sister on the bank, and of having
nothing to do: once or twice she had peeped into the book
her sister was reading, but it had no pictures or
conversations in it, "and what is the use of a book," thought
Alice, "without pictures or conversations?"</P>
<P>So she was considering in her own mind (as well as she
could, for the hot day made her feel very sleepy and
stupid) whether the pleasure of making a daisy-chain
would be worth the trouble of getting up and picking the
daisies, when suddenly a White Rabbit with pink eyes ran
close to her.</P>
</BODY>
</HTML>
```

Testing Cross-Browser Compatibility

Remember to always test your CSS style rules in multiple browsers. Figure 2-13 shows the document in Internet Explorer 5.5. Figure 2-14 shows the result in Opera 5.0.

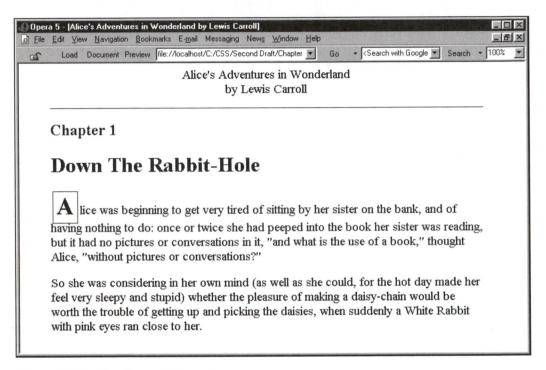

Figure 2-14   The Opera 5.0 result

Notice that there are some slight discrepancies between the Internet Explorer and Opera interpretations of the page, but the result is essentially the same. Figure 2-15 shows the result in Netscape 4.7, which has less support for the more advanced techniques. Still, the document is acceptable in this browser as well.

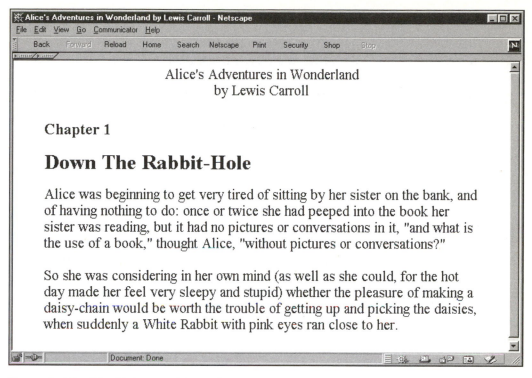

Figure 2-15   The Netscape 4.7 result

Netscape 6.0 offers much improved support for CSS, as the result in Figure 2–16 shows.

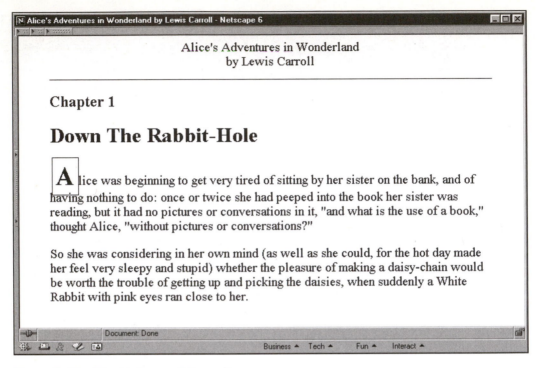

Figure 2-16   The Netscape 6.0 result

CSS2 SELECTORS

This section describes the newer CSS2 selection techniques. These techniques include using the following:

- Child selectors

- Adjacent siblings

- :first-child, dynamic, and :lang pseudo-classes

- :before and :after pseudo-elements

- Attribute selectors

Although you may not be able to use these selection techniques immediately, they will become more widely supported as newer browsers are released. Table 2-1 shows browser support for the CSS2 selection techniques based on the author's testing for this section. Your results can vary based on the exact browser version, so remember to test these new selection techniques in multiple browsers to see how they affect your finished work. Note also that Netscape 4.0 supports none of these selectors, so it is not included in the table.

Table 2-1   CSS2 selector compatibility cross-reference

Selector	IE 5.5 PC	IE 5 Macintosh	Netscape 6	Opera 5.0
Child	N	Y	Y	Y
Adjacent sibling	N	Y	Y	Y
:first-child	N	Y	Y	N
Dynamic	:hover and :active only	:hover and :active only	:hover and :active only	:hover and :active only
.lang	N	N	N	N
Before and after	N	N	N	N
Attribute selectors	N	N	N	Y

Using the Child Selector

The child selector lets you apply a style rule to the child elements of any parent element. The following style rule selects the child <BLOCKQUOTE> elements within a <DIV> element. Note the use of the greater-than symbol (>) to indicate the parent/child relationship.

```
DIV > BLOCKQUOTE {font-weight: bold;}
```

Figure 2-17 shows the result in Netscape 6.0.

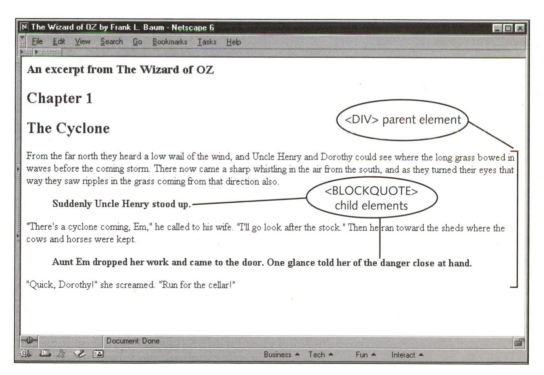

Figure 2-17   The child selector

Using the Adjacent Sibling Selector

The adjacent sibling selector lets you apply style rules to elements that share the same parent and are adjacent in the code. The code fragment in Figure 2-18 shows adjacent <H3> and <H2> elements.

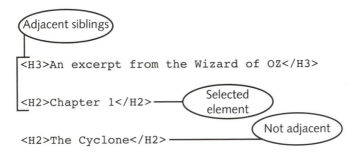

Figure 2-18   Adjacent sibling elements

The <H3> is the preceding sibling, whereas the first <H2> is the following sibling. Adjacent sibling selectors always apply the style rule to the following sibling, in this case the <H2>. The second <H2> element will not be affected because it is not an adjacent sibling to <H3>. The following code shows the style rule. Note the use of the plus sign (+) to indicate adjacent siblings.

```
H3 + H2 {background-color: gray;}
```

Figure 2-19 shows the result of the style rule in the document in Netscape 6.0.

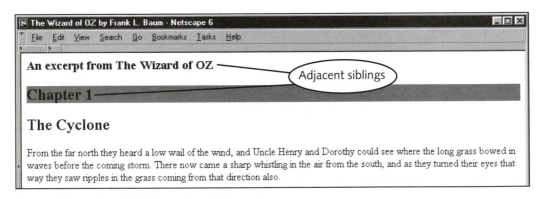

Figure 2-19   The adjacent sibling selector

Using the :first-child Selector

The :first-child selector lets you apply a style rule to the first child element of any parent element. For example, you can use :first-child to apply a first paragraph style to a <P> element. The following style rule selects the first child <P> element within a <DIV> element:

```
DIV > P:first-child {font-weight: bold;}
```

Figure 2-20 shows the result of the style rules in Netscape 6.0.

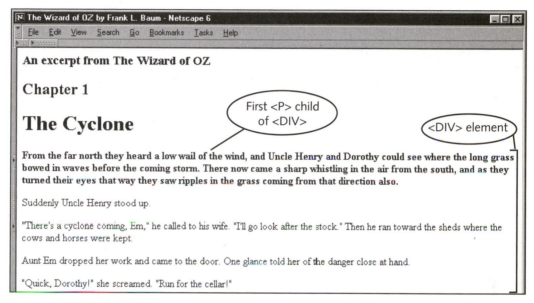

Figure 2-20   The :first-child selector

Using the Dynamic Pseudo-Class Selectors

The dynamic selectors apply styles to an element based on the user's actions. The dynamic pseudo-classes include:

- :hover - applies the style when the user designates an element; for example, by pointing to it with the mouse cursor

- :active - applies the style when the user has activated the element; for example, holding down the mouse button on a hypertext link

- :focus - applies the style when the element is accepting user input; such as in the text area of a <FORM> element

The current browsers support both the :active and :hover pseudo-class. Because both :active and :hover are very much alike, only :hover is demonstrated here.

Using the :hover Pseudo-Class

The :hover pseudo-class lets you apply a style that appears when the user points to an element with a pointing device. This is a useful navigation aid to add to the <A> element, with the result that the link appears highlighted when the user points to it with the mouse. The following style rule shows the :hover pseudo-class with the <A> element as the selector.

```
A:hover {background-color: gray;}
```

This style rule changes the background color of the link to gray, which makes the best contrast for the grayscale images in this book. On your Web pages, you might choose yellow as a more effective highlight color. Figure 2-21 shows the results of the style rule.

Using the :lang Pseudo-Class

The :lang pseudo-class lets you specify the human language for either an entire document or an element within a document. There are two situations where you can use the :lang pseudo-class:

- To provide different style sheets for different language versions of an HTML document
- To insert a different language section within a document

To determine the default language for a document, the Web server sends a two-letter language code along with the HTML file that is requested by the browser. For example, the letter code for English is EN, for Spanish, ES. The language codes are listed in Appendix A.

The following style selects all Spanish <P> elements and sets the font-style to italic.

```
P:lang(es) {font-style: italic;}
```

Of course, the browser cannot determine the type of language on its own. To specify the language, use the LANG attribute in the <P> elements that contain Spanish text:

```
<P LANG="es">This is a paragraph of Spanish text</P>
```

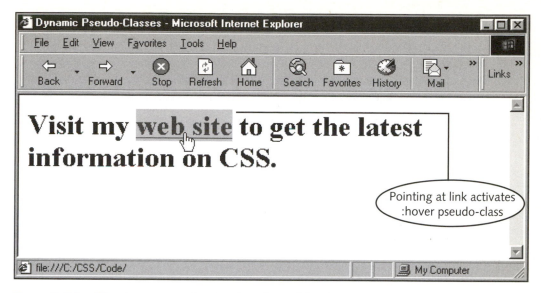

Figure 2-21   The :hover pseudo-class is activated by the mouse cursor

Using the :before and :after Pseudo-Classes

These two pseudo-class selectors let you insert content before or after an element. You define the content that is inserted within the style rule itself. Although not currently supported by any browser, these pseudo-classes will provide a method for inserting "boilerplate" information into a document—standard language that does not vary from one copy of the document to another. For example, assume that you have a document that is a series of questions and answers. You have designed <P> elements that have CLASS values of "question" and "answer" as shown below:

```
<P CLASS="question">Who sets the standards for HTML?</P>
<P CLASS="answer">The World Wide Web Consortium</P>
```

Suppose you want to include the words "Question" and "Answer" in bold type before each respective paragraph. The following style rules accomplish this effect:

```
P.question:before {content:"Question:"; font-weight: bold;}
P.answer:before {content:"Answer:"; font-weight: bold;}
```

Figure 2-22 shows the results of these style rules:

```
Question: Who sets the standards for HTML?

Answer: The World Wide Web Consortium
```

Figure 2-22   Using the :before pseudo-class

The :after pseudo-class works in the same way, inserting content after the element.

Using the Attribute Selectors

The attribute selectors let you apply styles based on the values of attributes in the HTML elements. This can be useful if you need to add style rules to HTML documents in which you do not want to alter the existing code by adding new elements, such as <DIV>, or new attributes, such as CLASS. If the attributes have been used consistently, you can apply style rules consistently. You can use attribute selectors based on two methods:

- The presence of the attribute
- The value of the attribute

Selecting on Attribute Value

You can select elements depending on whether an attribute appears within an element. The value of the attribute does not matter. The following code selects all elements that have the ALIGN attribute and sets the alignment to left.

```
[ALIGN] {text-align: left;}
```

Notice that the attribute name is enclosed within square brackets. To narrow down this selection, you can add the element selector to the rule. The following rule selects only <H1> elements that have an ALIGN attribute:

```
H1[ALIGN] {text-align: left;}
```

Selecting Based on Attribute Value

You can also select elements depending on the specific value of an attribute. The following rule selects <H1> elements that have the ALIGN attribute set to center:

```
H1[ALIGN="center"] {text-align: left;}
```

CHAPTER SUMMARY

In this chapter, you learned about the various methods of selecting elements and how to apply style rules in a variety of ways. You saw that the CSS basic selection techniques are often powerful enough to handle most document styling. The advanced selection techniques let you apply style in ways previously not possible on the Web, even allowing the application of elements that are not defined in HTML elements, such as the :first-child or :first-line pseudo-elements. Also, you learned that the CLASS and ID attributes let you create naming conventions for styles that are meaningful to your organization or information type. As browsers continue to evolve, you will be able to take advantage of the newer CSS2 selection techniques that allow even greater control over expression in document styling.

❑ Basic style rules let you apply style rules based on standard element selectors. You can combine the selectors and declarations to create more powerful style expressions. You can also select elements based on the contextual relationship of elements in the document tree.

2

❐ The advanced selection techniques allow you to use the CLASS and ID attribute selectors, which are often paired with the <DIV> and <SPAN> HTML elements. These elements have no style of their own but offer a convenient way of expressing style for any section of a document, whether block-level or inline. Additionally, CLASS and ID allow you to choose a meaningful naming convention for your style rules.

❐ The pseudo-class and pseudo-element selectors provide a method of styling characteristics of a document that are not expressed with standard HTML elements. These selection techniques offer advanced style effects that bring HTML documents closer to the capabilities of print-based publishing.

❐ The newer CSS2 selectors, although not yet widely supported, offer even more ways to add style rules.

REVIEW QUESTIONS

1. Write a basic style rule that selects <P> elements and sets the color property to red.
2. Add the <BLOCKQUOTE> element as an additional selector to the previous rule.
3. Add a font-size property to the rule, and set the size to 14 points.
4. Write a style rule that selects <UL> elements only when they appear within <P> elements, and set the color property to red.
5. Write the style rule for a CLASS selector named "note." Set the font-weight property to bold.
6. Restrict the previous rule so it can be used only with <P> elements.
7. Write the style rule for an ID selector named "footer." Set the font-size property to 10 points and the font-family property to sans-serif.
8. What characteristic makes ID different from CLASS?
9. What is the difference between <DIV> and <SPAN>?
10. Which pseudo-class selectors let you change the style for the <A> element?
11. Write a style rule that sets the default document text color to red.
12. What is the advantage of working with CLASS attribute?
13. What element does this selector choose? `P UL LI`
14. What element does this selector choose? `DIV P *`
15. What element does this selector choose? `BLOCKQUOTE.warning`
16. What element does this selector choose? `:link`
17. What element does this selector choose? `P.custom:first-line`
18. What are the three dynamic pseudo-classes?
19. How are the dynamic pseudo-classes activated?
20. What are the two methods of selecting by attribute?

HANDS-ON PROJECTS

1. Find an article from a magazine of your choice. Describe the style characteristics of the page. Does it use multiple heading styles? A different first paragraph style? A special footer style? Devise CLASS names for the different elements. Indicate the CLASS names on the magazine page.

2. Extend the project by listing the style properties that you want to state for each element on the page. You do not have to use the exact CSS style properties, but list the style characteristics in general terms, such as border, margin, font style, and so on.

3. Find a mainstream Web site, and discuss how you would standardize the look and feel of the site by adding CSS style rules. Think about the different levels of information and how you will use CSS selectors to effectively select the different elements within the pages of the site.

4. In this project, you will have a chance to test a few basic selection techniques on a standard HTML document and view the results in your browser. Save and view the file in your browser after completing each step.

   a. Using your HTML editor, create a simple HTML file (or open an existing file) that contains <BODY> <H1> <P> elements and so on. Save the file in your work folder as **csstest2.htm**.

   b. Add a <STYLE> element to the <HEAD> section, as shown in the following code.

   ```
   <HEAD>
   <TITLE>CSS Test Document</TITLE>
   <STYLE TYPE="text/css">
   </STYLE>
   </HEAD>
   ```

   c. Write a style rule that uses BODY as a selector and sets the color property to the color of your choice.

   d. Find two elements on the page, such as <H1> and <H2>, that can share the same characteristics. Write a single style rule that will apply to both elements. Set the color property to red and the margin property to 20px.

   e. Find one element that contains another, such as a <B> or <I> element within a <P> element. Write a descendant selector rule that affects the contained element and sets the color property to green.

5. In this project, you will have a chance to test a few advanced selection techniques on a standard HTML document and view the results in your browser. Save and view the file in your browser after completing each step.

   a. Using your HTML editor, create a simple HTML file (or open an existing file) that contains <BODY> <H1> <P> elements and so on. Save the file in your work folder as **csstest3.htm**.

   b. Add a <STYLE> element to the <HEAD> section, as shown in Exercise #4.

c. Write a rule for a CLASS selector named "heading." Set the color property to red and the font-size property to 36pt. Apply the heading class to an <H1> or <H2> element in the document.

d. Write a rule for a CLASS selector named "emphasis." Set the color property to yellow. In the document, add a <SPAN> element to a span of words that you want to highlight. Apply the emphasis class to the <SPAN> element.

e. Add a hypertext link in the document that points to *www.yahoo.com*, as shown in the following code:

```
<A HREF=http://www.yahoo.com>Yahoo Web Site</A>
```

f. Write a style rule that uses A:hover as the selector. Set the color property to yellow. After you save the file, test the hover capability of your browser by pointing at the hypertext link. The background color of the link should turn yellow.

CASE STUDY

Revisit your project proposal, and try to add as much detail to each category as possible, concentrating on the content, goals, and style considerations. Carefully consider any feedback you have received from your instructor and fellow students. Decide where you can make changes that help focus the content to match your user's needs.

Start visualizing the page design for your site by sketching out mock layouts for different page designs and levels of information in your site. You do not have to determine the exact look of the different page components. At this stage you are trying to build a rough idea of the site's look and feel. Think about your navigation choices and how you will present these to the user. Consider the following questions:

- Will navigation links be graphics, text, or both?
- How many columns of text will there be on a page?
- How many images will there be on a page?
- How many different page designs are needed?

Start to organize your content by working on a site map. Create a visual diagram or flowchart that includes the main page and other pages of the site. Indicate the links between the pages and the file naming conventions for the site. Think about how your users will access your content—will they be able to quickly find the information they desire?

3

USING THE FONT AND TYPE PROPERTIES

When you complete this chapter, you will be able to:

♦ Understand how to use type effectively

♦ Understand how to use the CSS measurement values

♦ Use the CSS font properties

♦ Use the CSS text spacing properties

Type is the basic building block of any Web page. You can use typography to enhance the display of information on your Web site, to communicate relative importance of items, and to guide the reader's eye. HTML offers only basic type controls, forcing many designers to use graphics to add interesting text effects to a Web page, with the unfortunate side effect of increasing user download times. As you will see in this chapter, the CSS font and text properties let you add a wide range of desktop publishing effects to your Web site without increasing user download times.

USING TYPE EFFECTIVELY

The CSS font and type properties allow a much greater range of typographic expression than available with standard HTML. With so many properties available, it is tempting to use as many as possible. Remember that restraint is the key to effective type design. Here are the guidelines for using type to communicate your message on a Web page:

- Choose fewer fonts and sizes
- Choose available fonts
- Design for legibility

Choose Fewer Fonts and Sizes

Your pages look cleaner when you choose fewer fonts and sizes of type. Decide on a typeface for each different level of topic importance, such as page headings and section headings. Communicate the hierarchy of information with changes in the size, weight, or color of the face. For example, a page heading might have a larger, bolder type, while a section heading would appear in the same face, only lighter or smaller.

Pick a few sizes and weights in a family. For example, you might choose three sizes, such as 24 points for headings, 18 points for subheadings, and 12 points for body text. You can vary these styles by changing the font weight; for example, use 12-point bold for topic headings within text. Consistently apply the same fonts and the same combination of styles throughout your site. Avoid making random changes in your use of type conventions. Consistency develops a strong visual identity on your pages.

Choose Available Fonts

Fonts are often a problem in HTML because font information is client based. The user's browser and operating system determine how a font is displayed or if it is displayed at all. If you design your pages using a font that your user doesn't have installed, then the browser defaults to Times (Times New Roman on a PC). To make matters worse, even the most widely available fonts appear in different sizes on different operating systems. Unfortunately, there's not much you can do about this except test on multiple platforms to judge the effect on your pages.

Table 3-1 lists the most common fonts on the PC, UNIX, and Macintosh systems.

This table shows that Times (Times New Roman on the PC) is available on all three operating systems. It is the default browser font. Courier is the default monospace font. Arial or Helvetica are the default sans-serif fonts. Arial and Verdana come with Internet Explorer 4.0 and up, so many users, both Mac and PC, have them installed. Some Macintosh users only have Helvetica, so it's a good idea to specify it as an alternate choice when you are using sans-serif fonts.

Table 3-1   Common installed fonts

Common PC Fonts	Common UNIX Fonts	Common Macintosh Fonts
Arial	Helvetica	Helvetica
Courier New	Courier	Courier
Times New Roman	Times	Times
Verdana		Verdana
		Palatino
		Arial

Design for Legibility

Figure 3-1 shows the same paragraph in Times, Arial, Helvetica, and Verdana at the default browser size.

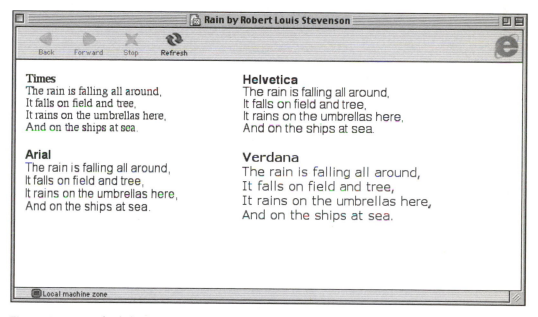

Figure 3-1   Default browser sizes in the common fonts

In these examples, line length varies based on the font. Times at the default size can be hard to read. Some find Arial more legible online. Helvetica is available on Macintosh computers and some PCs. Verdana is an expanded font—each letter takes up more horizontal space than Arial or Times. This makes the text easier to read online, but takes much more space on the Web page.

The size and face of the type you use on your pages determine the legibility of your text. The computer monitor has a lower resolution than the printed page, compounding the difficulty of reading online. Fonts that are legible on paper can be more difficult to read on a monitor. Keep fonts big enough to be legible, and avoid specialty fonts that degrade when viewed online. To aid the reader, add more white space to the page around your blocks of text. Consider more white space between lines as well. Test your content with both serif and sans-serif body text (discussed later in this chapter). Finally, make sure that you provide enough contrast between your text color and any background colors you use. In general, dark text on a light background is easiest to read.

UNDERSTANDING CSS MEASUREMENT UNITS

CSS offers a variety of measurement units, including absolute units, such as points; relative units, such as pixels; and percentages of the base font. The measurement values you choose depend on the destination medium for your content. For example, if you are designing a style sheet for printed media, you can use absolute units of measurement, such as points or centimeters. When you are designing a style sheet for a Web page, you can use relative measurement values that adapt to the user's display type, such as ems or pixels. In this section, you will learn about the following CSS measurement units. These units are detailed in Table 3–2.

- Absolute units
- Relative units
- Percentage

Table 3-2   CSS measurement units

Unit	Unit Abbreviation	Description
Absolute Units		
Centimeter	cm	Standard metric centimeter
Inch	in	Standard U.S. inch
Millimeter	mm	Standard metric millimeter
Pica	pc	Standard publishing unit equal to 12 points
Point	pt	Standard publishing unit, with 72 points in an inch
Relative Units		
Em	em	The width of the capital M in the current font, usually the same as the font size
Ex	ex	The height of the letter x in the current font
Pixel	px	The size of a pixel on the current monitor
Percentage	For example: 150%	Sets a font size relative to the base font size; 150% equals one-and-one-half the base font size

3

Absolute Units

CSS lets you use absolute measurement values that specify a fixed value. The measurement values require a number followed by one of the unit abbreviations listed in Table 3-2. The numeric value can be a positive value, negative value, or fractional value. For example, the following rule sets margins to 1.25 inches:

```
P {margin: 1.25in;}
```

You generally want to avoid using absolute units for Web pages because they cannot be scaled to the individual user display type. They are better used when you know the exact measurements of the destination medium. For example, if you know a document will be printed on 8.5 × 11-inch paper, you can plan your style rules accordingly because you know the physical dimensions of the finished document. Absolute units are better suited to print destinations than Web destinations. Although the point (pt) is the standard unit of measurement for type sizes, it is not the best measurement value for the Web. Because computer displays vary widely in size, they lend themselves better to relative units of measurement that can adapt to different monitor sizes and screen resolutions.

Relative Units

The relative units are designed to let you build scalable Web pages that adapt to different display types and sizes. The designers of CSS2, Hakon Lie and Bert Bos, recommend that you always use relative sizes (specifically, the em value) to set font sizes on your Web pages. This practice ensures that your type sizes will display properly relative to each other or to the default font size set for the browser.

The em Unit

The **em** is a printing measurement, traditionally equal to the horizontal length of the capital letter M in any given font size. In CSS the em is equal to the font size of an element. It can be used for both horizontal and vertical measurement. In addition to stating font sizes, em is useful for padding and margins as well. You can read more about this in the chapter titled "Using the Box Properties."

The size of the em is equivalent to the font size of the element. For example, if the default paragraph font size is 12-point text, the em equals 12 points. Stating a text size of 2 em would create 24-point text—two times the default size. This is useful because it means that measurements stated in em are always relative to their environment. For example, assume that you want a larger size heading on your page. If you set the <H1> element to 24 points, it will always remain that size. If a user sets his or her default font size to 24 points, the headings will be the same size as the text. However, if you use the relative em unit, the heading will always be sized based on the size of the default text. The following rule sets heading divisions to twice the size of the default text:

```
DIV.heading {font-size: 2em;}
```

The ex Unit

The ex unit is equal to the height of the lowercase letter x in any given font. As shown in Figure 3-2, the height of the lowercase letter x varies widely from one type face to another.

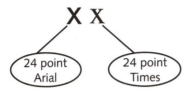

Figure 3-2   Differences in height of the ex unit

Ex is a less reliable unit of measurement than em because the size of the letter x changes in height from one font family to another, and the browser cannot always calculate the difference correctly. Most browsers simply set the ex value to one-half the value of the font's em size.

The px unit

Pixels are the basic picture element of a computer display. The size of the pixel is determined by the display resolution. **Resolution** is the measure of how many pixels fit on a screen. The standard display resolutions are 640 × 480, 800 × 600, and 1024 × 768. As the resolutions grow in value, the individual pixel size gets smaller, making the pixel relative to the individual display settings. Pixel measurements work well for computer displays, but they are not so well suited to other media, such as printing, because some printers cannot accurately determine the size of the pixel.

Percentages

Percentage values are always relative to another value. For example the following rule sets the font size for the <BODY> element to one-and-one-half of the browser default:

```
BODY {font-size: 150%;}
```

Child elements inherit the percentage values of their parents. For example, the <B> text in the following example will be 125% larger than the <P> that contains it:

```
P {font-size: 12pt;}
P B {font-size: 125%;}
```

The first rule establishes the font size for the <P> element. The second rule selects any <B> elements within <P> elements. Because the <P> element has the font size set to 12 points, the <B> text will display at 15 points, or 125% larger than its parent.

How to Read the Property Descriptions

The property descriptions are used throughout the book to provide key information about each CSS property. A property description looks like the following:

border-width property description

Value: thin | medium | thick | <length>

Initial: medium

Applies to: all elements

Inherited: no

Percentages: N/A

Table 3-3 lists the five property description categories.

Table 3-3   Property description categories

Category	Definition
Value	The valid keyword or variable values for the property; variable values are set between angle brackets; for example, <length> means enter a length value; Table 3-4 lists the value notation symbols
Initial	The initial value of the property
Applies to	The elements to which the property applies
Inherited	Indicates if the property is inherited from its parent element
Percentages	Indicates if percentage values are allowed

Table 3-4 lists the value category notation.

Table 3-4   Value category notation

Notation	Definition
< >	Words between angle brackets specify a variable value; for example, <length>
|	A single vertical bar separates two or more alternatives, one of which must occur; for example, thin | medium | thick
||	Two vertical bars separate options; one or more of the values can occur in any order; for example, underline || overline || line-through
[ ]	Square brackets group parts of the property value together; for example, none | [underline || overline || line-through] means that the value is either none or one of the values within the square brackets
?	A question mark indicates that the preceding value or group of values is optional

USING THE FONT PROPERTIES

The CSS font properties allow you to control the appearance of your text. These properties describe how the letter forms look. The CSS text properties, described later in this chapter, describe the spacing around the text rather than affecting the actual text itself. In this section, you will learn about the following properties:

- font-family
- font-size
- font-style
- font-variant
- font-weight
- font-stretch
- font (shorthand property)

Specifying Font Family

font-family property description

Value: <family-name> | <generic-family>

Initial: depends on user agent

Applies to: all elements

Inherited: yes

Percentages: N/A

The font-family property lets you state a generic font family name, such as sans-serif, or a specific font family name, like Helvetica. You can also string together a list of font families, separated by commas, supplying a selection of fonts that the browser can attempt to match.

To make your pages display more consistently, think in terms of font families, such as serif and sans-serif typefaces, rather than specific styles. Because of the variable nature of fonts installed on different computers, you can never be sure that the user will see the exact font you have specified. You can, however, use font substitution to specify a variety of fonts within a font family, such as Arial or Helvetica, which are both common sans-serif fonts.

Using Generic Font Families

You can use the following generic names for font families:

- **Serif** fonts are the traditional letter form, with strokes (or serifs) that finish off the top and bottom of the letter. The most common serif font is Times.

- **Sans-serif** fonts have no serifs. They are block letters. The most common sans-serif fonts are Helvetica and Arial.

- **Monospace** fonts are fixed-width fonts. Every letter has the same horizontal width. Monospace is commonly used to mimic typewritten text or for programming code. The style rules in this book are printed in a monospace font.

- **Cursive** fonts are designed to resemble handwriting. This is a less well-supported font family.

- **Fantasy** fonts are primarily decorative. Like cursive, fantasy is not a well-supported font family.

The ability to use generic names ensures greater portability across browsers and operating systems, because it does not rely on a specific font being installed on the user's computer. The following rule sets <P> elements to the default sans-serif font:

```
P {font-family: sans-serif;}
```

Of course, if you don't specify any font family, the browser displays the default font, usually some version of Times.

Using Specific Font Families

In addition to generic font families, the font-family property lets you declare a specific font family, such as Futura or Garamond. The user must have the font installed on his or her computer; otherwise, the browser uses the default font.

The following rule specifies Arial as the font family for the <P> element:

```
P {font-family: arial;}
```

Specifying Font Substitution

You can specify a list of alternate fonts using commas as a separator. The browser will attempt to load each successive font in the list. If no fonts match, the browser uses its default font. The following code tells the browser to use Arial; if Arial is not present, use Helvetica.

```
P {font-family: arial, helvetica;}
```

This rule uses a common font substitution string that produces a sans-serif font on both PCs that have Arial installed and Macintosh computers that have Helvetica installed. To further ensure the portability of this rule, add a generic font family name to the list, as shown in the following rule:

```
P {font-family: arial, helvetica, sans-serif;}
```

This rule ensures that the <P> element will be displayed in some type of sans-serif font, even if it is not Arial or Helvetica.

Specifying Font Size

font-size property description

Value: <absolute-size> | <relative-size> | <length> | <percentage>

Initial: medium

Applies to: all elements

Inherited: the computed value is inherited

Percentages: refer to parent element's font size

The font-size property gives you control over the specific sizing of your type. You can choose from length units, such as em or pixels, or a percentage value that is based on the parent element's font size.

The following rule sets the <BLOCKQUOTE> element to 18-point Arial:

```
BLOCKQUOTE {font-family: arial; font-size: 18pt;}
```

To specify a default size for a document, use BODY as the selector. This rule sets the text to 14-point Arial:

```
BODY {font-family: arial; font-size: 14pt;}
```

You can also choose from a list of absolute size and relative size keywords, described in the following sections.

Absolute Font Size Keywords

These keywords refer to a table of sizes that is determined by the browser. The keywords are:

- xx-small
- x-small
- small
- medium
- large
- x-large
- xx-large

The CSS2 specification recommends a scaling factor of 1.2 between sizes for the computer display. Therefore, if the medium font is 10 points, the large font would be 12 points ($10 \times 1.2 = 12$). Figure 3-3 shows the different absolute sizes in the browser.

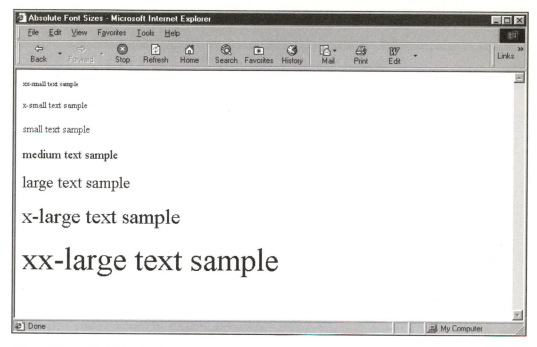

Figure 3-3 Absolute font sizes

Relative Font Size Keywords

The relative size keywords refer to the table of sizes kept by the browser listed in the previous section. The keywords, listed below, are relative to the parent element's absolute font size.

- smaller
- larger

For example, if the parent element's size is large, and the current element's size is set to larger, the current font size will be x-large. In the following example, the <BODY> element is set to medium, and the <BLOCKQUOTE> element is set to smaller. <BLOCKQUOTE> elements will appear one size smaller than medium, which is size small.

```
BODY {font-size: medium;}
BLOCKQUOTE {font-size: smaller;}
```

Specifying Font Style

---

font-style property description

Value: normal | italic | oblique

Initial: normal

Applies to: all elements

Inherited: yes

Percentages: N/A

The font-style property lets you specify italic or oblique text. The difference between italic and oblique text is subtle. The italic form of a typeface is designed with different letterforms to create the slanted font, while the oblique form is simply normal text slanted to the right. In print-based typography, oblique text is considered inferior to italic. On the Web however, current browsers cannot make the distinction between the two—either value will create slanted text. The following example sets italicized text for a CLASS attribute "note."

```
.note {font-style: italic;}
```

Here is the "note" class applied to a <DIV> element:

```
<DIV CLASS="note">A note to the reader:</DIV>
```

The text contained in the <DIV> will appear italicized in the browser. Remember that italic text is hard to read on a computer display. Use italics for special emphasis, rather than for large blocks of text.

Specifying Font Variant

---

font-variant property description

Value: normal | small-caps

Initial: normal

Applies to: all elements

Inherited: yes

Percentages: N/A

The font-variant property lets you define small capitals, which are often used for chapter openings, acronyms, and other special purposes. Small capitals are intended to be a different type style than regular capital letters, but this is not supported in all browsers, some of which will simply downsize the regular capital letters. Internet Explorer 5.0 for the Macintosh does support the true small capitals shown in Figure 3-4.

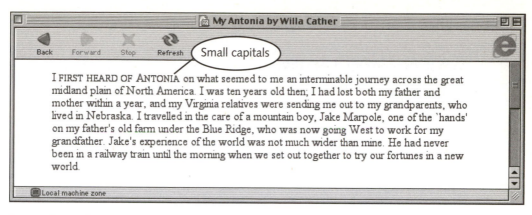

Figure 3-4 Small capitals

In this example, a <SPAN> element contains the text that is converted to small capitals, as shown in the following code fragment:

```
<SPAN STYLE="font-variant: small-caps;">I first heard of
Antonia</SPAN> on what seemed to be…
```

This style rules shows the use of the <SPAN> element to affect the style for an inline span of words within a block of text. The STYLE attribute lets you test the style on this one element before adding it to your style sheet.

Specifying Font Weight

font-weight property description

Value: normal | bold | bolder | lighter | 100 | 200 | 300 | 400 | 500 | 600 | 700 | 800 | 900

Initial: normal

Applies to: all elements

Inherited: yes

Percentages: N/A

The font-weight property lets you set the weight of the typeface. The numeric values express nine levels of weight from 100 to 900, although most browser and fonts do not support such a wide range of weights. The default type weight is equal to 400, with bold text equal to 700. Bolder and lighter are relative weights based on the weight of the parent element. Using the bold value will produce the same weight of text as the <B> element. The following style rule sets the "warning" class to bold:

```
.warning {font-weight: bold;}
```

Specifying Font Stretching

```
font-stretch property description

Value: normal | wider | narrower | ultra-condensed | extra-condensed
| condensed | semi-condensed | semi-expanded | expanded |
extra-expanded | ultra-expanded
Initial: normal
Applies to: all elements
Inherited: yes
Percentages: N/A
```

The font-stretch property is not supported by any of the current browsers. When implemented, it will allow fonts to be condensed or expanded to a narrower or wider face. In addition to the absolute values, the "wider" and "narrower" keywords are based on the parent element in which they are applied.

Using the Font Shortcut Property

```
font property description

Value: [[<'font-style'> || <'font-variant'> || <'font-weight'> ]?
<'font-size'> [ / <'line-height'> ]? <'font-family'> ]
Initial: see individual properties
Applies to: all elements
Inherited: yes
Percentages: allowed on 'font-size' and 'line-height'
```

The font property is a shortcut that lets you specify the most common font properties in a single statement. The syntax of this property is based on a traditional typographical shorthand notation to set multiple properties related to fonts.

As shown in the previous value listing, the font property lets you state the font-style, font-variant, font-weight, font-size, line-height, and font-family in one statement. The only two values that are required are font-size and font-family, which must be in the correct order for the style rule to work. The following rules are examples of the most basic use of the font property:

```
P {font: 12pt arial;}
H1 {font: 2em sans-serif;}
```

The font properties other than font-size and font-family are optional and do not have to be included unless you want to change their default. If you want to include line-height, note that it must always follow a slash after the font-size. The following rule sets 12-point Arial text on 18-point line height:

```
P {font: 12pt/18pt arial;}
```

The font shortcut property lets you abbreviate from the more verbose individual property listings. For example, both of the following rules produce the same result:

```
P {font-weight: bold;
   font-size: 18pt;
   line-height: 24pt;
   font-family: arial
}
P {font: bold 18pt/24pt arial;} /* Same rule as above */
```

Although the font shortcut property is a convenience, you may prefer to state explicitly the font properties as shown in the more verbose rule, because they are easier to understand.

USING THE TEXT SPACING PROPERTIES

The CSS text properties let you adjust the spacing around and within your text. The properties in this section let you create distinctive text effects that are not possible with standard HTML. In this section, you will learn about the following properties:

- text-indent
- text-align
- text-decoration
- line-height
- vertical-align
- letter-spacing
- word-spacing
- text-shadow
- text-transform
- white-space

Specifying Text Indents

text-indent property description

Value: <length> | <percentage>

Initial: 0

Applies to: block-level elements

Inherited: yes

Percentages: refer to width of containing block

Use the text-indent property to set the amount of indentation for the first line of text in an element, such as a paragraph. You can specify a length or percentage value. The percentage is relative to the width of the containing element. If you specify a value of 15%, the indent will be 15% of the width of the element. Negative values let you create a hanging indent. Figure 3-5 shows two different text-indent effects.

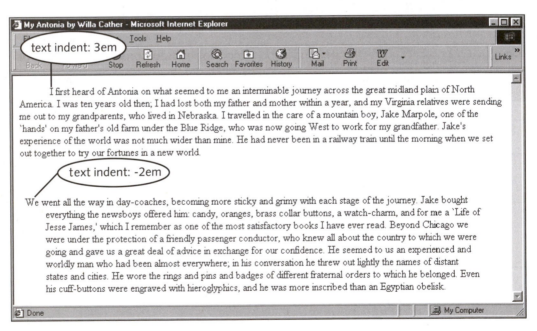

Figure 3-5   Text indents

The following rules set an indent of 3 em for the <P> element and −2 em for the <BLOCKQUOTE> element:

```
P {text-indent: 2em;}
BLOCKQUOTE {text-indent: -2em;}
```

Indents are sensitive to the language specification for the document. To determine the default language for a document, the Web server sends a two-letter language code (Appendix A contains a list of language codes) along with the HTML file that is requested by the browser. In left-to-right reading languages (such as English), the indent is added to the left of the first line; in right-to-left reading languages (such as Hebrew), the indent is added to the right of the first line.

Indents are inherited from parent to child elements. For example, the following rule sets a 2-em text indent to a <DIV> element:

```
DIV {text-indent: 2em;}
```

Any block-level elements, such as <P>, that are contained within this division will have the 2-em text indent specified in the rule for the parent <DIV>.

Specifying Text Alignment

text-align property description

Value: left | right | center | justify
Initial: depends on user agent and language
Applies to: block-level elements
Inherited: yes
Percentages: N/A

Use the text-align property to set horizontal alignment for the lines of text in an element. You can specify four alignment values: left, center, right, and justify. The justify value lines up the text on both horizontal margins, adding white space between the words on the line, like a column of text in a newspaper. The following style rule sets the <P> element to justified alignment:

```
P {text-align: justify;}
```

Figure 3-6 shows a sample of all four alignment values.

When choosing an alignment value, keep the default settings for the language and the user's preferences in mind. For example, most western languages read from left to right, and the default alignment is left. Unless you are trying to emphasize a particular section of text, use the alignment with which most readers will be comfortable. Both right and center alignment are fine for short sections of text, but they make reading difficult for lengthier passages.

Justified text lets you create newspaper-like alignment where the lines of text all have the same length. The browser inserts white space between the words of the text to adjust the alignment so both margins of the text align, as shown in Figure 3-6. Justify is not supported by all browsers, and different browsers might justify the text differently.

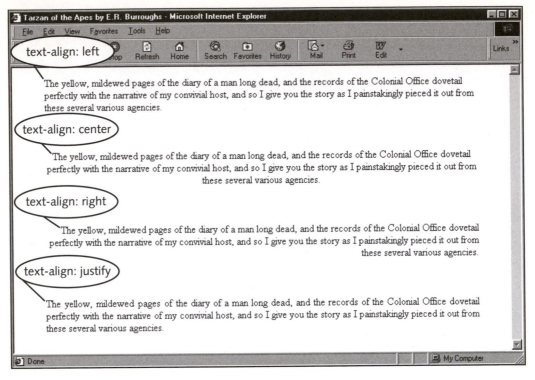

Figure 3-6   Text alignments

Specifying Text Decoration

---
text-decoration property description

Value: none | [underline || overline || line-through || blink]

Initial: none

Applies to: all elements

Inherited: no

Percentages: N/A

The text-decoration property lets you add line decorations to text. You can add or remove underlining, over-lining, and lines through the text. The following rule sets the text-decoration property value to line-through for the <EM> element:

```
EM {text-decoration: line-through;}
```

Text decoration lets you underline text, an effect that has particular meaning in a hypertext environment. Your users know to look for underlined words as the indicators for hypertext links. Any text you underline will appear to be a hypertext link. Except for text links, underlining is an inappropriate text style for a Web page.

Text-decoration also supports the blink value, which creates blinking text. Although you might be tempted to use this effect, most users find the constantly blinking text distracting. The CSS2 specification does not require all browsers to support the blink value. Figure 3-7 shows the different text decorations, except for the blink value.

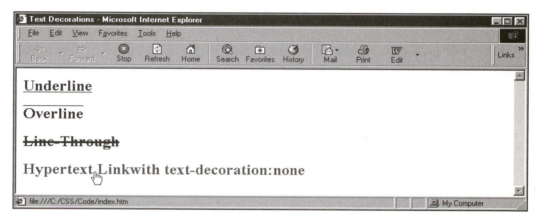

Figure 3-7   Text decorations

As Figure 3-7 shows, the text-decoration property lets you remove the underlining from the <A> element. As you read earlier, the user commonly relies on the underlining text to indicate a hypertext link. However, some Web sites choose to remove link underlining, indicating links with a color different from the standard text color. You can remove the underlining from your anchor elements with the following rule:

```
A {text-decoration: none;}
```

Users with sight disabilities can have trouble finding the links in your content if you choose to remove the underlining. Alternately, a user can override the author's style rules by setting preferences in his or her browser or applying his or her own style sheet.

Specifying Line Height

---

line-height property description

Value: normal | <number> | <length> | <percentage>

Initial: normal

Applies to: all elements

Inherited: yes

Percentages: refer to the font size of the element itself

CSS allows you to specify either a length or percentage value for the line height, which is more commonly called **leading**, the white space between lines of text. The percentage is based on the font size. Setting the value to 150% with a 12-point font size will result in a line height of 18 points. The following rule sets the line height to 150%:

```
P {line-height: 150%;}
```

Figure 3-8 shows the default line height and various adjustments in line height. A gray background color for the Web page and white background color for the text highlight the line box around each line. Notice that the line height is evenly divided between the top and bottom of the element.

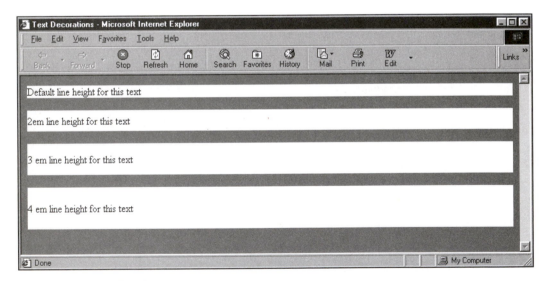

Figure 3-8   Line height

The line-height property can increase the legibility of your text. Adding to the default line height inserts additional white space between the lines of text. On the computer monitor, increasing the white space helps guide the user's eyes along the line of text and provides rest for the eye. Figure 3-9 shows two paragraphs; one with the standard line height and one with the line height set to 1.5 em. The increased line height adds to the legibility of the text.

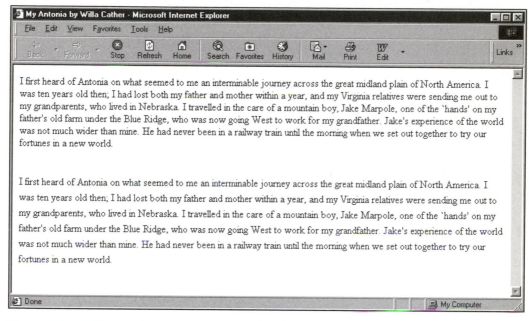

Figure 3-9   Adjusting line height increases legibility

Specifying Vertical Alignment

vertical-align property description

Value: baseline | sub | super | top | text-top | middle | bottom |
text-bottom | <percentage> | <length>

Initial: baseline

Applies to: inline-level and 'table-cell' elements

Inherited: no

Percentages: refer to the 'line-height' of the element itself

The vertical-align property lets you adjust the vertical alignment of text within the line box. Vertical-align works on inline elements (described in the "Using the Box Properties" chapter) only. You can use this property to superscript or subscript characters above or below the line of text and to align images with text. Table 3-5 defines the different vertical-align values. The baseline, sub, and super values are the most evenly supported by the different browsers.

Table 3-5 Vertical-align property values

Value	Definition
baseline	Align the baseline of the text with the baseline of the parent element
sub	Lower the baseline of the box to the proper position for subscripts of the parent's box; this value does not automatically create a smaller font size for the subscripted text
middle	The CSS2 specification defines "middle" as "the vertical midpoint of the box with the baseline of the parent box plus half the x-height of the parent;" realistically, this means the middle-aligned text is aligned to half the height of the lowercase letters
super	Raise the baseline of the box to the proper position for superscripts of the parent's box; this value does not automatically create a smaller font size for the superscripted text
text-top	Align the top of the box with the top of the parent element's font
text-bottom	Align the bottom of the box with the bottom of the parent element's font
top	Align the top of the box with the top of the line box
bottom	Align the bottom of the box with the bottom of the line box

The following rule sets superscripting for a CLASS named "superscript":

```
.superscript {vertical-align: super;}
```

Figure 3-10 shows different types of vertical alignments.

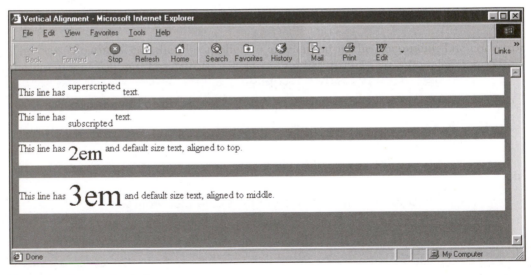

Figure 3-10 Vertical alignments

You can also use vertical alignment to align text with graphics. The following rule, added to the <IMG> element with the STYLE attribute, sets the vertical alignment to top:

```
<IMG src="image.gif" style="vertical-align: text-top;">
```

Figure 3-11 shows various alignments of images and text. Note that the vertical alignment affects only the one line of text that contains the graphic, because the graphic is an inline element. If you want to wrap a paragraph of text around an image, use the float property, described in the chapter titled "Using the Box Properties."

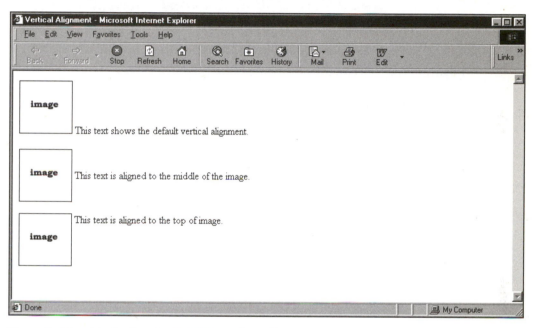

Figure 3-11   Vertically aligning text and graphics

Specifying Letter Spacing

letter-spacing property description

Value: normal | <length>

Initial: normal

Applies to: all elements

Inherited: yes

Percentages: N/A

The letter-spacing property lets you adjust the white space between letters. In publishing terminology, this adjustment is called **kerning**. The length you specify in the style rule is added to the default letter spacing. The following code sets the letter spacing to 4 points:

```
H1 {letter-spacing: 4pt;}
```

Figure 3-12 shows samples of different letter spacing values.

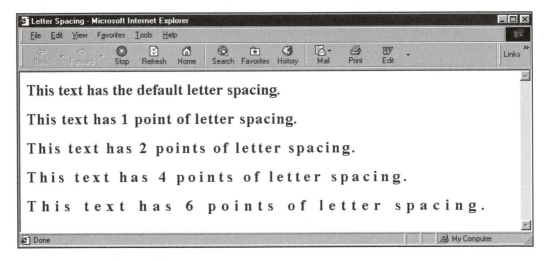

Figure 3-12   Adjusting letter spacing

Specifying Word Spacing

word-spacing property description

Value: normal | <length>

Initial: normal

Applies to: all elements

Inherited: yes

Percentages: N/A

The word-spacing property lets you adjust the white space between words in the text. The length you specify in the style rule is added to the default word spacing. The following code sets the word spacing to 2 em:

```
H1 {word-spacing: 2em;}
```

Figure 3-13 shows the result of the word-spacing property.

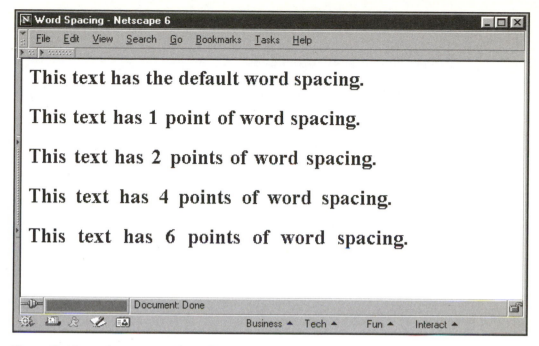

Figure 3-13   Adjusting word spacing

Specifying Text Shadows

text-shadow property description

Value: none | [<color> || <length> <length> <length>? ,] [<color> ||
<length> <length> <length>?]
Initial: none
Applies to: all elements
Inherited: no
Percentages: N/A

The text-shadow property lets you add decorative shadow effects. This property is not supported in any current browser. When this property is supported, you will be able to add shadows to letters by setting the shadow offset, blur radius, and color.

Transforming Text Case

text-transform property description
Value: capitalize | uppercase | lowercase | none
Initial: none
Applies to: all elements
Inherited: yes
Percentages: N/A

The text-transform property lets you transform the case of text. You saw this property applied in the chapter titled "Understanding CSS Selection Techniques" with the :first-line pseudo-class:

```
P.intro:first-line {text-transform: uppercase;}
```

The other values are capitalize, which capitalizes the first letter of every word, and lowercase, which forces all text to lowercase letters. Figure 3-14 shows samples of text transformation.

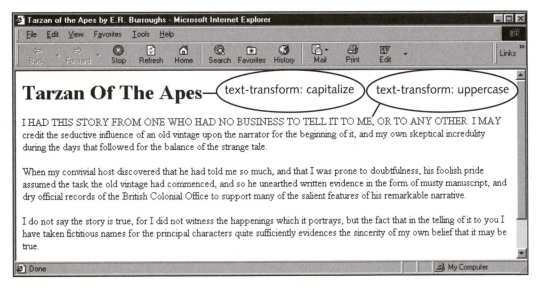

Figure 3-14   Text transformations

Here is the code fragment for the <H1> and first <P> element in the HTML file in Figure 3-14. Notice that the <H1> element text is lowercase and that the first line of the <P> element is sentence case:

```
<H1>tarzan of the apes</H1>
<P class="intro">
```

```
I had this story from one who had no business to tell it to
me, or to any other. I may credit the seductive influence
of an old vintage upon the narrator for the beginning of
it, and my own skeptical incredulity during the days that
followed for the balance of the strange tale.</P>
```

The style rules apply the text transformation shown in Figure 3-14 to this text, capitalizing the <H1> text and applying uppercase to the first line of the <P>element.

Here are the style rules that created the text transformations:

P. intro: first-line {text-transform: uppercase;}

H1 {text-transform: capitalize; page;}

Controlling Element White Space

white-space property description

Value: normal | pre | nowrap

Initial: normal

Applies to: block-level elements

Inherited: yes

Percentages: N/A

The white-space property lets you control the white space properties of an element. This property is currently not supported by Internet Explorer 5.5.

If you have used the <PRE> element in HTML, you are familiar with the capabilities of this property. In most elements, the browser collapses additional white space, preserving only a single space between words. In the <PRE> element, however, the exact amount of white space is preserved in the browser. The white-space property lets you apply this type of white space handling to any element. For example, you might want to format a poem in a particular way in the browser. The following style rule applies the pre white-space value to a <DIV> element with a class of "poem":

```
DIV.poem {white-space: pre;}
```

Here is the poem division in the HTML code:

```
<DIV class="poem">
          Rain
The rain is falling all around,
    It falls on field and tree,
        It rains on the umbrellas here,
            And on the ships at sea.
</DIV>
```

Figure 3-15 shows the result of the code in Opera 5.0.

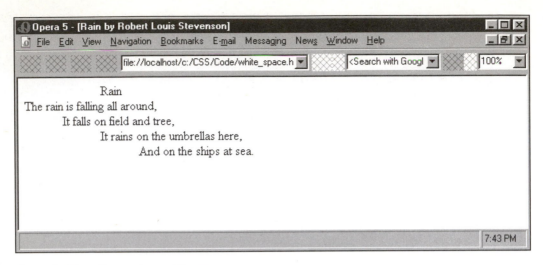

Figure 3-15   Preserving white space

USING THE FONT AND TEXT PROPERTIES

In the following set of steps, you will build a style sheet that uses the typographic techniques you learned about in this chapter. Save your file, and test your work in the browser as you complete each step.

To build the style sheet:

1. Open the file **webnews.htm** in your HTML editor, and save it in your work folder as **webnews1.htm**.

2. In your browser, open the file **webnews1.htm**. When you open the file, it looks like Figure 3-16.

3. Examine the code. Notice that the Web page uses common HTML elements, including a <FONT> element, to style the text. HTML table elements build the structure of the layout. For this exercise, the style rules will affect only the content within the table, not the table itself. Comments are included to help you locate the various page components. The complete code for the page follows:

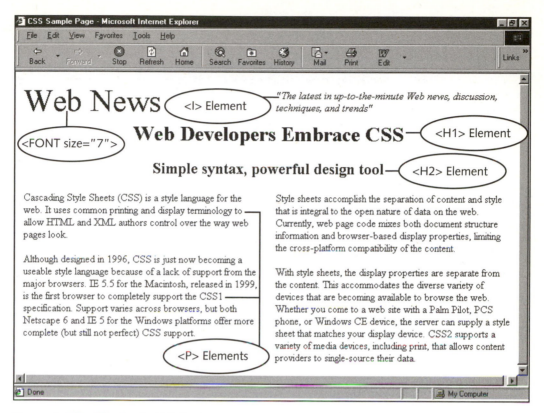

Figure 3-16   The basic HTML document

```
<HTML>
<HEAD>
<TITLE>CSS Sample Page</TITLE>
</HEAD>
<BODY>
<TABLE WIDTH=765>
<!-- First Row contains banner and tagline-->
<TR>
<TD WIDTH=50%><FONT SIZE=7>Web News</FONT></TD>
<!-- spacer cell -->
<TD> </TD>
<TD WIDTH=50%><I>"The latest in up-to-the-minute
Web news, discussion, techniques, and trends"</I></TD>
</TR>
<!-- Second Row contains headline-->
<TR>
<TD COLSPAN=3>
<H1 ALIGN="CENTER">Web Developers Embrace CSS</H1></TD>
</TR>
<!-- Third Row contains sub-head -->
```

```
<TR><TD COLSPAN=3>
<H2 ALIGN="CENTER">Simple syntax, powerful design tool
</H2></TD>
</TR>
<!-- Fourth row contains article columns -->
<TR VALIGN=TOP>
<TD>
<P>Cascading Style Sheets (CSS) is a style language
for the web. It uses common printing and display
terminology to allow HTML and XML authors control over
the way web pages look.</P>
<P>Although designed in 1996, CSS is just now becoming a
useable style language because of a lack of support from
the major browsers. IE 5.5 for the Macintosh, released in
1999, is the first browser to completely support the CSS1
specification. Support varies across browsers, but both
Netscape 6 and IE 5 for the Windows platforms offer more
complete (but still not perfect) CSS support.</P>
</TD>
<!-- Spacer cell -->
<TD>    </TD>
<TD><P>Style sheets accomplish the separation of
content and style that is integral to the open nature of
data on the web. Currently, web page code mixes both
document structure information and browser-based
display properties, limiting the cross-platform
compatibility of the content.</P>
<P>With style sheets, the display properties are
separate from the content. This accommodates the diverse
variety of devices that are becoming available to browse
the web. Whether you come to a web site with a Palm
Pilot, PCS phone, or Windows CE device, the server can
supply a style sheet that matches your display device.
CSS2 supports a variety of media devices, including
print, that allows content providers to single-
source their data.</P>
</TD>
</TR>
</TABLE>
</BODY>
</HTML>
```

Naming the Style Classes

The first step in building a style sheet for this document is to name the logical document sections to which you can apply styles. You can then use these document section names as class names and apply the style using <DIV> elements and CLASS attributes. Figure 3-17 shows the basic document with the class names that will be used to apply styles.

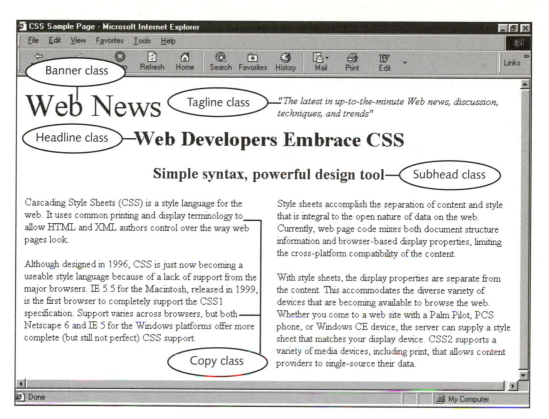

Figure 3-17   Logical document sections

Adding the <STYLE> Section

Because you are working on a single document, you can use a <STYLE> element in the <HEAD> section to contain your style rules.

To add the <STYLE> section:

1. Add a <STYLE> element in the <HEAD> section to contain your style rules as shown in the following code.

2. Leave a few lines of white space between the <STYLE> tags to contain the style rules.

```
<HEAD>
<TITLE></TITLE>
<STYLE type="text/css">

</STYLE>
</HEAD>
```

Styling the Banner Class

The banner currently uses a <FONT> element to make the text as large as possible within standard HTML. <FONT> is a **deprecated** element. Deprecated elements are elements that the W3C has identified as obsolete. The <FONT> element is deprecated specifically in favor of CSS style rules.

To style the banner class:

1. Write a style rule that selects the class named "banner." Set the font-size to 4 em and the font-style to italic, as shown in the following code:

```
<STYLE type="text/css">
.banner {font-size: 4em; font-style: italic;}
</STYLE>
```

2. Locate the banner text within the file. Remove the <FONT> elements highlighted in the following code:

```
<!— First Row contains banner and tagline-->
<TR>
<TD WIDTH=50%><FONT SIZE=7>Web News</FONT></TD>
```

3. Replace the <FONT> elements with <DIV> elements. Specify "banner" as the class attribute value as shown below:

```
<!— First Row contains banner and tagline-->
<TR>
<TD WIDTH=50%><DIV class="banner">Web News</DIV></TD>
```

Figure 3-18 shows the complete banner style.

Styling the Tagline Class

The tagline element currently uses an <I> element to make the text italicized. Italic text is hard to read on a computer display. You will write a rule that makes the tagline text stand out and easier to read.

To style the tagline class:

1. Write a style rule that selects the class named "tagline." Set the font-family to monospace and the text-weight to bold as shown in the following code:

```
<STYLE type="text/css">
.banner {font-size: 4em; font-style: italic;}
.tagline {font-family: monospace; font-weight: bold;}
</STYLE>
```

2. Locate the tagline text within the file. Remove the <I> elements highlighted in the following code:

```
<TD WIDTH=50%><I>"The latest in up-to-the-minute
Web news, discussion, techniques, and trends"</I></TD>
```

3. Replace the <I> elements with <DIV> elements. Set the CLASS attribute to "tagline," as shown in the following code:

```
<DIV class="tagline">"The latest in up-to-the-minute
Web news, discussion, techniques, and trends"</DIV>
```

Figure 3-18   The banner style

Figure 3-19 shows the result of the tagline style rules. The monospace text is associated with computers and thus is appropriate for this page.

Styling the Headline

The headline currently uses <H1> elements to make the text as large and bold as possible. You will write a style rule that applies five different properties to the headline text.

To style the headline:

1. Write a style rule that selects the class named "headline." Set the font-family to Arial, and use font substitution to ensure that Arial, Helvetica, or the default sans-serif font apply.

```
<STYLE type="text/css">
```

```
.banner {font-size: 4em; font-style: italic;}
.tagline {font-family: monospace; font-weight: bold;}
.headline {font-family: arial, helvetica, sans-serif;}
</STYLE>
```

Figure 3-19   The tagline style

2. Add more properties to the rule. Set the font-size to 2.5 times the size of the default font. Set text-align to center and set the line-height to 2.5 em. Because this style rule is more complex, you can place the properties on separate lines to make the rule easier to read, as shown in the following code:

```
<STYLE type="text/css">
.banner {font-size: 4em; font-style: italic;}
.tagline {font-family: monospace; font-weight: bold;}
.headline {font-family: arial, helvetica, sans-serif;
        font-size: 2.5em;
        text-align: center;
        line-height: 2.5em;}
</STYLE>
```

3. Finally, set the letter spacing to .25 em to provide extra white space between the headline letters to make the headline more legible. Note the closing curly bracket is now on its own line.

```
<STYLE type="text/css">
.banner {font-size: 4em; font-style: italic;}
.tagline {font-family: monospace; font-weight: bold;}
.headline {font-family: arial, helvetica, sans-serif;
           font-size: 2.5em;
           text-align: center;
           line-height: 2.5em;
           letter-spacing: .25em;
}
</STYLE>
```

4. Locate the headline text within the file. Remove the <H1> elements highlighted in the following code:

```
<!— Second Row contains headline—>
<TR>
<TD COLSPAN=3>
<H1 ALIGN="CENTER">Web Developers Embrace CSS</H1></TD>
</TR>
```

5. Replace the <H1> elements with <DIV> elements. Set the CLASS attribute to headline as shown in the following code:

```
<DIV class="headline">Web Developers Embrace CSS</DIV>
```

Figure 3-20 shows the result of the style rule. The line height and letter spacing add distinctive white space to the text, setting it off from the rest of the page.

Styling the Subhead

The subhead mimics the headline style, but on a smaller scale. It also uses Arial as the primary font family, with Helvetica and sans-serif as substitutes.

To style the subhead:

1. Write a style rule that selects the class named "subhead". Set the font-family to Arial, and use font substitution to ensure that Arial, Helvetica, or the default sans-serif font applies.

```
<STYLE type="text/css">
.banner {font-size: 4em; font-style: italic;}
.tagline {font-family: monospace; font-weight: bold;}
.headline {font-family: arial, helvetica, sans-serif;
           font-size: 2.5em;
           text-align: center;
           line-height: 2.5em;
           letter-spacing: .25em;
}
```

```
                          .subhead {font-family: arial, helvetica,
                          sans-serif;}
          </STYLE>
```

Figure 3-20   The headline style

2. Set font-size to 1.5 times the default font size. Set text-align to center, and set the line-height to 1.75 em, as shown in the following rule:

```
<STYLE type="text/css">
.banner {font-size: 4em; font-style: italic;}
.tagline {font-family: monospace; font-weight: bold;}
.headline {font-family: arial, helvetica, sans-serif;
          font-size: 2.5em;
          text-align: center;
          line-height: 2.5em;
          letter-spacing: .25em;
}
.subhead {font-family: arial, helvetica, sans-serif;
          font-size: 1.5em;
          text-align: center;
          line-height: 1.75em;
```

```
}
</STYLE>
```

3. Locate the subhead text within the file. Remove the <H2> elements high-lighted in the following code:

```
<!— Third Row contains sub-head —>
<TR><TD COLSPAN=3>
<H2 ALIGN="CENTER">Simple syntax, powerful design tool
</H2></TD>
</TR>
```

4. Replace the <H2> elements with <DIV> elements. Set the CLASS attribute to "subhead," as shown in the following code:

```
<DIV class="subhead">Simple syntax, powerful @Code in NL
2nd:design tool</DIV>
```

Figure 3-21 shows the result of the style rule.

Figure 3-21   The subhead style

Styling the Body Copy

The body copy is the article text in the columns. This text will display using the browser's default font. You will write a style rule to enhance the legibility of the text.

To style the body copy:

1. Write a style rule that selects the class named "copy". Set the line-height property to 1.25 em to aid the legibility of the text.

2. Set the text-indent property to 2 em to set an indent for each paragraph. The style rule follows:

   ```
   .copy {line-height: 1.25em; text-indent: 2em;}
   ```

3. Locate the <P> elements that contain the body copy.

4. Add CLASS attributes to the <P> elements, and specify "copy" as the attribute value, as shown in the following sample paragraph:

   ```
   <P CLASS="copy">Style sheets accomplish the separation of
   content and style that is integral to the open nature of
   data on the web. Currently, web page code mixes both
   document structure information and browser-based
   display properties, limiting the cross-platform
   compatibility of the content.</P>
   ```

Figure 3-22 shows the result of the style rule.

Adding a Small Caps Span

The final style to add is a <SPAN> element that contains the first few words of the article. You will use the font-variant property to set the words in small capitals.

To style the banner class:

1. Locate the first few words in the first paragraph of the article, as shown in the following code:

   ```
   <P CLASS="copy">Cascading Style Sheets (CSS) is a style
   language for the web. It uses common printing and
   display terminology to allow HTML and XML authors
   control over the way web pages look.</P>
   ```

2. Add the <SPAN> element around the selected words, as shown in the following code:

   ```
   <P CLASS="copy"><SPAN>Cascading Style Sheets (CSS)</SPAN>
   is a style language for the web. It uses common
   printing and display terminology to allow HTML and XML
   authors control over the way web pages look.</P>
   ```

Figure 3-22   The copy style

3. Add the style rule in a STYLE attribute to the <SPAN> element. Set the font-variant property to small-caps, as shown below:

```
<P CLASS="copy"><SPAN STYLE="font-variant: small-
caps;">Cascading Style Sheets (CSS)</SPAN> is a style
language for the web. It uses common printing and
display terminology to allow HTML and XML authors
control over the way web pages look.</P>
```

Figure 3-23 shows the result of the font-variant property.

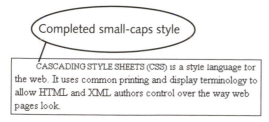

Figure 3-23   Adding small capitals

The finished Web page is shown in Figure 3-24.

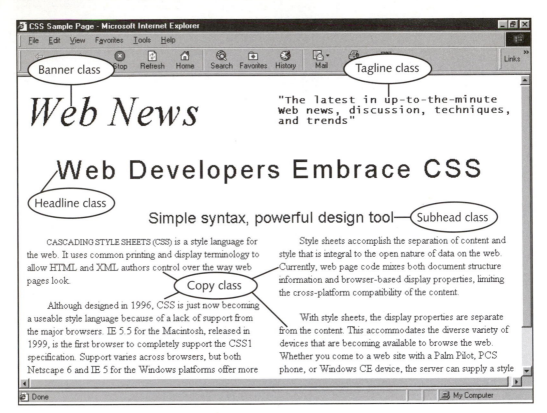

Figure 3-24   The finished Web page

CHAPTER SUMMARY

In this chapter, you learned how to control Web typography with CSS font and text spacing properties. You learned about different type considerations for the Web, including how to choose the correct fonts and plan for the legibility of your text. You saw how CSS provides a wide variety of different measurement values that adapt to different destination media. With the CSS font properties you learned how to control the appearance of text, including the font family, size, and weight. With the CSS text properties you saw how to manipulate the spacing around and within type text, allowing you to create interesting text effects. Finally, you applied combined font and text spacing properties to logical classes within an HTML document.

❑ Use type effectively by choosing available fonts and sizes. Design for legibility and use text to communicate information about the structure of your material.

◻ Choose the correct measurement unit based on the destination medium. For the computer screen, ems, pixels, or percentage measurements will scale to the user's preferences.

◻ Use the font properties to control the look of your letter forms. Specify font substitution values to ensure that your text displays properly across different platforms.

◻ The font shortcut property lets you combine a number of the font properties in one concise statement.

◻ Use the text spacing properties to create more visually interesting and legible text.

3

REVIEW QUESTIONS

1. What is the default browser font?

2. What are the three types of CSS measurement units?

3. What is the best destination for absolute units of measurement?

4. Why would you use relative or percentage values for a Web page?

5. What is the size of the em?

6. What determines the size of a pixel?

7. What selector would you use to set default text properties for a document?

8. What is the font size for the <H1> in the following style rules?

   ```
   DIV {font-size: 10pt}
   DIV H1 {font-size: 150%}
   ```

9. What is the advantage of the generic font families?

10. Write a font-family substitution string that selects Arial, Helvetica, or any sans-serif font for a <P> element.

11. Write a style rule for an <H2> element that specifies bold text that is twice the size of the default font size.

12. Rewrite the following rule using the font shortcut property:

    ```
    BLOCKQUOTE    {font-style:italic; font-size 12pt; line-
    height:18pt; font-family:times, serif}
    ```

13. How do you specify a hanging indent?

14. What is the distinguishing characteristic of justified text?

15. Why should you avoid underlining text on a Web page?

16. What is the common printing terms for line height and letter spacing?

17. What is a benefit of increasing the standard text line height?

18. What is the size of the text indent and line height in the following style rule?

    ```
    P {font-size: 12pt; text-indent:3em; line-height:150%}
    ```

HANDS-ON PROJECTS

1. Browse the Web and choose a site that you feel exhibits good typographic design. Write a short design critique of why the typographic techniques work effectively.

2. Browse the Web for examples of poor typographic design. Choose a Web page and write a short design critique of why the typographic techniques are confusing or difficult to read.

3. Expand upon the previous exercise by writing a design proposal for upgrading the existing design. Suggest new fonts, sizing, and spacing that will enhance the appearance of the content.

4. In this project you will have a chance to test the font and text properties on paragraphs of text. Save and view the file in your browser after completing each step.

    a. Using your HTML editor, create a simple HTML file (or open an existing file) that contains multiple <P> elements and so on. Save the file in your work folder as fonts1.htm.

    b. Add a <STYLE> element to the <HEAD> section, as shown in the following code.

    ```
    <HEAD>
    <TITLE>CSS Test Document</TITLE>
    <STYLE TYPE="text/css">

    </STYLE>
    </HEAD>
    ```

    c. Write a style rule that uses P as a selector and sets the font-family to a sans-serif font. You can use a generic font family, or choose one of the fonts available on your computer.

    d. Specify a list of alternate fonts to ensure that your font choice will display properly across a range of computers.

    e. Specify a text indent for the <P> elements. Use the em value as the measurement unit.

    f. Add the line-height property to the style rule. Experiment with different line heights until you find one that you feel enhances the legibility of the paragraph text.

5. In this project you will have a chance to test the font and text properties by building a customized heading element. Save and view the file in your browser after completing each step.

    a. Using your HTML editor, create a simple HTML file (or open an existing file) that contains at least one <H1> element. Save the file in your work folder as fonts2.htm.

    b. Add a <STYLE> element to the <HEAD> section, as shown in Exercise #4 previously.

3

   c. Write a rule that selects the <H1> element. Set the font size to 2.5 times the size of the default text.

   d. Add the font-variant property to the rule, and set the value to small-caps.

   e. Add the letter-spacing property to adjust the kerning of the heading. Set the value to 4 points. Experiment with different letter-spacing values until you are happy with the results.

6. In this project you will have a chance to test the font and text properties by building a series of style rules and applying them in a document using class names. You can use an existing HTML file of your own, or open any one of the book's supplied text files for this project.

   a. Define the logical classes for the file. Name the classes to reflect the usage of each class, such as heading, footnote, and so on.

   b. Build and test the style rules for the classes.

   c. Apply the classes to the document elements.

   d. Refine the styles until you are happy with the results.

   e. Submit both the finished Web page and an essay that describes the typographic choices you have made and why you made them and the different classes and their styles.

CASE STUDY

Design the type hierarchy for the project Web site. Create a type specification HTML page that shows examples of the different typefaces and sizes and how they will be used. This can be a mocked-up page that uses generic content but demonstrates the overall typographic scheme. Consider the following questions:

- What will be the style for the body type?

- How many levels of headings are necessary?

- What are the different weights and sizes of the headings?

- How will text be emphasized?

- Will hypertext links be standard or custom colors?

CHAPTER

4

USING THE BOX PROPERTIES

When you complete this chapter, you will be able to:

♦ Understand the CSS visual formatting model
♦ Use the margin properties
♦ Use the padding properties
♦ Use the border properties
♦ Use the special box properties to create floating elements

In this chapter, you will explore the CSS box properties. These properties let you control the margin, padding, and border characteristics of block-level elements. To understand how these properties work, you will first learn about the CSS visual formatting model and box model. These models control the way content is displayed on a Web page. Then you will learn about the margin, padding, and border properties and how you can use them to enhance the display of content in the browser. Finally, you will see how the special box properties—width, height, float, and clear—let you create floating elements.

THE VISUAL FORMATTING MODEL

The CSS **visual formatting model** describes how the element content boxes should be displayed by the browser. The visual formatting model is based on the hierarchical structure of the HTML document (see the "Introducing Cascading Style Sheets" chapter) and the element display type. In HTML, elements fall into three display type categories:

- **Block**: Block-level elements display visually as blocks, such as paragraphs. Block elements contain inline boxes that contain the element content.

- **Inline**: Inline-level elements contain the content within the block-level elements. They do not form new blocks of content.

- **List-item**: List-item elements create a surrounding containing box and list-item inline boxes.

Figure 4-1 shows three different block-level elements—<BODY>, <H1>, and <P>. The <H1> and <P> elements contain inline content boxes.

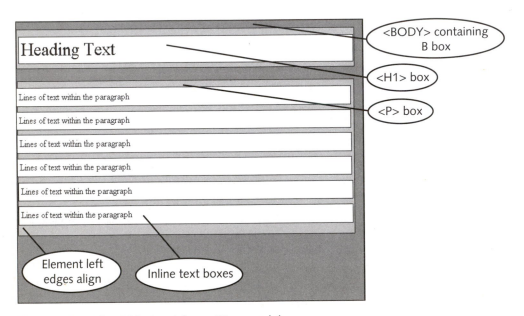

Figure 4-1 The CSS visual formatting model

Figure 4-1 also shows that parent elements contain child elements. The parent element is called the **containing box**. You can see that <BODY> is the containing box for the elements of a Web page. All other element boxes reside within <BODY>. In Figure 4-1, the <BODY> element is the containing box for the <H1> and <P> elements. The <P> element is the containing box for the inline text that comprises the paragraph text.

CSS lets you specify margin, border, and padding values for all block-level elements. In some instances, the values you specify will be dependent on the containing box that is the parent of the element you want to affect. For example, if you choose a percentage value for a margin, the percentage value is based on the containing box. In Figure 4-1, a 10% margin value for the <P> element would create margins that are 10% of the width of the containing box, in this case, the <BODY> element.

Specifying Element Display Type

display property description

Value: block | inline | list-item | none

Initial: inline

Applies to: all elements

Inherited: no

Percentages: N/A

The CSS display property determines the display type of an element. When you are working with HTML, you will probably not use the display property very often because the browser contains default element display information for each HTML element. For example, <H1>, <P>, and <BLOCKQUOTE> elements are block-level elements; <B> and <I> are inline elements. In most cases, you want the browser to display each element using the default element type. However, there may be times when you want to manipulate this property. The following style rule changes the default display type for an <H1> element from "block" to "inline."

```
H1 {display: inline;}
```

The result of this style rule is an <H1> element that behaves like an inline element, as shown in Figure 4-2.

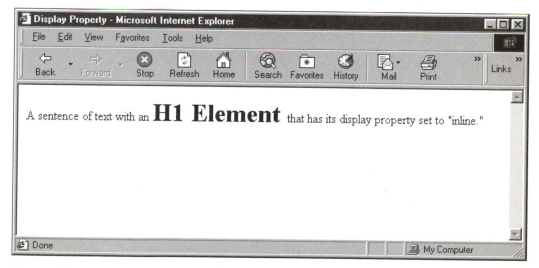

Figure 4-2   Manipulating the display property

The display property "none" value lets you hide an element so that it does not display in the browser. This could be useful in a style sheet where you may want to display only some of the information on a page.

CSS Box Model

The CSS **box model** describes the rectangular boxes that contain content on a Web page. Each block-level element you create is displayed as a box containing content in the browser window. Each content box can have margins, borders, and padding, as shown in Figure 4–3.

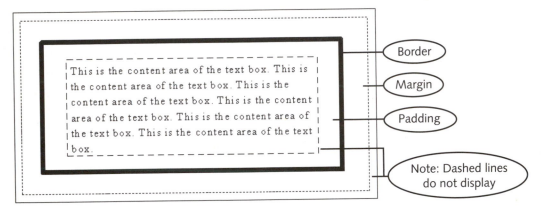

Figure 4-3   The CSS box model

As Figure 4–3 illustrates, the content box is the innermost box, surrounded by the padding, border, and margin areas. The padding area has the same background color as the content element, in which the margin area is always transparent. The border separates the padding and margin areas.

Figure 4-4 shows the box model areas in a paragraph element. This paragraph has 2-em padding, a thin black border, and 2-em margins. Notice that the margin area is transparent.

The following code shows the style rule for the paragraph in Figure 4-4:

```
P {   margin: 2em;
      padding: 2em;
      border: solid thin black;
      background: white;
  }
```

The margin and padding properties set the length to 2 em for all four sides of the box. The border property is a shorthand property (like the font property) that sets the border-style to solid, border-weight to thin, and border-color to black. The background property sets the paragraph background color to white. You will learn about the background properties in the "Using the Color and Background Properties" chapter.

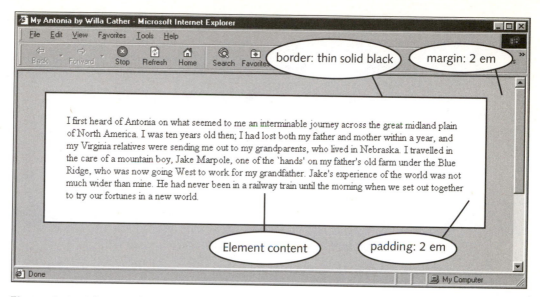

Figure 4-4   The CSS box model areas in a <P> element

CSS lets you specify margin, padding, and border properties individually for each side of the box. Figure 4-5 shows that each area has a left, right, top, and bottom side. Each one of the sides can be referred to individually. If the browser supports the individual properties, you can select, for example, the padding-bottom, border-top, or margin-left if you prefer. Netscape 4.x does not support the individual properties, but Opera 5.0, Netscape 6.0, and Internet Explorer 5.5 do.

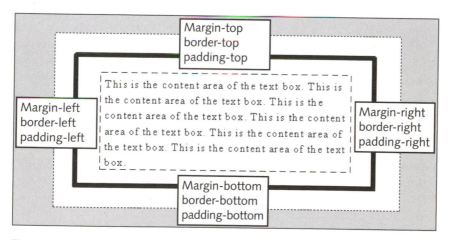

Figure 4-5   The CSS box model individual sides

Figure 4-6 shows the same paragraph with margin-left and margin-right set to 2 em, padding-left and padding-right set to 2 em, and border-left and border-right set to solid thin black.

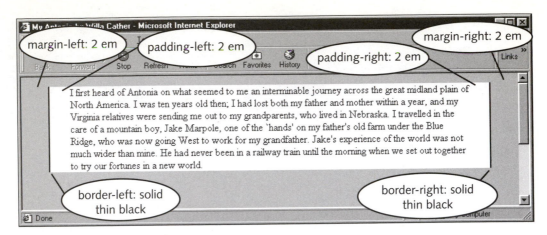

Figure 4-6   The CSS box model individual sides in a <P> element

The style rule for the paragraph follows:

```
P {    margin-left: 2em;
       margin-right: 2em;
       padding-left: 2em;
       padding-right: 2em;
       border-left: solid thin black;
       border-right: solid thin black;
       background: white;
   }
```

Measurement Values

The margin, border, and padding properties let you state two types of measurement values—either a length or a percentage. (For a full discussion of measurement values, see the "Using the Font and Text Properties" chapter.) If you use a percentage value, the percentage is based on the width of the containing box, as described previously. If you choose a length, you have to decide whether to use an absolute or relative value. As with font sizes, you are better off using relative units such as ems or pixels when you are stating margin, border, or padding sizes. The relative measurement values let you build scalable Web pages. In some instances, it's preferable to use the absolute values, such as the point, but these are generally more useful when you know the exact measurements of the output device.

Margin Properties

The margin properties let you control the margin area of the box model. Margins are always transparent, showing the background of their containing element. You can use margins to enhance the legibility of text, create indented elements, and add white space around images.

Specifying Margins

---

margin property description

Value: <length> | <percentage>

Initial: 0

Applies to: all elements

Inherited: no

Percentages: refer to width of containing block

The margin property is a shorthand property that lets you set all four individual margins with one property. You can specify either a length or percentage value. The most commonly supported usage of the margin property is to state one value for all four margin sides, as shown in the following style rule:

```
P {margin: 2em;}
```

You also can choose to state individual margin settings within this same rule. This can be confusing, because the individual margin settings change based on the order within the rule. Table 4-1 shows how the syntax works.

Table 4-1   Shorthand notation for margin property

Number of Values	Example	Description
1 value	P {margin: 1em}	All four margins will be 1 em
2 values	P {margin: 1em 2em}	Top and bottom margins will be 1 em; left and right margins will be 2 em
3 values	P {margin: 1em 2em 3em}	Top margin will be 1 em; right and left margins will be 2 em; bottom margin will be 3 em
4 values	P {margin: 1em 2em 3em 4em}	Top margin will be 1 em; right margin will be 2 em; bottom margin will be 3 em; left margin will be 4 em

To make your style rules more specific and easy to read, you can use the individual margin properties, such as margin-left, rather than the shorthand notation. The individual margin properties are described in the next section.

Figure 4-7 shows two paragraph elements. The first paragraph has the margin set to 2 em, and the second has the default margin setting.

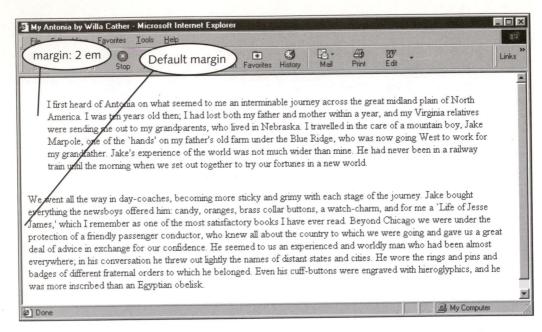

Figure 4-7   Using the margin property

Notice that the increased margins enhance the legibility of the text. However, only the horizontal margins on the left and right side of the paragraph are beneficial. The extra vertical margin between the paragraphs is too large and breaks up the flow of the text. To solve this problem, you can use the individual margin properties described next.

Specifying the Individual Margin Properties

> **margin-left, margin-right, margin-top, margin-bottom individual property descriptions**
>
> Value: \<length\>|\<percentage\>
>
> Initial: 0
>
> Applies to: all elements
>
> Inherited: no
>
> Percentages: refer to width of containing block

The individual margin properties let you control each of the individual margins: margin-left, margin-right, margin-top, and margin-bottom. The following style rule sets the left and right margins for the paragraph element:

```
P {    margin-left: 2em;
       margin-right: 2em;
}
```

As Figure 4-8 shows, both paragraphs now have the default vertical margins with 2-em left and right horizontal margins.

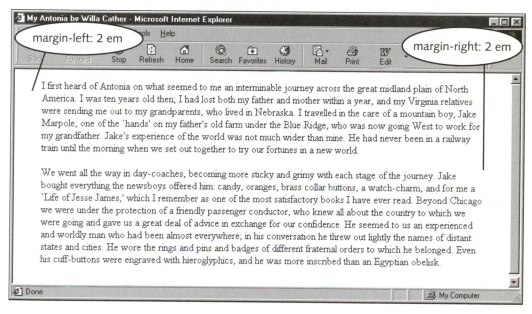

Figure 4-8   Using the individual margin properties

Negative Margins

You can set negative margin values to achieve special effects. For example, you can override the default browser margin by setting a negative value. Although it varies by browser, the default left margin is approximately 10 px. The following rule sets a negative value of –10 px:

```
P {margin-left: -10px;}
```

Figure 4-9 shows two paragraphs, one with the default margin and one with a negative margin.

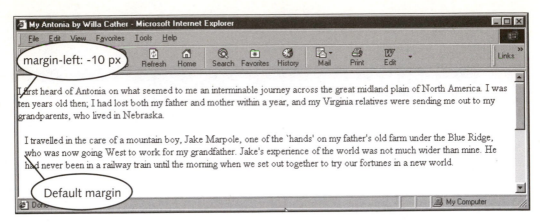

Figure 4-9 A <P> element with negative left margin

You can also use negative margins to remove the default margins from other elements. Figure 4-10 shows two <H1> elements, one with the default margins and one with the bottom margin set to a negative value.

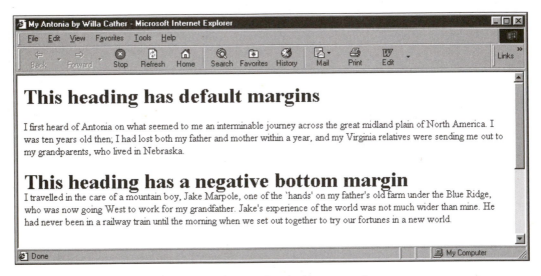

Figure 4-10 An <H1> element with negative bottom margin

Although neither of the above negative margin results really enhances the legibility of the text, you might someday encounter a design problem that requires a negative margin solution; it's helpful to know that CSS allows you to do this.

Collapsing Margins

To ensure that the spacing between block-level elements is consistent, the browser will collapse the vertical margins between elements. The vertical margins are the top and bottom element margins. The browser does not add the value of the two, but picks the greater value and applies it to the space between the adjoining elements. To illustrate this, consider the following rule:

```
P {margin-top: 15px; margin-bottom: 25px;}
```

If the browser did not collapse the vertical margins, the paragraphs would have 40 px of space between each paragraph. Instead, the browser collapses the margin. Following the CSS convention, the browser sets the vertical margin between paragraphs to 25 px, the greater of the two values. Figure 4-11 shows the results of collapsing the margins with the above style rule.

4

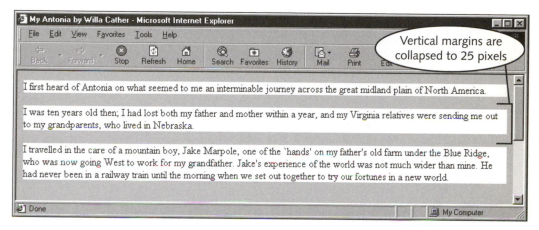

Figure 4-11   The browser collapses vertical margins

PADDING PROPERTIES

The CSS padding properties let you control the padding area in the box model. The padding area is between the element content and the border. The padding area inherits the background color of the element, so if a <P> element has a white background, the padding area will be white as well. If you add a border to an element, you will almost always want to use padding to increase the white space between the content and the border, as shown in Figure 4-12.

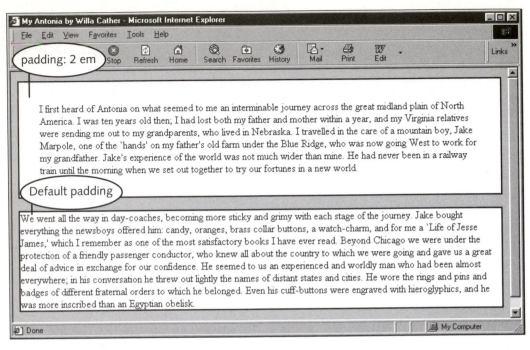

Figure 4-12   Default padding and 2-em padding

Specifying Padding

---

padding property description

Value: <length> | <percentage>

Initial: 0

Applies to: all elements

Inherited: no

Percentages: refers to width of containing block

The padding property is a shorthand property that lets you set all four individual padding values with one rule. You can specify either a length or a percentage value. Unlike margins, you cannot collapse the padding area or set negative padding values.

The most common usage of the padding property is to state one value for all four padding sides, as shown in the following style rule:

```
P {padding: 2em;}
```

You can also choose to state individual padding settings in the padding property. Like the margin shorthand property described previously, the individual padding settings change based on the order within the rule. Table 4-2 shows how the syntax works.

Table 4-2   Shorthand notation for padding property

Number of Values	Example	Description
1 value	P { padding: 1em}	All four side's padding will be 1 em
2 values	P { padding: 1em 2em}	Top and bottom padding will be 1 em; left and right padding will be 2 em
3 values	P { padding: 1em 2em 3em}	Top padding will be 1 em; right and left padding will be 2 em; bottom padding will be 3 em
4 values	P { padding: 1em 2em 3em 4em}	Top padding will be 1 em; right padding will be 2 em; bottom padding will be 3 em; left padding will be 4 em

Specifying the Individual Padding Properties

---

padding-left, padding-right, padding-top, padding-bottom individual property descriptions

Value: <length> | <percentage>

Initial: 0

Applies to: all elements

Inherited: no

Percentages: refer to width of containing block

The individual padding properties let you control the individual padding areas: padding-left, padding-right, padding-top, and padding-bottom. The following style sets the top and bottom padding areas for the paragraph, along with complementing borders and a white background:

```
P {   padding-top: 2em;
      padding-bottom: 2em;
      border-top: solid thin black;
      border-bottom: solid thin black;
      background-color: #ffffff;
}
```

As Figure 4-13 shows, the paragraph now has the default left and right padding with 2-em top and bottom padding.

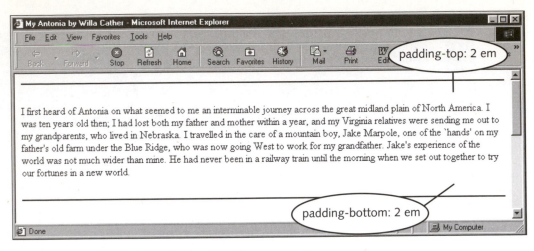

Figure 4-13   Using the individual padding properties

BORDER PROPERTIES

The border properties let you control the appearance of borders around elements. The border area resides between the margin and padding. You can set 20 border properties, many of which are too specific for common use. You will most likely use the five border shorthand properties, which include:

- border
- border-left
- border-right
- border-top
- border-bottom

These shorthand properties let you state border-style, border-color, and border-width for all four borders or for any of the individual sides of the box. However, you can also state much more specific borders by using the border properties separately. Table 4-3 lists the entire range of 20 border properties.

Table 4-3   Border properties

Description	Property Name		
Overall shorthand property	border		
Individual side shorthand properties	border-left, border-top, border-right, border-bottom		
Specific shorthand property	border-style	border-width	border-color
Individual properties	border-left-style border-right-style border-top-style border-bottom-style	border-left-width border-right-width border-top-width border-bottom-width	border-left-color border-right-color border-top-color border-bottom-color

To use the shorthand properties you must first understand the three border characteristics—border style, border color, and border width. Then you will learn how to use the border shorthand properties.

Specifying Border Style

border-style property description

Value: <border-style>

Initial: none

Applies to: all elements

Inherited: no

Percentages: N/A

The border-style is the most important border property because it must be stated to make a border appear. The border-style property lets you choose from one of the following border style keywords:

- none – no border on the element; this is the default setting

- dotted – dotted border

- dashed – dashed border

- solid – solid line border

- double – double line border

- groove – 3-dimensional border that appears to be embossed into the page

- ridge – 3-dimensional border that appears to extend outward from the page

- inset – 3-dimensional border that appears to set the entire box into the page

- outset – 3-dimensional border that appears to extend the entire box outward from the page

The following code shows an example of the border-style property in use:

```
P {border-style: solid;}
```

Figure 4-14 shows examples of the borders. The gray background for this page enhances the display of the 3-dimensional styles, which do not look the same on a white background. Not all borders are supported by all browsers, so test your work carefully. If you specify a border style that is not supported, the border will default to solid.

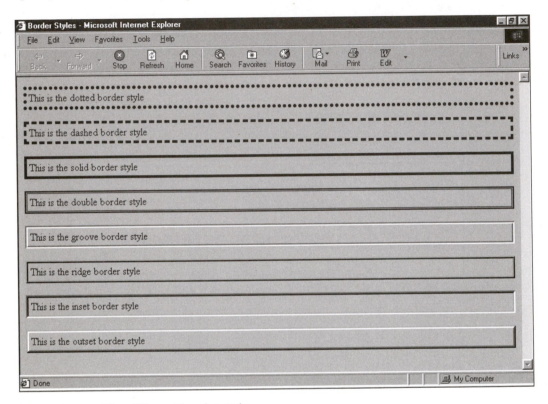

Figure 4-14   The different border styles

You can also choose to state border styles for individual sides using the border-style property. The individual border style settings change based on the order within the rule. Table 4-4 shows how the syntax works.

Table 4-4   Shorthand notation for border-style property

Number of Values	Example	Description
1 value	`P {border-style: solid}`	All four borders will be solid
2 values	`P {border-style: solid double}`	Top and bottom borders will be solid; left and right borders will be double
3 values	`P {border-style: solid double dashed}`	Top border will be solid; right and left borders will be double; bottom border will be dashed
4 values	`P {border-style: solid double dashed dotted}`	Top border will be solid; right border will be double; bottom border will be dashed; left border will be dotted

4

Of course, if you examine the rules in Table 4-4, you can see they will create odd effects. For example, a paragraph with a different border style for each side is not a common design technique. Remember to use restraint and keep the user in mind when working with border styles.

Individual Border Styles

You can also specify individual borders styles with the following border-style properties:

- border-left-style
- border-right-style
- border-top-style
- border-bottom-style

These properties let you single out one border and apply a style. The following rule applies only to the left border of the element:

```
P {border-left-style: double;}
```

Specifying Border Width

border-width property description

Value: thin | medium | thick | <length>

Initial: medium

Applies to: all elements

Inherited: no

Percentages: N/A

The border-width property lets you state the width of the border with either a keyword or a length value. You can use the following keywords to express width:

- thin
- medium (default)
- thick

The width of the rule when you use these keywords is based on the browser. The length values let you state an absolute or relative value for the border; percentages are not allowed. Using a length value lets you create anything from a hairline to a very thick border. The following code shows an example of the border-width property in use:

```
P {border-width: 1px; border-style: solid;}
```

Remember that the border will not display unless the border-style property is stated. Figure 4-15 shows examples of different border widths.

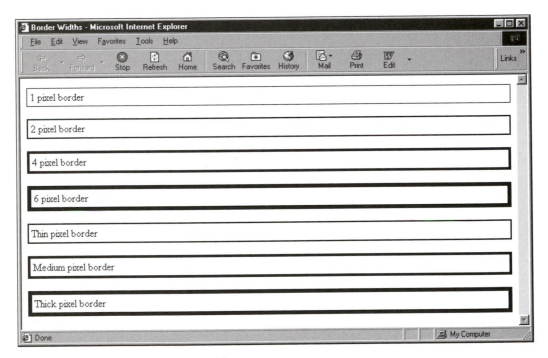

Figure 4-15   Different border widths

You can also choose to state individual border widths in the border-width property. The individual border width settings change based on the order within the rule. Table 4-5 shows how the syntax works.

Table 4-5   Shorthand notation for border-width property

Number of Values	Example	Description
1 value	`P {border-width: 1px}`	All four borders will be 1 pixel wide
2 values	`P {border-width: 1px 2px}`	Top and bottom borders will be 1 pixel wide; left and right borders will be 2 pixels wide
3 values	`P {border-width: 1px 2px 3px}`	Top border will be 1 pixel wide; right and left borders will be 2 pixels wide; bottom border will be 3 pixels wide
4 values	`P {border-width: 1px 2px 3px 4px}`	Top border will be 1 pixel wide; right border will be 2 pixels wide; bottom border will be 3 pixels wide; left border will be 4 pixels wide

Individual Border Widths

You can also specify individual borders widths with the following border-width properties:

- border-left-width
- border-right-width
- border-top-width
- border-bottom-width

These properties let you single out one border and apply a width. The following rule applies only to the left border of the element:

```
P {border-left-width: thin;}
```

Specifying Border Color

border-color property description

Value: <color>

Applies to: all elements

Inherited: no

Percentages: N/A

The border-color element lets you set the color of the element border. The value can be either a hexadecimal value, RGB value, or one of the 16 predefined color names listed in Table 4-6. You will learn about hexadecimal and RGB color values in the "Using the Color and Background Properties" chapter.

Table 4-6 Predefined color names

Aqua	Navy	Gray	Silver
Black	Olive	Green	Teal
Blue	Purple	Lime	White
Fuschia	Red	Maroon	Yellow

To set a border color, use the property as shown in the following rule:

```
P {border-color: red; border-width: 1px;
border-style: solid;}
```

The default border color is the color of the element content. For example, the following style rule sets the element color to red. The border will also be red because a border color is not specified.

```
P {color: red; font: 12pt arial; border: solid;}
```

You can also choose to state individual border colors in the border-color property. The individual border color settings change based on the order within the rule. Table 4-7 shows how the syntax works.

Table 4-7 Shorthand notation for border-color property

Number of Values	Example	Description
1 value	P {border-color: black}	All four borders will be black
2 values	P {border-color: black red}	Top and bottom borders will be black; left and right borders will be red
3 values	P {border-color: black red green}	Top border will be black; right and left borders will be red; bottom border will be green
4 values	P {border-color: black red green blue}	Top border will be black; right border will be red; bottom border will be green; left border will be blue

Individual Border Colors

You can also specify individual border colors with the following border-color properties:

- border-left-color
- border-right-color
- border-top-color
- border-bottom-color

These properties let you single out one border and apply a color. The following rule applies only to the left border of the element:

```
P {border-left-color: red; border-style: solid;}
```

Using the Border Shorthand Properties

The shorthand properties are the most common and easiest way to express border characteristics. When you use these shorthand properties, you are stating the style, color, and width of the border in one concise rule.

4

Specifying Borders

> **border property description**
>
> Value: <border-width> | <border-style> | <color>
> Initial: see individual properties
> Applies to: all elements
> Inherited: no
> Percentages: N/A

The border property lets you state the properties for all four borders of the element. You can state the border-width, border-style, and border-color in any order. Border-style must be included for the border to appear. If you do not include border-width, the width will default to medium. If you do not include border-color, the border will appear in the same color as the element. The following example rules show different uses of the border property.

The following rule sets the border style to solid. The border weight defaults to medium. The border color will be the same as the color of the <P> element. Because no color is stated, the border color will be black.

```
P {border: solid;}
```

The following rule sets the border style to solid. The border weight is 1 px. The border color will be red.

```
P {border: solid 1px red;}
```

The following rule sets the border style to double. The border weight is thin. The border color will be blue. Notice that the order of the values does not matter.

```
P {border: double blue thin;}
```

Specifying Individual Borders

---

border-top, border-right, border-bottom, border-left individual property descriptions

Value: <border-top-width> || <border-style> || <color>

Initial: see individual properties

Applies to: all elements

Inherited: no

Percentages: N/A

You can set individual border properties using the individual border shorthand properties. These let you state border-style, border-width, and border-color in one statement that selects a single element border. For example, the following rule sets the border style to solid and the border weight to thin for both the left and right borders. Because no color is stated, the borders default to the element color.

```
P {border-left: solid thin; border-right: solid thin;}
```

The following rule sets the border style to double and the border color to red for the top border. Because no border weight is stated, the weight defaults to medium.

```
P {border-top: double red;}
```

SPECIAL BOX PROPERTIES

The special box properties let you float an image or box of text to the left or right of content on the page. You can use these properties to create newspaper-type layouts where text can flow around the floated box, as shown in Figure 4-16. You will also use these properties when you use the CSS positioning properties (described in the "Using the Positioning Properties" chapter).

In this section, you will learn about the following special box properties:

- width
- height
- float
- clear

After you have learned about the four properties, you will see how they are used to create a floating text box, like the one shown in Figure 4-16.

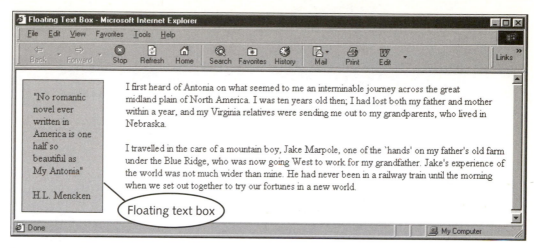

Figure 4-16   A floating text box

Width

> **width property description**
>
> Value: <length> | <percentage>
>
> Initial: auto
>
> Applies to: all elements but nonreplaced inline elements, table rows, and row groups
>
> Inherited: no
>
> Percentages: refer to width of containing block

The width property lets you set the horizontal width of an element. Width is not intended for normal block-level elements, but you can use it to create floating text boxes or positioned elements (see the "Using the Positioning Properties" chapter). In most cases, you will set the padding or margins of the elements rather than explicitly stating a width.

The width property accepts either a length value or a percentage. The percentage value is based on the width of the containing element box. By default, the value of width is set to auto, which is based on the content of the element minus the padding, border, and margins if applicable. The following is an example of width property usage:

```
DIV {width: 200px;}
```

Use percentages or relative measurement values, such as pixels, to ensure that your widths will be portable across different screen resolutions.

Height

> **height property description**
>
> Value: <length> | <percentage>
> Initial: auto
> Applies to: all elements but nonreplaced inline elements, table columns,
> and column groups
> Inherited: no
> Percentages: N/A

The height property lets you set the vertical height of an element. Like width, height is not intended for normal block-level elements, but you can use it to create floating text boxes or with images. In most cases, you will set the padding or margins of the elements rather than explicitly stating a height.

The height property accepts either a length value or a percentage. The percentage value is based on the height of the containing element box. By default, the value of height is set to auto, which is based on the content of the element minus the padding, border, and margins if applicable. The following is an example of height property usage:

```
DIV {height: 150px;}
```

Float

> **float property description**
>
> Value: left | right | none
> Initial: none
> Applies to: all elements except positioned elements and generated content (see
> Appendix B "Generated Content")
> Inherited: no
> Percentages: N/A

The float property lets you position an element to the left or right edge of its parent element. Float is most commonly used for <IMG> elements, allowing alignment of an image to the left or right of text. You can also use the float property to align a text box to the left or right edge of its parent.

Floating Images

The float property can be used to float an image to the left or right of text. The following style rules create two classes of <IMG> elements, one of which floats to the left of text; the other floats to the right.

```
img.left {float: left;}
img.right {float: right;}
```

You can apply these rules to an image using the CLASS attribute within the <IMG> element, as shown in the following code fragment:

```
<IMG SRC="sample.gif" CLASS="left">
```

Figure 4-17 shows two floating images within a page.

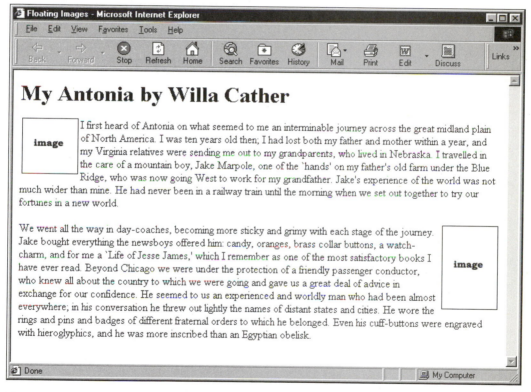

Figure 4-17   Floating images

Floating Text Boxes

The float property can also be used to float a text box to the left or right of text. Used with the width and height properties, you can create a text box of the type shown in Figure 4-18. The advantage to this type of layout is that no HTML tables are used to create the design; rather a simple CSS rule is all that is necessary.

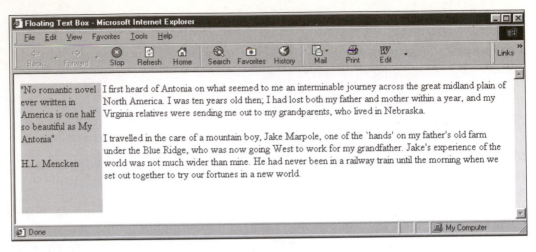

Figure 4-18   Floating text box

The rule for the left-floating text box looks like this:

```
.floatbox {width: 125px;
          height: 200px;
          float: left;
          background-color: #CCCCCC; /* gray */
             }
```

This rule states a class named "floatbox." The rule sets the width, height, and float properties of the element and sets the background color to a hexadecimal color value that is a light gray.

The class "floatbox" can then be applied to an element in the document. The code from the document follows. The "floatbox" class is applied to the first <P> element.

```
<BODY>
<P class="floatbox">
"No romantic novel ever written in America is one half so
beautiful as My Antonia"<BR><BR>H.L. Mencken
</P>
<P>I first heard of Antonia on what seemed to me an
interminable journey across the great midland plain of North
America. I was ten years old then; I had lost both my
father and mother within a year, and my Virginia
relatives were sending me out to my grandparents, who
lived in Nebraska.</P>
<P>
I traveled in the care of a mountain boy, Jake Marpole,
one of the 'hands' on my father's old farm under the Blue
Ridge, who was now going West to work for my grandfather.
Jake's experience of the world was not much wider than
mine. He had never been in a railway train until the
```

```
morning when we set out together to try our fortunes in a
new world.
</P>
</BODY>
```

The float box can be enhanced by adding some of the other properties you learned about in this chapter. The following rule adds 1-em padding for the entire element, a 2-em right margin, and a 1-px solid black rule.

```
.floatbox    {
              width: 125px;
              height: 200px;
              float: left;
              background-color: #CCCCCC; /* gray */
              padding: 1em;
              margin-right: 2em;
              border: solid black 1px;

}
```

The enhanced float box is much more legible and enhances the page layout. Figure 4-19 shows the result of the new properties added to the rule.

Float is supported by Internet Explorer 5.x, Opera 5.0, and Netscape 6. The float property is not supported in Internet Explorer 4.0 or Netscape 4.x.

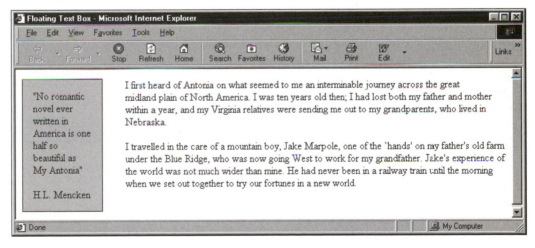

Figure 4-19   The enhanced floating text box

Clear

---

clear property description

Value: none | left | right | both

Applies to: block-level elements

Inherited: no

Percentages: N/A

The clear property lets you control the flow of text around floated elements. You will only use the clear property when you are using the float property. Clear lets you force text to appear beneath a floated element, rather than next to it. Figure 4-20 shows an example of normal text flow around an element.

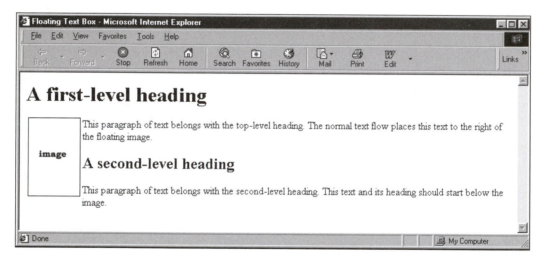

Figure 4-20   Normal text flow around a floating image

This figure shows an image with the float property set to "left." The text flows down around the image on the right, which is the correct behavior. The second-level heading and paragraph, however, do not appear in the correct position. They should be positioned beneath the floating image. To correct this problem, use the clear property. In this instance, the <H2> should display clear of any left-floating images. Add this style rule directly to the <H2> element with the style attribute as follows:

```
<H2 STYLE="clear: left;">
```

Figure 4-21 shows the result of adding the clear property.

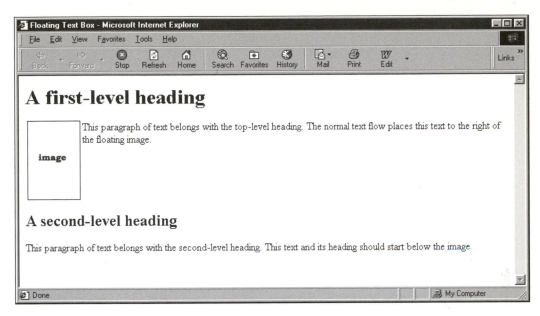

Figure 4-21   Using the clear property

The code for this page follows:

```
<HTML>
<HEAD>
<TITLE>Floating Text Box</TITLE>
<STYLE TYPE="text/css">
IMG.left {float: left;}
</STYLE>
</HEAD>
<BODY>
<H1>A first-level heading</H1>
<P>
<IMG SRC="120pximg.gif" class="left">This paragraph of
text belongs with the top-level heading. The normal text
flow places this text to the right of the floating image.
</P>
<H2 STYLE="clear: left;">A second-level heading</H2>
<P>
This paragraph of text belongs with the second-level
heading. This text and its heading should start below the
image.
</P>
</BODY>
</HTML>
```

Notice that the clear property lets you clear from either left- or right-floating images using the "left" and "right" values. The "both" value lets you control text flow in the event you have floating images on both the left and right sides of the text.

APPLYING THE BOX PROPERTIES

In the following steps, you have a chance to apply some of the properties you learned about in this chapter. As you work through the steps, refer to Figure 4-22 to see the results you will achieve. Save your file, and test your work in the browser as you complete each step.

To apply the box properties:

1. Open the file **boxtest.htm** in your HTML editor, and save it in your work folder as **boxtest1.htm**.

2. In your browser, open the file **boxtest1.htm**. When you open the file, it looks like Figure 4-22. Notice the text in the file is Latin filler text.

Figure 4-22   The original HTML document

3. Examine the code. Notice the <STYLE> section of the file. It contains three basic style rules that center the <H1>, <H2>, and <H3> element. The complete code for the page follows:

```
<HTML>
<HEAD>
<TITLE>CSS Sample Page</TITLE>
<STYLE TYPE="text/css">
H1 {text-align: center;}
H2 {text-align: center;}
H3 {text-align: center;}
</STYLE>
```

```
</HEAD>
<BODY>
<H1>Web News</H1>
<H2>Web Developers Embrace CSS</H2>
<H3>Simple syntax, powerful design tool</H3>
<P>This is the first line of the article. This is the
rest of the copy. Lorem ipsum dolor sit amet,
consectetuer adipiscing elit, sed diem nonummy nibh
euismod tincidunt ut lacreet dolore magna aliguam erat
volutpat.  Ut wisis enim ad minim veniam quis nostrud
exerci tution ullamcorper suscipit lobortis nisl ut
aliquip ex ea commodo consequat.
</P>
<P>Lorem ipsum dolor sit amet, consectetuer adipiscing el
it, sed diem nonummy nibh euismod tincidunt ut lacreet do
lore magna aliguam erat volutpat.  Ut wisis enim ad minim
veniam quis nostrud exerci tution ullamcorper suscipit
lobortis nisl ut aliquip ex ea commodo consequat.</P>
</BODY>
</HTML>
</STYLE>
```

4. Start by styling the <H1> element with a 1-em margin. Add the margin property to the existing <H1> style rule:

```
H1 {text-align: center; margin: 1em;}
```

5. The <H2> element has a bottom-margin of 1 em. Add this property to the existing style rule:

```
H2 {text-align: center; margin-bottom: 1em;}
```

6. The <H3> has the most complex style effects, so break the style rule into separate lines. Start by adding .5 em of padding to the top and bottom of the element. Add the properties to the existing style rule:

```
H3 {  text-align: center;
      padding-top: .5em;
      padding-bottom: .5em;
}
```

7. Now add top and bottom borders to the <H3>. Set the style to solid and the weight to thin. Because the finished rules are black, you do not have to state a color:

```
H3 {  text-align: center;
      padding-top: .5em;
      padding-bottom: .5em;
      border-top: solid thin;
      border-bottom: solid thin;
}
```

8. Finish the <H3> by setting the left and right margins to 40 px:

```
H3 {   text-align: center;
       padding-top: .5em;
       padding-bottom: .5em;
       border-top: solid thin;
       border-bottom: solid thin;
       margin-left: 40px;
       margin-right: 40px;
}
```

9. Finish styling the document by setting the <P> left and right margins to 40 px to line up with the borders of the <H3>:

```
P {margin-left: 40px; margin-right: 40px;}
```

10. Figure 4-23 shows the results of the style rules.

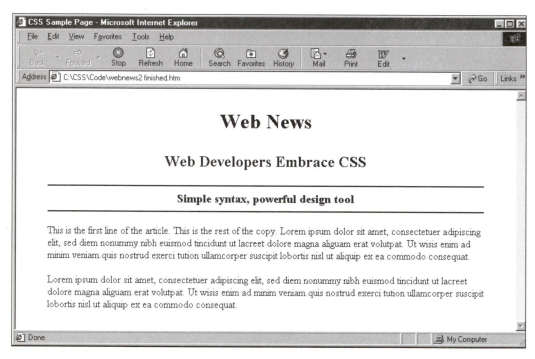

Figure 4-23   The finished Web page

CHAPTER SUMMARY

In this chapter, you learned about the concepts of the CSS box and visual formatting models. You saw how the margin, padding, and border properties let you control the space around block-level elements on a Web page. By using these properties judiciously, you can enhance the legibility of your content. You also learned how the special box properties let you create interesting text effects, like floating text boxes, without the use of HTML table elements.

❏ The CSS box model lets you control spacing around the element content.

❏ You can state values of margin, border, and padding for all four sides of the box or individual sides.

❏ To build scalable Web pages, choose relative length units such as ems or pixels.

❏ The browser collapses vertical margins to ensure even spacing between elements.

❏ Margins are transparent, showing the color of the containing element's background color. Padding takes on the color of the element to which it belongs.

❏ The border properties let you add borders to all individual sides or all four sides of an element. The three border characteristics are style, color, and width. Style must be stated to make the border appear.

❏ The special box properties let you create floating images or text boxes.

❏ Remember to use margin, border, and padding properties judiciously to enhance the legibility of your content, rather than just for novelty effects.

REVIEW QUESTIONS

1. What are the three space areas in the box model?
2. Which space area is transparent?
3. What does the visual formatting model describe?
4. What is the visual formatting model based on?
5. What are percentage measurement values based on?
6. What are the preferred length units for margins and padding?
7. In the following rule, what is the size of the vertical margins between paragraphs?

```
P {margin-top: 15px; margin-bottom: 10px;}
```

8. Where is the padding area located?
9. What are the five most common border properties?
10. What is the default border style?
11. What is the default border weight?
12. What is the default border color?
13. What are the two types of color values?
14. What does the float property let you do?
15. What does the clear element let you do?
16. Write a style rule for a <P> element that sets margins to 2 em, padding to 1 em, and a black solid 1-px border.

17. Write a style rule for an <H1> element that sets top and bottom padding to .5 em with a dashed thin red border on the bottom.

18. Write a style rule for a <P> element that creates left and right padding of 1 em, a left margin of 30 px, and a left double black medium border.

HANDS-ON PROJECTS

1. Browse the Web and choose a site that you feel exhibits good handling of white space to increase the legibility of the content. Write a short design critique of why the white space works effectively.

2. Browse the Web and choose a site that can benefit from the box properties available in CSS. Print out a copy of the page, and indicate where you would change the spacing and border properties. Write a short essay that describes the changes you want to achieve and how they increase the legibility of the page content.

3. In this exercise, you will create a floating text box.

    a. Open the file **float.htm** in your HTML editor, and save it in your work folder as **float1.htm**.

    b. In your browser, open the file **float1.htm**. When you open the file, it looks like Figure 4-24.

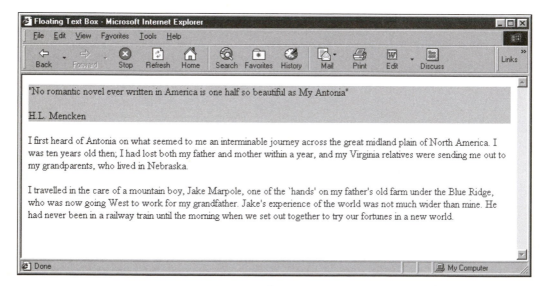

Figure 4-24   The original HTML file for Project 3

    c. Examine the page code. Notice that there is an existing style rule that sets a background color for a class "floatbox," as shown in the following code fragment:

```
.floatbox    {background-color:#cccccc;}
```

d. This class is applied to the first <P> element in the document, as shown in Figure 4-24. Your goal is to use a variety of box properties to create a finished page that looks like Figure 4-25.

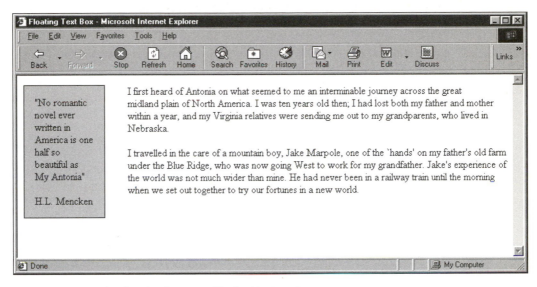

Figure 4-25   The finished HTML file for Project 3

e. You will need to use the following properties to create the finished floating text box:

- ◻ width
- ◻ height
- ◻ float
- ◻ padding
- ◻ margin-right
- ◻ border

f. Experiment with the different properties until you achieve results that look as close to the finished page as possible.

4. In this exercise, you will create floating images.

a. Open the file **floatimg.htm** in your HTML editor, and save it in your work folder as **floatimg1.htm**.

b. Copy the image **testimg.gif** into your work folder, or the image will not display in the browser.

c. In your browser, open the file **floatimg1.htm**. When you open the file, it looks like Figure 4-26.

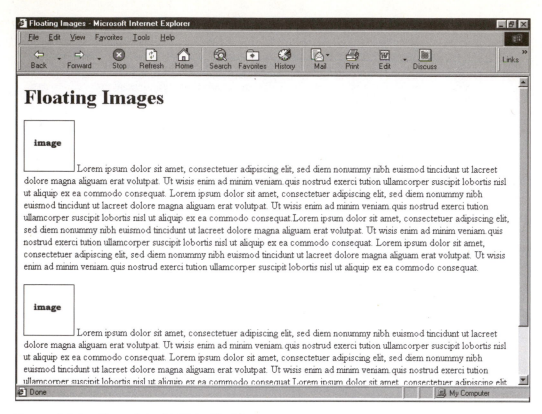

Figure 4-26 The original HTML file for Project 4

   d. Your goal is to use the float and margin properties to achieve the results shown in Figure 4–27.

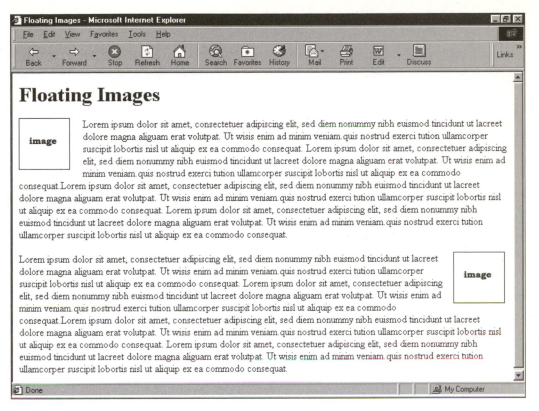

Figure 4-27   The finished HTML file for Project 4

    e. Create class names such as the following for the two different types of images:

```
img.left
img.right
```

    f. Experiment with the different properties until you achieve results that look as close to the finished page as possible.

5. In this project, you will have a chance to test the border properties. Save and view the file in your browser after completing each step.

    a. Using your HTML editor, create a simple HTML file (or open an existing file) that contains heading and paragraph elements. Save the file in your work folder as **borders.htm**.

    b. Add a <STYLE> element to the <HEAD> section, as shown in the following code:

```
:<HEAD>
<TITLE>CSS Test Document</TITLE>
<STYLE TYPE="text/css">

</STYLE>
</HEAD>
```

c. Experiment with the different border styles. Start by applying any of the following style rules to your document's elements:

```
H1 {border: solid 1px black;}
H2 {border-top: solid 1px; border-bottom: solid 3px;}
P {border-left: double red; border-right: solid 1px;}
```

d. Experiment with adding padding properties to your style rules to offset the borders from the text. The following style rules have sample padding properties to try:

```
H1 {border: solid 1px black; padding: 20px;}
H2 {border-top: solid 1px; border-bottom:
solid 3px; padding-top 15px; padding-bottom; 30px;}
P {border-left: double red; border-right: solid 1px;
padding-left: 30px; padding-right: 20px;}
```

e. Continue to experiment with the border and padding properties. Try adding color and margin properties to see how the elements display. Save your file when you're finished.

CASE STUDY

Create the box element spacing conventions for your Web site. Build on the typographic classes you created in the "Using the Font and Text Properties" chapter. Think about the different spacing requirements for your content, and decide how the legibility can be enhanced using the box properties. Add this information to the type specification HTML page that shows examples of the different typefaces and sizes and how they will be used. Decide on margins, padding, and borders and which elements will benefit from their use. Create before and after sample HTML pages that reflect the enhanced design.

5

COLOR AND BACKGROUNDS

When you complete this chapter, you will be able to:

♦ Understand the basics of computer color and its variable nature in the Web environment

♦ Express color values using a color name, hexadecimal value, or RGB value

♦ Use the color property to specify the color of element content and link colors

♦ Use the background properties to set background color, images, and background image position

In this chapter, you will explore the CSS color and background properties. These properties let you control the text color and backgrounds of any element on a Web page. The CSS color property replaces the obsolete <FONT> element in HTML and gives you much more precise control over element color on your Web pages. The CSS background properties provide far greater control over background images than was previously available with the HTML background attribute. You can now control the tiling and positioning of images in the background of a Web page or any element contained within the page. Along with the precision that CSS provides with these properties comes a measure of responsibility as well. Remember to choose colors and backgrounds that enhance, not degrade, the presentation of your content.

WORKING WITH COLOR

A computer monitor displays color by mixing three basic colors of light: red, green, and blue. Each of these three basic colors is called a **color channel**. The monitor can express a range of intensity for each color channel, from 0 (absence of color) to 100% (full intensity of color). With the CSS color properties, you can select a specific color from the range of colors the monitor can display. Colors are relative to the specific environment in which they are viewed. What looks like red on one monitor can look orange on another monitor. Colors vary widely based on monitor location, the user's individual preferences, and equipment brand.

The range of colors a computer monitor can display is based on the color depth of the monitor. The **color depth** is the amount of data used to create the color. Most computer monitors can display 8-bit, 16-bit, and 24-bit color depths. The higher the color depth, the more colors the monitor can display. The problem when choosing colors for a Web page is that you never know the color depth of the user's monitor. If you specify a color that the monitor does not support, the browser will attempt to mix the color, which can create unreliable results. Therefore, you should use colors that will appear correctly at different color depths and on different monitor types. The palette of colors that will display faithfully is called the **browser-safe palette**. This palette contains 216 colors that display properly across both PC and Macintosh platforms at the lowest color depth setting. The Companion Web site contains links to a variety of Web sites and tools that will help you specify and use browser-safe colors.

Because of the variable nature of color on the Web, be sure to test the colors you choose, and use restraint when adding color to your design. Remember that colors will not look the same on different monitor brands and operating systems. When used properly, color can enhance the presentation of your information, providing structural and navigation cues to your user. Conversely, poor use of color distracts from your content and can annoy your users. Dark backgrounds, clashing colors, and unreadable links are just a few examples of the unrestrained use of the HTML color attributes that are common on the Web. Because CSS allows you to easily apply color to any element does not mean that you should apply color haphazardly. Remember that many of your users might have accessibility issues that prevent them from seeing color the way you do. The user's ability to navigate, read, and interact with your content should always determine the choices and use of color in a Web site.

Specifying CSS Color Values

In this section, you will learn about the different ways to express color using CSS properties. CSS lets you specify color values in one of three ways:

- Color names
- RGB color values
- Hexadecimal color values

Which color value method should you use? Hexadecimal numbers probably should be your first choice because they are already supported by most browsers. Both hexadecimal and RGB values are more specific and let you express a wider range of color than the color names. Whichever method you choose, make sure to use that method consistently throughout your entire Web site.

Using Color Names

The color name values let you quickly state color using common names. The valid CSS color name values are the 16 basic color names stated in the W3C HTML 4.0 specification, listed in Table 5-1.

Table 5-1   Color names recognized by most browsers (bolded colors are browser safe)

Color Name	Hex	Color Name	Hex	Color Name	Hex
Aqua	**00FFFF**	**Lime**	**00FF00**	Silver	C0C0C0
Black	**000000**	Maroon	800000	Teal	008080
Blue	**0000FF**	Navy	000080	**White**	**FFFFFF**
Fuschia	**FF00FF**	Olive	808000	**Yellow**	**FFFF00**
Gray	808080	Purple	800080		
Green	008000	**Red**	**FF0000**		

Although the color names are easy to use, they allow only a small range of color expression. To use a wider variety of available color, you must use a more specific value, such as RGB or hexadecimal.

Using RGB Colors

The RGB color model is used to specify numerical values that express the blending of the red, green, and blue color channels. When you specify RGB values, you are mixing the three basic colors to create a fourth color. Each of the three color channels can be specified in range from 0 to 100%, with 0 representing the absence of the color, and 100% representing the full brilliance of the color. If all three values are set to 0, the resulting color is black, which is the absence of all color. If all three color values are set to 100%, the resulting color is white, which is the inclusion of all colors.

The syntax for specifying RGB is the keyword rgb followed by three numerical values in parentheses—the first for red, the second for green, the third for blue. The following rule states a percentage RGB value:

```
P {color: rgb(0, 100%, 100%);}
```

RGB color values can be specified as an integer value as well. The integer scale ranges from 0 to 255 with 255 equal to 100%. The following rules specify the same color:

```
P {color: rgb(0%, 100%, 100%);} /* percentages */
P {color: rgb(0, 255, 255);}  /* integers */
```

5

Using Hexadecimal Colors

HTML uses hexadecimal numbers to express RGB color values, and you can use them in CSS as well. Hexadecimal numbers are a base-16 numbering system, so the numbers run from 0 through 9 and then A through F. When compared to standard base-10 numbers, hexadecimal values look strange because they include letters in the numbering scheme. Hexadecimal color values are six-digit numbers; the first two define the red value, the second two define the green, and the third two define the blue. The hexadecimal scale ranges from 00 to FF with FF equal to 100%. Hexadecimal values are always preceded by a pound sign (#). The following rules specify the same color:

```
P {color: #00FFFF;} /* hexadecimal */
P {color: rgb(0%, 100%, 100%);}      /* percentages */
P {color: rgb(0, 255, 255);}  /* integers */
```

 Browser-safe hexadecimal colors are always made up of the following two-digit color values: 00, 33, 66, 99, CC, and FF. Therefore, 0066FF is a browser-safe color; 0F66FF is not.

Understanding Element Layers

The color and background properties you will learn about in this chapter let you control three different layers of any element. You can imagine these layers as three individual pieces of tracing paper laid over each other to complete the finished Web page. Each layer is transparent until you add a color or an image. These are the three layers listed in order from back to front:

- **Background color layer** — the backmost layer, specified by the background-color property

- **Background-image layer** — the middle layer, specified by the background-image property

- **Content layer** — the frontmost layer; this is the color of the text content; specified by the color property

Figure 5-1 shows the three layers applied to the <BODY> element. Using BODY as the selector applies these effects to the entire content area of the Web page. The background color layer is gray. It lays behind all of the other layers. The background image layer has an image tiled vertically along the left side of the browser. It overlays the background color. The frontmost layer contains the content. Notice that the content layer overlays both the background image and background color layers.

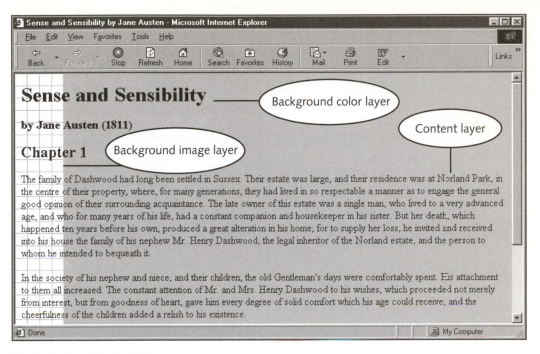

Figure 5-1   Page layers

Specifying Color

Color property description

Value: <color>

Initial: depends on browser

Applies to: all elements

Inherited: yes

Percentages: N/A

The color property lets you specify the foreground color of any element on a Web page. This property sets the color for both the text and the border of the element unless you have specifically stated a border color with one of the border properties (see the "Using the Box Properties" chapter).

The value for the color property is a valid color keyword or numerical representation, either hexadecimal or RGB (described earlier in the "Using RGB Colors" section). The following style rules show the different methods of specifying a color:

```
P {color: blue;}      /* color name */
P {color: #0000ff;}     /* hexadecimal value */
P {color: rgb(0,0,255);}    /* RGB numbers */
P {color: rgb(0%,0%,100%);}    /* RGB percentages */
```

Figure 5-2 shows a <P> element with the color set to gray. By default, the element's border is the same color as the element content.

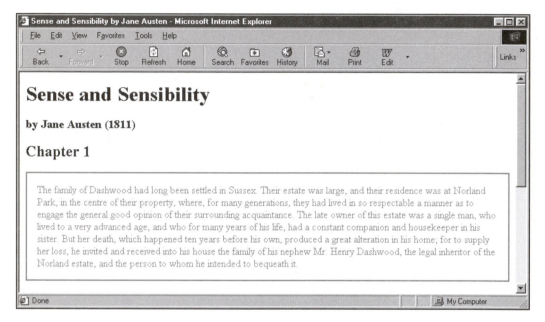

Figure 5-2   The element border defaults to the element color

Here is the style rule for the paragraph. Notice that the border color is not specified, so the element's border is the same color as the content.

```
P {color: gray; border: solid thin; padding: 1em;}
```

Setting the Default Text Color

Color is inherited from parent to child elements. If you set the color for <BODY>, all elements on the page will inherit their color from the <BODY> element, effectively setting the default text color for the entire Web page. The following rule sets the color for the <BODY> element:

```
BODY {color: #006633;}
```

Changing Link Colors

You can change the colors of hypertext links by using the link pseudo-classes, which are fully described in the "CSS Selection Techniques" chapter. You can affect the new link, active link, and visited link colors, as shown in the following style rules:

```
A:link {color: #000000;} /* new links are black */
A:active {color: #FF0000;} /* active links are red */
A:visited {color: #CCCCCC;} /* visited links are gray */
```

The active link color is activated by the user pressing and holding the mouse button when pointing at a link.

The familiar blue (for new links) and purple (for visited links) colors are one of the most recognizable navigation cues for users visiting your site. If you choose to change link colors, make sure to choose colors that have enough contrast so users can tell the difference between new and visited links. Keep in mind that some users might have sight disabilities, such as color blindness, that could prevent them from seeing your Web pages in the way you intend.

5

WORKING WITH BACKGROUNDS

The background properties let you control the background color and background images in any element. In this section, you will learn about the following CSS background properties:

- background-color
- background-image
- background-repeat
- background-position
- background-attachment
- background shortcut property

Background-color

background-color property description
Value: <color>
Initial: transparent
Applies to: all elements
Inherited: no
Percentages: N/A

The background-color property lets you set the background color of any element on a Web page. The background color includes any padding area (explained in the "Using the Box Properties" chapter) that you have defined for the element. Figure 5-3 shows <P> elements with background color and different padding values.

The 4.x version of the Netscape browser has a significant problem displaying the background color property, as shown in Figure 5-4.

The background-color property can be applied to both block-level and inline elements. The following style rule uses descendant selection (described in the "Understanding CSS Selection Techniques" chapter) to select <B> elements only when they reside within <P> elements and apply a background-color:

```
P B {background-color: #cccccc;}
```

This rule selects the bold text in the paragraph and applies the background color as shown in Figure 5-5.

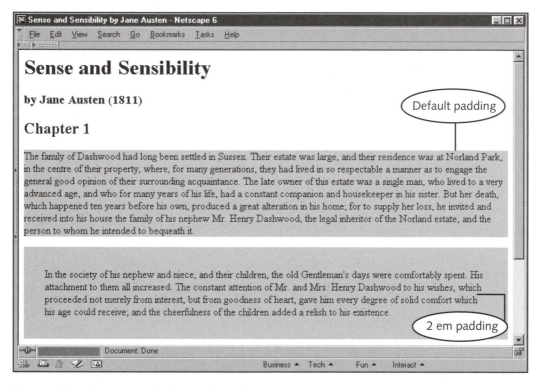

Figure 5-3 Background color and padding

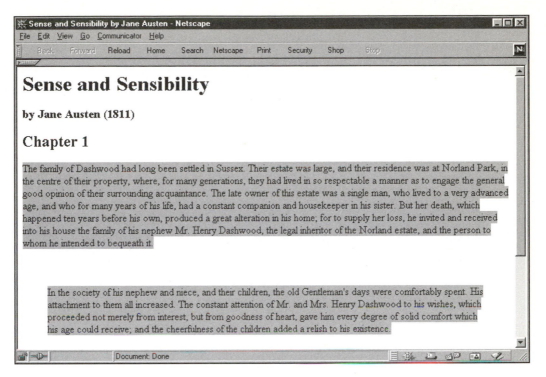

Figure 5-4   Background color and padding in Netscape 4.75

Setting the Page Background Color

To set the page background color, use BODY as the selector. This sets the background color for the content area of the Web page. By default, the background color of any element is transparent. Therefore, all elements will show the page background color unless background-color is specifically stated. The following rule sets a background color for the <BODY> element:

```
BODY {background-color: #cccccc;}
```

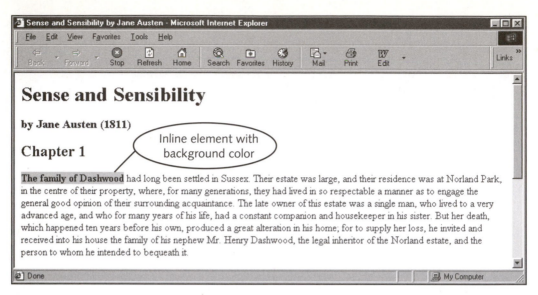

Figure 5-5   An inline element with a background color

In Figure 5-6, notice that the first two headings have their background color set to white, whereas the remainder of the elements show the background color of the <BODY> element.

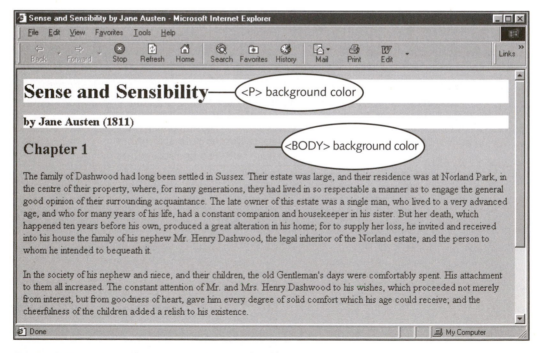

Figure 5-6   Setting the page background color

It is always a good practice to include a page background color because some users might have a default background color that is different from the color you chose in your design. Even if you plan on a white page background, you can never be sure that all users will have their default set to white, so include the background-color property rather than relying on the user's settings.

Creating a Text Reverse

A **reverse** is a common printing effect where the background color, which is normally white, and the text color, which is usually black, are reversed. On the Web you can do this in your choice of color. Reverses are usually reserved for headings rather than the regular body text. You can easily create a reverse with a style rule. The following rule sets the background color of the <H1> element to gray, and the text color to white:

```
H1 {color: #ffffff; background-color: gray;
padding:.25em;}
```

The element padding is set to .25 em to increase the background color area. Figure 5-7 shows the result of the style rule.

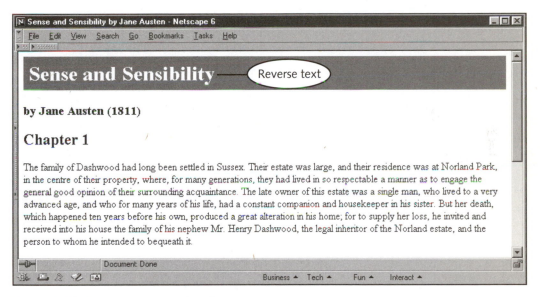

Figure 5-7   Reverse text in a heading

Specifying a Background Image

---

background-image property description

Value: <url>

Initial: none

Applies to: all elements

Inherited: no

Percentages: N/A

The background-image property lets you add a background image to an entire Web page or to a single element. When you combine background-image with the other CSS background properties described later, you will see that you can gain significant control over the behavior of background images to create interesting background effects.

With standard HTML, the only behavior of background images is to tile completely across the browser background. This is also the default behavior with the CSS background-image property. Figure 5-8 shows a document with an image tiled across the background.

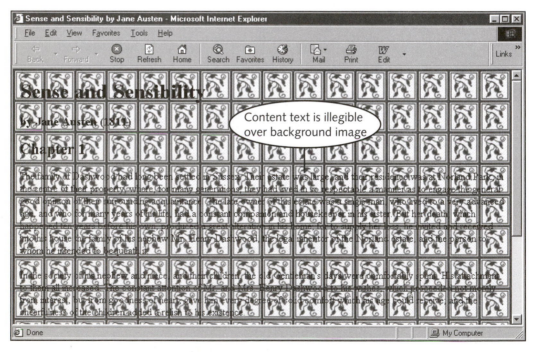

Figure 5-8   Default background image behavior

The background image from this example is shown in Figure 5-9. It is tiled repeatedly both vertically and horizontally.

Figure 5-9   The individual background image

5

In Figure 5-8, the text that is displayed over this busy background is illegible. When choosing page backgrounds, keep the legibility of your text in mind. Avoid overly busy and distracting backgrounds that make your content difficult to read.

Specifying the Background Image URL

To specify a page background image, use the <BODY> element as the selector, because <BODY> is the parent element of the content area. To use an image in the background, you must specify the relative location of the image in the style rule. CSS has a special notation for specifying a URL, as shown in Figure 5-10.

Creating a Page Background

To tile an image across the entire background of the Web page use BODY as the selector, as shown in the following rule. This is the style rule that was used to create Figure 5-8.

```
body {background-image: url(grayivy.jpg);}
```

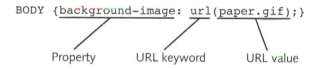

Figure 5-10   URL value syntax

Creating an Element Background

You can also use the background-image property to apply an image to the background of any element. The following rule sets a background image for the <H1> element:

```
H1 {background-image: url(bluetex.jpg); padding: .25em;}
```

The padding property adds extra space around the <H1> element to show an additional area of the background image. Figure 5-11 shows the result of the style rule.

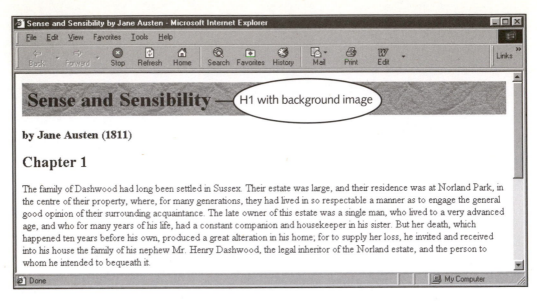

Figure 5-11   Background image applied to an element

Specifying Background Repeat

---

background-repeat property description

Value: repeat | repeat-x | repeat-y | no-repeat | inherit

Initial: repeat

Applies to: all elements

Inherited: no

Percentages: N/A

The background-repeat property lets you control the tiling of background images across the document or element background. A background image must be specified for this property to work, so you will always use the background-image property with the background-repeat property. Table 5-2 lists the background-repeat values.

Table 5-2   Background-repeat property values

Value	Background Image Behavior
repeat	The image is repeated across the entire background of the element; this is the default behavior
Repeat-x	The image is repeated across the horizontal (x) axis of the document only
Repeat-y	The image is repeated across the vertical (y) axis of the document only
No-repeat	The image is not repeated; only one instance of the image is shown in the background

Creating a Vertical Repeat

The repeat-y value of the background-repeat property lets you create a vertical repeating background graphic. Figure 5-12 shows an example of this effect.

The style rules for this Web page follow. Notice the use of the margin-left property to align the heading and paragraph elements properly with the background image.

```
BODY {background-image: url(grayivy.jpg);
      background-repeat: repeat-y;
      }
H1, H2, H3, P {margin-left: 70px;}
```

5

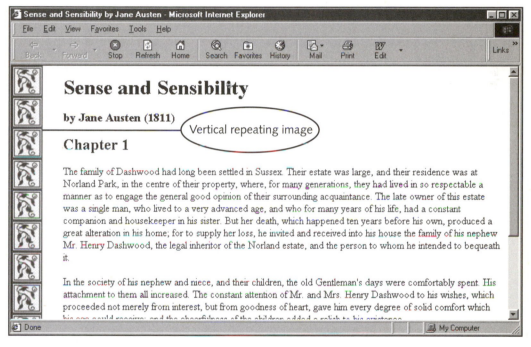

Figure 5-12   Vertical repeating background image

Creating a Horizontal Repeat

The repeat-x value of the background-repeat property lets you create a horizontal repeating background graphic. Figure 5-13 shows an example of this effect.

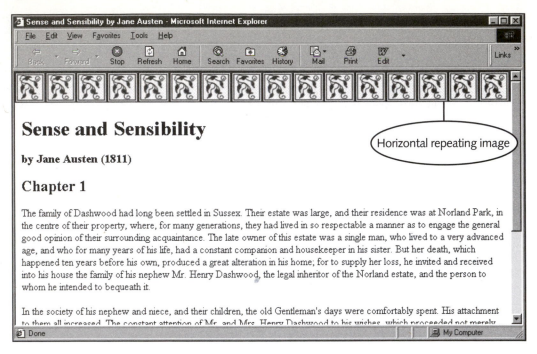

Figure 5-13 Horizontal repeating background image

The style rules for this Web page follow. Notice the use of the margin-top property to align the <H1> element properly with the background image.

```
BODY {background-image: url(grayivy.jpg);
      background-repeat: repeat-x;
      }
H1 {margin-top: 70px;}
```

Creating a Nonrepeating Background Image

The no-repeat value of the background-repeat property lets you create a single instance of an image in the background. This is useful if you want to apply a watermark effect on your page. As you will see, the no-repeat value can be enhanced by using it in combination with the background-position property, described in the next section.

Figure 5-14 shows an example of a nonrepeating background image.

The following style rule shows the use of the no-repeat value:

```
BODY {background-image: url(grayivy.jpg);
      background-repeat: no-repeat;
      }
H1 {margin-top: 50px;}
```

In this style sheet, the margin-top property is set to 50 px to properly align the <H1> element beneath the single background image. To position this single background image elsewhere on the page, you can use the background-position property.

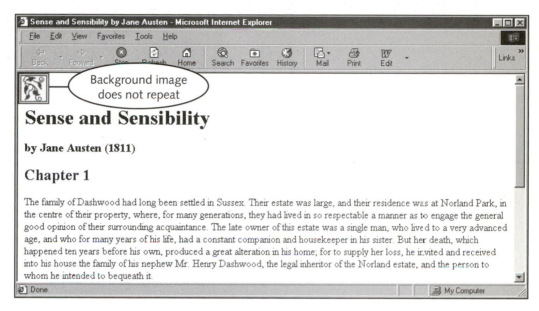

Figure 5-14   Nonrepeating background image

Specifying Background Position

background-position property description
Value: [[<percentage> | <length>]{1,2} | [[top | center | bottom] || [left | center | right]]]
Initial: 0% 0%
Applies to: block-level and replaced elements
Inherited: no
Percentages: refer to the size of the box itself

The background-position property lets you use three types of values: percentage, length, or keywords. Table 5-3 lists the values and their meanings. Figure 5-15 shows the keyword positions in the element box and their equivalent percentage values.

Creating a Centered Background Image

You can use the background-position property to place either vertical, horizontal, or non-repeating images. Probably one of the most popular uses of the background-position property is to combine it with the background-repeat property to create a centered background image, which mimics a printed watermark on the Web page. Figure 5-16 shows this effect.

LEFT TOP 0% 0%	CENTER TOP 50% 0%	RIGHT TOP 100% 0%
LEFT CENTER 0% 50%	CENTER 50% 50%	RIGHT CENTER 100% 50%
LEFT BOTTOM 0% 100%	CENTER BOTTOM 50% 100%	RIGHT BOTTOM 100% 100%

Figure 5-15   Keyword and percentage background positions

Table 5-3   Background-position property values

Value	Background Image Behavior
percentage	The percentage values are based on the starting point of the upper-left corner of the containing element's box. The first percentage value is horizontal; the second is vertical. For example, the value "45% 30%" places the background image 45% from the left edge and 30% from the top edge of the containing box.
length	Length values work in much the same way as percentages, starting from the upper-left corner of the element's containing box. The first length value is horizontal; the second is vertical. For example, the value "100px 200px" places the background image 100 pixels from the left edge and 200 pixels from the top edge of the containing box.
keywords	The keywords are: ■ left ■ center ■ right ■ top ■ bottom You can use these keywords alone ("left") or in combination ("left top") to position the background image. Figure 5-15 shows the nine keyword positions and their percentage equivalents. The keywords can be used interchangeably, so the values "left top" and "top left" are the same.

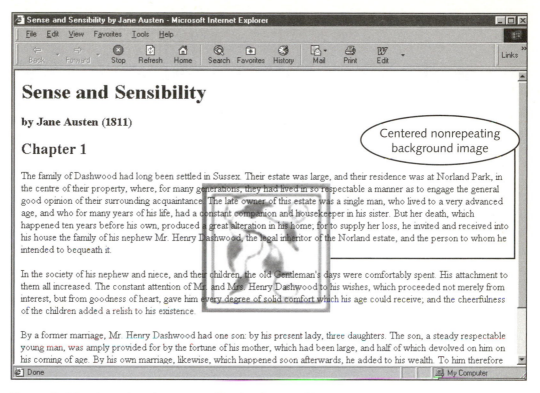

Figure 5-16   A centered nonrepeating background image

The image in Figure 5-16 has been altered in a graphics program for use in the background. It is larger and lighter than the original shown in Figure 5-9. The following style rule centers the nonrepeating background image:

```
BODY {background-image: url(lgivy.jpg);
      background-repeat: no-repeat;
      background-position: center;
      }
```

Positioning Vertical and Horizontal Background Images

You can also position images that repeat on either the horizontal or vertical axis of the Web page. The following style rule positions the vertical repeating image background along the right side of the browser window:

```
BODY {background-image: url(grayivy.jpg);
      background-repeat: repeat-y;
      background-position: right;
      }
P  {margin-right: 70px;}
```

As in previous examples, the <P> element right margin must be adjusted to keep the text from running over the background. Figure 5-17 shows the result of the style rule.

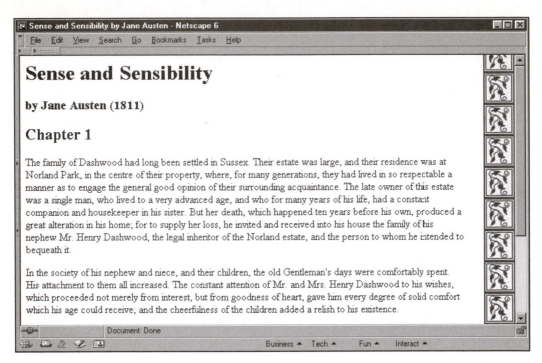

Figure 5-17   Positioning a vertical repeating background image

You can also position a horizontal repeating image. The following rule positions a horizontal repeating background image along the bottom of the browser window:

```
BODY {background-image: url(grayivy.jpg);
      background-repeat: repeat-x;
      background-position: bottom;
      }
P {margin-right: 70px;}
```

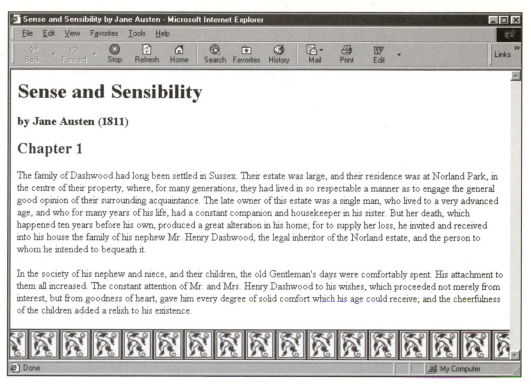

Figure 5-18   Positioning a horizontal repeating background image

Specifying Background Attachment

background-attachment property description

Value: scroll | fixed

Initial: scroll

Applies to: all elements

Inherited: no

Percentages: N/A

The background-attachment property lets you determine the scrolling behavior of the background image. For example, in Figure 5-16, the background graphic normally scrolls with the text. If the user scrolls down the page, the background graphic scrolls along with the content. By using the background-attachment property, you can set the background graphic to remain fixed, allowing the content to scroll over the graphic. This dynamic effect cannot be demonstrated in print. You can view the example files on the Companion Web site to see the results of background-attachment property.

The following style rule creates a fixed background image:

```
BODY {background-image: url(lgivy.jpg);
     background-repeat: no-repeat;
     background-position: center;
     background-attachment: fixed;
     }
```

Using the Background Shorthand Property

background property description
Value: [<'background-color'> || <'background-image'> || <'background-repeat'> || <'background-attachment'> || <'background-position'>]
Initial: see individual properties
Applies to: all elements
Inherited: no
Percentages: allowed on 'background-position'

The background property is a shorthand property that lets you set all of the background properties in one statement. You can express the following background properties in any order:

- background-color
- background-image
- background-repeat
- background-position
- background-attachment

For example, consider the following rule stated with the individual properties:

```
BODY {background-color: #ffffff;
     background-image: url(lgivy.jpg);
     background-repeat: no-repeat;
     background-position: center;
     background-attachment: fixed;
     }
```

You can state these same properties using the background shortcut property as follows:

```
BODY {background: #ffffff url(lgivy.jpg) no-repeat center
fixed;}
```

You can state any or all of the background properties. If you leave out any of the properties, the default values are applied. The background shortcut property lets you write simple rules like the following:

```
BODY {background: #ffffff;}
```

APPLYING THE COLOR AND BACKGROUND PROPERTIES

In this set of steps, you have a chance to apply some of the properties you learned about in this chapter. As you work through the steps, refer to Figure 5-20 to see the results you will achieve. Save your file and test your work in the browser as you complete each step.

5

To build the style sheet:

1. Open the file **mars.htm** in your HTML editor, and save it in your work folder as **mars1.htm**.

2. In your browser, open the file **mars.htm**. When you open the file, it looks like Figure 5-19.

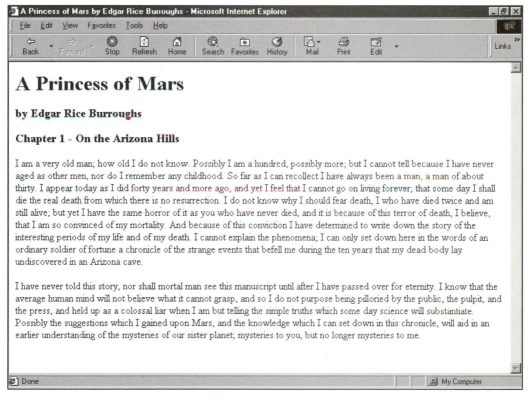

Figure 5-19   The beginning Web page

3. Examine the code. Notice the <STYLE> section of the file. It currently contains no style rules. The complete code for the page follows:

```
<HTML>
<HEAD>
<TITLE>A Princess of Mars by Edgar Rice
Burroughs</TITLE>
<STYLE TYPE="text/css">
</STYLE>
</HEAD>
<BODY>
<H1>A Princess Of Mars</H1>
<H3>by Edgar Rice Burroughs</H3>
<H3>Chapter 1 - On the Arizona Hills</H3>
<P>I am a very old man; how old I do not know.
Possibly I am a hundred, possibly more; but I cannot
tell because I have never aged as other men, nor do I
remember any childhood. So far as I can recollect I
have always been a man, a man of about thirty.  I
appear today as I did forty years and more ago, and yet
I feel that I cannot go on living forever; that some
day I shall die the real death from which there is no
resurrection.  I do not know why I should fear death, I
who have died twice and am still alive; but yet I have
the same horror of it as you who have never died, and
it is because of this terror of death, I believe, that
I am so convinced of my mortality. And because of this
conviction I have determined to write down the story of
the interesting periods of my life and of my death.  I
cannot explain the phenomena; I can only set down here
in the words of an ordinary soldier of fortune a chron-
icle of the strange events that befell me during the
ten years that my dead body lay undiscovered in an
Arizona cave.</P>
<P>I have never told this story, nor shall mortal man
see this manuscript until after I have passed over for
eternity.  I know that the average human mind will not
believe what it cannot grasp, and so I do not purpose
being pilloried by the public, the pulpit, and the
press, and held up as a colossal liar when I am but
telling the simple truths which some day science will
substantiate.  Possibly the suggestions which I gained
upon Mars, and the knowledge which I can set down in
this chronicle, will aid in an earlier understanding of
the mysteries of our sister planet; mysteries to you,
but no longer mysteries to me.</P>
</BODY>
</HTML>
```

4. Start by setting the background color for the Web page. Because the finished design uses a white background, you want to force a white background regardless of the user's browser background color. Write a style rule that uses BODY as the selector and sets the background-color property to white:

```
<STYLE TYPE="text/css">
BODY {background-color: #ffffff;}
</STYLE>
```

5. Next, build the style for the <H1> element, which is a text reverse. Use H1 as the selector, and specify a background color of #cccccc (gray) and a text color of #ffffff (white):

```
H1 {color: #ffffff; background-color: #cccccc;}
```

6. Add a background image for the Web page. Copy glyph.jpg into your work folder. Add the background-image property to the existing style rule for the <BODY> element, because you want to apply the background image to the entire Web page.

```
BODY {background-color: #ffffff;
      background-image:url(glyph.jpg);
      }
```

7. When you test the new style rule you added in Step 6, you see that the background image tiles across the entire background of the Web page. You want to restrict the tiling of the background graphic to the left margin of the browser. To accomplish this, use the background-repeat property set to repeat-y. Add this property to the existing style rule:

```
BODY {background-color: #ffffff;
      background-image:url(glyph.jpg);
      background-repeat: repeat-y;
      }
```

8. The background now repeats correctly on the left side of the browser window, but the content text is illegible against it. To fix this problem, add a margin-left property for all of the elements that contain text: <H1>, <H2>, <H3>, and <P>. Specify a value of 125 px, as shown in the following rule:

```
H1, H2, H3, P {margin-left: 125px;}
```

9. Finally, write a style rule to style the background for the chapter number. Because this content is inline within an <H3> element, you can use a <SPAN> element to add the style. Write the style rule first, using the SPAN selector with a class of "chapter". Set the background-color to #cccccc.

```
SPAN.chapter {background-color: #cccccc;}
```

10. Finish styling the document by adding the <SPAN> element to the chapter number within the <H3> element as shown:

```
<H3><SPAN class="chapter">Chapter 1</SPAN> - On the
Arizona Hills</H3>
```

11. The finished code follows. Figure 5-20 shows the completed Web page.

```
<HTML>
<HEAD>
<TITLE>A Princess of Mars by Edgar Rice
Burroughs</TITLE>
<STYLE TYPE="text/css">
BODY {background-color: #ffffff;
      background-image:url(glyph.jpg);
      background-repeat: repeat-y;
}
H1    {color: #ffffff;
      background-color: #cccccc;
}
H1, H3, P {margin-left: 125px;}
SPAN.chapter {background-color: #cccccc;}
</STYLE>
</HEAD>
<BODY>
<H1>A Princess Of Mars</H1>
<H3>by Edgar Rice Burroughs</H3>
<H3><SPAN class="chapter">Chapter 1</SPAN> - On the
Arizona Hills</H3>
<P>I am a very old man; how old I do not know.
Possibly I am a hundred, possibly more; but I cannot
tell because I have never aged as other men, nor do I
remember any childhood. So far as I can recollect I
have always been a man, a man of about thirty.  I
appear today as I did forty years and more ago, and yet
I feel that I cannot go on living forever; that some
day I shall die the real death from which there is no
resurrection.  I do not know why I should fear death, I
who have died twice and am still alive; but yet I have
the same horror of it as you who have never died, and
it is because of this terror of death, I believe, that
I am so convinced of my mortality. And because of this
conviction I have determined to write down the story of
the interesting periods of my life and of my death.  I
cannot explain the phenomena; I can only set down here
in the words of an ordinary soldier of fortune a chron-
icle of the strange events that befell me during the
ten years that my dead body lay undiscovered in an
Arizona cave.</P>
<P>I have never told this story, nor shall mortal man
see this manuscript until after I have passed over for
eternity.  I know that the average human mind will not
believe what it cannot grasp, and so I do not purpose
being pilloried by the public, the pulpit, and the
press, and held up as a colossal liar when I am but
telling the simple truths which some day science will
substantiate.  Possibly the suggestions which I gained
```

```
upon Mars, and the knowledge which I can set down in
this chronicle, will aid in an earlier understanding of
the mysteries of our sister planet; mysteries to you,
but no longer mysteries to me.</P>
</BODY>
</HTML>
```

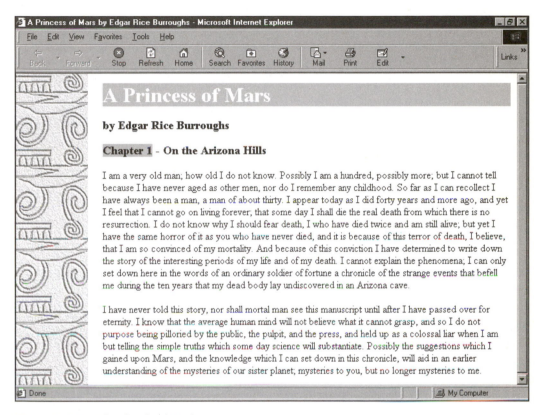

Figure 5-20   The finished Web page

CHAPTER SUMMARY

In this chapter, you learned about the basics of computer color and how you can apply color to your Web page content. You saw that CSS lets you specify color in a variety of ways, including color names, RGB, and hexadecimal values. You learned that there are three layers you can affect with the color and background properties. You examined each of the color and background properties and saw how they can be combined to create interesting effects, such as watermarks and tiling background images.

❐ Remember that color is widely variable on the Web. Different monitors and operating systems display colors differently.

❑ Test your colors carefully to make sure that the widest variety of users will be able to access your content. Consider restricting your color palette to the colors available in the browser-safe palette to ensure the greatest portability of your Web pages.

❑ Color names are not always the best way to specify color values because of their variable nature. Consider using RGB or the more common hexadecimal values instead.

❑ Use the color property to set foreground colors for elements. Remember that the element border defaults to the element color unless you specifically state a border color.

❑ Background colors affect any padding areas in the element. They can be applied to both block-level and inline elements.

❑ Choose background images that will not detract from the legibility of your content. Use the background-repeat and background-position properties to control the appearance of images in the background.

REVIEW QUESTIONS

1. What are the three basic colors a computer monitor can display?
2. What are these three basic colors called?
3. What term refers to the amount of data a monitor uses to display color?
4. What is the browser-safe palette?
5. What are the three different ways to express color values in CSS?
6. What color does the following rule specify?
   BODY {background-color: rgb(100%, 100%, 100%);}
7. State the same color in Question 6 as a hexadecimal value.
8. Which property controls the backmost layer of the Web page?
9. Which selector lets you apply styles to the entire Web page?
10. How is the default border color of an element determined?
11. What selector would you use to set a default text color for a Web page?
12. What are the three special selectors that let you change link colors?
13. To what type of elements can you apply a background color?
14. What is a text reverse?
15. What is the default background image behavior?
16. What is the background repeat value for a horizontally repeated image?
17. Does the order of values affect the background shortcut property?

HANDS-ON PROJECTS

1. Browse the Web and choose a site that you feel exhibits positive use of color, both in content and backgrounds. Write a short design critique that describes how the use of color enhances the legibility of the site and improves user access to information.

2. Browse the Web and choose a mainstream (not amateur) site that can benefit from a change in color scheme. Look for problems with legibility of text over background colors, use of nonstandard linking colors, etc. Write a short essay that describes the changes you want implemented to improve the use of color on the site.

3. Using the Web as a research tool, write a paper describing the variable nature of color on the Web and the problems it poses for designers. Discuss color depth, how colors display on different operating systems, and the browser-safe palette. Make sure to include information on how color issues will change as the Web evolves.

4. Write a persuasive paper arguing for or against the use of different link colors on the Web. Discuss pros and cons for user navigation, and back up your argument with research you have gathered on the Web. Cite mainstream Web sites, Web designers, and usability studies that back up your argument.

5. In this exercise, you will experiment with background images.

    a. Open the file bkgrnd.htm in your HTML editor, and save it in your work folder as bkgrnd1.htm.

    b. Copy the image grid.jpg into your work folder, or the image will not display in the browser.

    c. In your browser, open the file bkgrnd1.htm. When you open the file, it looks like Figure 5-21.

    d. Your goal is to use the background properties to achieve the results shown in Figure 5-22. In addition to using the background properties, you will have to use a margin property (see the "Using the Box Properties" chapter) to indent the text to the right of the background image.

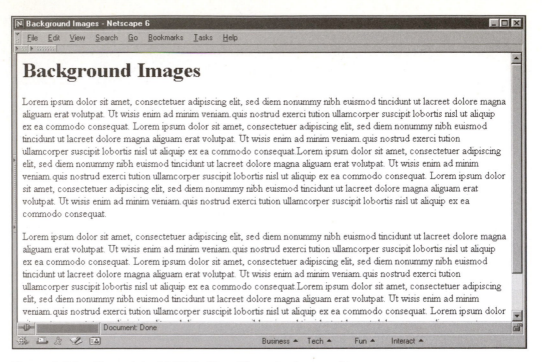

Figure 5-21   The original HTML file with no background images

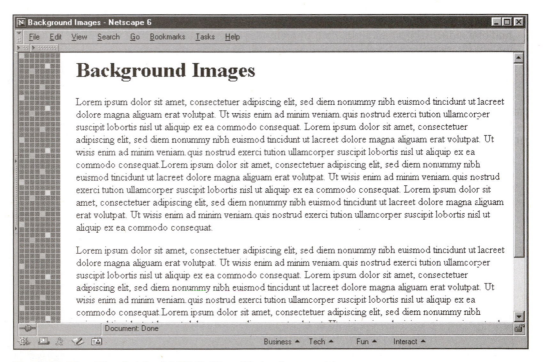

Figure 5-22   The finished HTML file with background image

6. In this exercise, you will experiment with positioning background images.

a. Open the file bkgrnd.htm in your HTML editor, and save it in your work folder as bkgrnd2.htm.

b. Copy the image grid.jpg into your work folder, or the image will not display in the browser.

c. In your browser, open the file bkgrnd2.htm. When you open, the file it looks like Figure 5-21.

d. Your goal is to use the background properties to achieve the results shown in Figure 5-23. In addition to using the background properties, you will have to use a margin property (see the "Using the Box Properties" chapter) to wrap the text to the left of the background image.

5

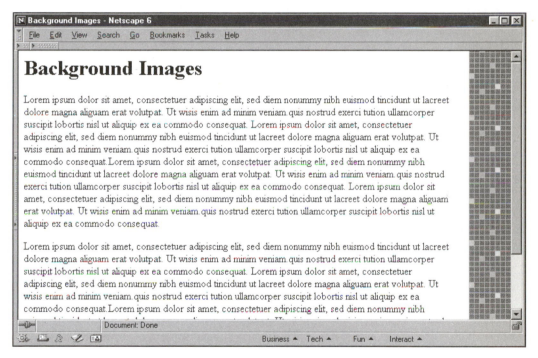

Figure 5-23   The finished HTML file with positioned background image

7. In this exercise, you will experiment with color.

a. Open the file colors.htm in your HTML editor, and save it in your work folder as colors1.htm.

b. In your browser, open the file colors1.htm. When you open the file, it looks like Figure 5-24.

c. Use your HTML editor to examine the code. Notice that there are existing style rules:

```
<STYLE TYPE="text/css">
P {margin-left: 40px;}
H1 {padding-left: 10px;}
H3 {padding-left: 10px;}
</STYLE>
```

d. Your goal is to use the color and background-color properties to achieve the results shown in Figure 5-25. You can use the hexadecimal color codes indicated in the Figure 5-25, or try your own combinations.

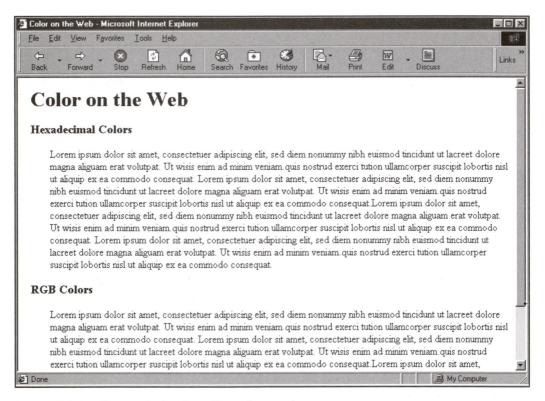

Figure 5-24   The original HTML file without color

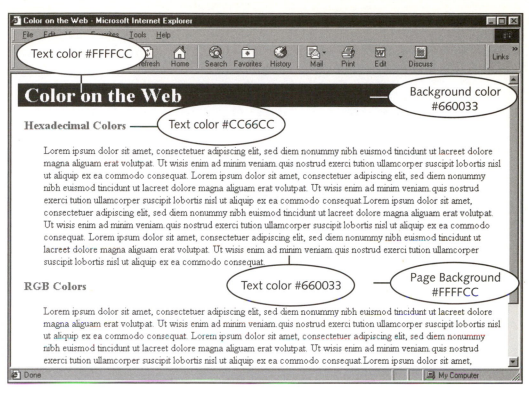

Figure 5-25   The finished HTML file with color

CASE STUDY

You will create the color and background conventions for your Web site. Think about the different color requirements for your content, and decide how the legibility can be enhanced. Can color communicate information about the structure of your information? Add color information to the type specification HTML page that shows examples of the different typefaces, sizes, and colors and how they will be used. Decide on page backgrounds and element background conventions and which elements will benefit from their use. Create before and after sample pages that reflect the enhanced design.

6

WORKING WITH TABLES AND LISTS

When you complete this chapter, you will be able to:

♦ Understand basic HTML table code

♦ Apply CSS rules to table elements

♦ Build a page layout table

♦ Understand the CSS2 table model

♦ Use the CSS list-item style properties

HTML provides both table and list elements for organizing and stating relationships between data. If you have ever built a Web site, then you have probably worked with the HTML table elements. Although originally designed for displaying tabular data, most Web designers use tables to build page templates that control positioning of elements and create columns of text. This chapter covers the use of CSS properties within tables both as a way to organize data and as a way to control page layout. You will see how the CSS2 table model expands on the usage and definition of table elements. You will also learn how to use the list-item properties, especially with list elements such as <UL> and <OL>. The list elements let you organize data in bulleted or ordered lists. CSS expands on the HTML list elements by letting you customize the look and behavior of list-item elements.

UNDERSTANDING TABLE BASICS

The table elements made their debut in HTML 2.0. Their primary purpose was to let HTML authors have more control over tables of data. Previously, the only way to organize a table was to use the somewhat limited <PRE> element. With the advent of the table elements, authors could add borders to table cells, adjust cell spacing and padding, and set both horizontal and vertical alignment within cells. Additionally, special table elements allowed the creation of captions and table header rows.

Designers who had been struggling with the limited page layout capabilities of HTML seized the table elements as a method of laying out a page rather than only tables of data. Tables quickly became the preferred method of building Web pages, allowing designers (most of whom had migrated from the print world) to create pages with familiar columns and gutters. Today the Web page is a table-oriented medium. Although the CSS positioning properties (discussed in the "Using the Positioning Properties" chapter) will eventually allow Web page design without resorting to tables, the current state of the Web demands that you know how to apply CSS style rules to content that is contained within tables.

Working with the Table Elements

The <TABLE> element is the parent element for the table structure, which consists of table row elements <TR> and individual table data cells <TD>. These are the three elements you will use most frequently when you are building tables. Figure 6-1 shows a basic table that uses these three table elements.

The basic table is the result of the following code:

```
<TABLE BORDER>
<TR><TD>Breed</TD><TD>Description</TD><TD>Group</TD></TR>
<TR><TD>French Bulldog</TD><TD>Lovable companion</TD><TD>
Non-sporting</TD></TR>
<TR><TD>Wheaten Terrier</TD><TD>
High-energy, friendly</TD><TD>Terrier</TD></TR>
<TR><TD>English Setter</TD><TD>Hunting companion</TD><TD>
Sporting</TD></TR>
<TR><TD>Shetland Sheepdog</TD><TD>Guarding, herding</TD>
<TD>Working</TD></TR>
</TABLE>
```

The <TABLE> element contains the rows and cells that make up the table. The <TR> tag signifies the four rows of the table. Notice that the <TR> tag contains the table cell element <TD>. The <TD> elements signify the table cells, which contain the table content. The BORDER attribute displays the default border around the table and between each cell.

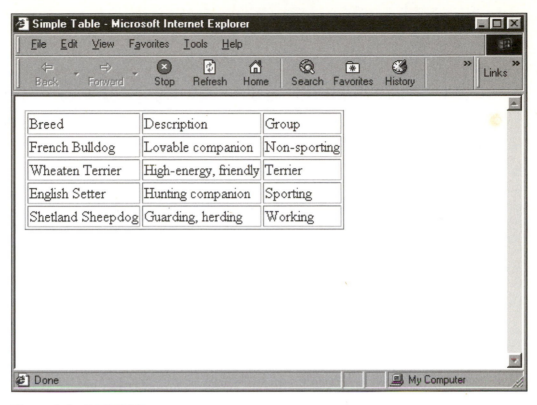

Figure 6-1   Basic table

You might also occasionally use <TH> elements when creating tables. The <TH> tag lets you create a table header cell that presents the cell content as bold and centered. In a data table, the <TH> elements provide descriptions of the data that follows. Figure 6-2 shows the same table with table header cells replacing the table data cells in the first row.

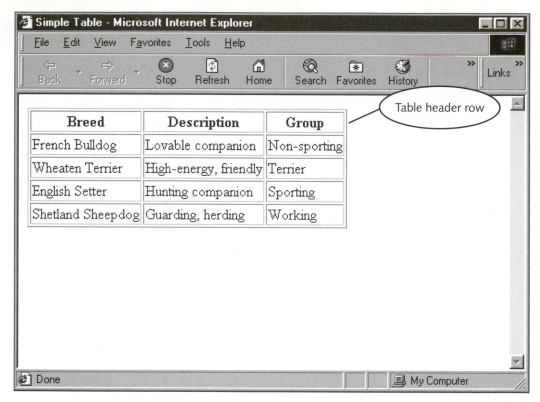

Figure 6-2 Table with table header row

The following table code shows the addition of the <TH> elements:

```
<TABLE BORDER>
<TR><TH>Breed</TH><TH>Description</TH><TH>Group</TH></TR>
<TR><TD>French Bulldog</TD><TD>Lovable companion</TD><TD>
Non-sporting</TD></TR>
<TR><TD>Wheaten Terrier</TD><TD>High-
energy, friendly</TD><TD>Terrier</TD></TR>
<TR><TD>English Setter</TD><TD>Hunting companion</TD><TD>
Sporting</TD></TR>
<TR><TD>Shetland Sheepdog</TD><TD>Guarding, herding</TD>
<TD>Working</TD></TR>
</TABLE>
```

Finally, many tables contain cells that span either multiple columns or rows of the table. In the following example, a new row has been added to the table that contains one cell. This cell has the COLSPAN attribute set to 3, making the cell span all three columns of the table. The cell contains an <H2> element that is horizontally aligned to the center of the cell.

```
<TABLE BORDER>
<TR><TD COLSPAN="3"><H2 ALIGN=CENTER>Table of Dog Breeds
</H2></TD></TR>
<TR><TH>Breed</TH><TH>Description</TH><TH>Group</TH></TR>
<TR><TD>French Bulldog</TD><TD>Lovable companion</TD><TD>
Non-sporting</TD></TR>
<TR><TD>Wheaten Terrier</TD><TD>High-energy, friendly</TD>
<TD>Terrier</TD></TR>
<TR><TD>English Setter</TD><TD>Hunting companion</TD><TD>
Sporting</TD></TR>
<TR><TD>Shetland Sheepdog</TD><TD>Guarding, herding</TD>
<TD>Working</TD></TR>
</TABLE>
```

Figure 6-3 shows the result of adding the new cell and its contents. In the next section, you will see how to apply CSS style rules to this table.

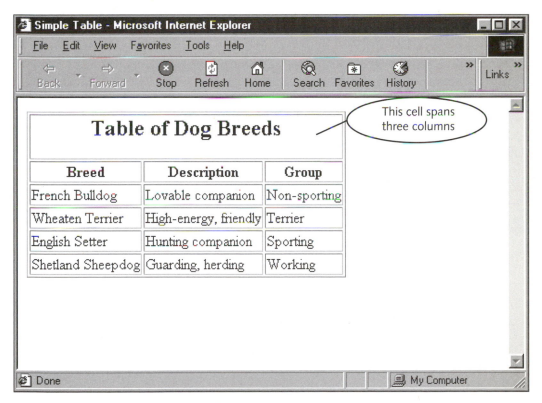

Figure 6-3   Table with COLSPAN cell

APPLYING STYLE RULES TO TABLES

Traditional styling of tables and table contents involves the use of many <FONT> elements and table attributes, such as ALIGN, VALIGN, and BGCOLOR, that are being phased out by the W3 in favor of CSS. As you will see in this section, CSS lets you select and apply styles to table contents in a variety of ways.

Selecting Table Elements

You can use the table elements as selectors to which you can apply styles. Table 6-1 lists the common table elements and their effect on the table when used as selectors.

Table 6-1   Common table elements

Table Element	Description
TABLE	The style rule is applied across the entire table
TR	The style rule is applied to the table rows
TH	The style rule is applied to the table header cells
TD	The style rule is applied to the table data cells

As you will see later in this section, you can further define the exact range of selection and how styles are applied by using more specific selection techniques, such as classes or descendant selection (See the "Understanding CSS Selection Techniques" chapter for more selector information).

Applying Styles to the Entire Table

You can apply styles to the entire table by using the <TABLE> element as the selector. The following style rule sets font family and background color values for the table you examined earlier in the chapter.

```
TABLE {font-family: arial, helvetica;
    background-color: #cccccc;
}
```

Figure 6-4 shows the result of the style rule.

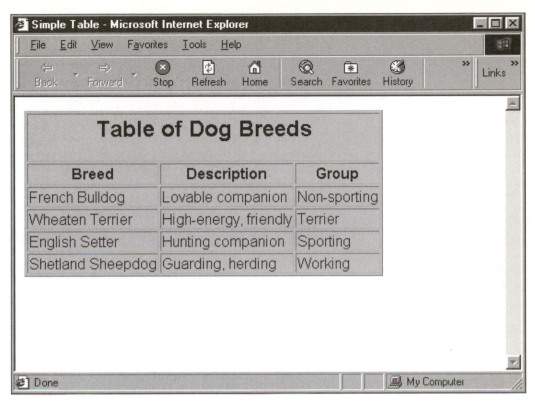

Figure 6-4   Style applied to the <TABLE> element

Using the <TABLE> element as the selector provides a convenient way to set styles and apply them globally throughout the table. Most style properties behave as you would expect when applied at the TABLE level, with a few exceptions. For example, margin values (discussed in "Using the Box Properties" chapter) are applied to the entire table, not the individual cells. Setting a 1-em margin, for example, adds the margin around the outside of the entire table. Padding values (also discussed in the "Using the Box Properties" chapter) applied at the TABLE level will not affect the table or the individual cells. Border properties (see "Using the Color and Background Properties" chapter) are applied only to the outside border of the table, not the individual cells. As always, remember to carefully test your work in multiple browsers to ensure that the user sees the results you intended.

 If you want your table contents to have the same style as the rest of the page content, apply the styles using BODY as the selector. The table will inherit the styles applied to the <BODY> element.

Applying Styles to Table Rows

You can use the table row element <TR> as a selector to apply styles across all cells contained within a row. Because all table content is contained in cells within rows, the effect of applying a style to the table row will mimic using TABLE as the selector. To narrow down the selection and only affect specific rows, you can use a class selector. For example, the following style rule selects table rows with a CLASS value of "highlight."

```
TR.highlight {background-color: #ffff00;}
```

This style is applied to <TR> elements with the CLASS attribute as shown in the following fragment of the table code:

```
<TR CLASS="highlight"><TD>French Bulldog</TD><TD>Lovable
companion</TD><TD>Non-sporting</TD></TR>
```

In the table example, this class attribute is applied to every other row in the table. Figure 6-5 shows the result of the new style rules.

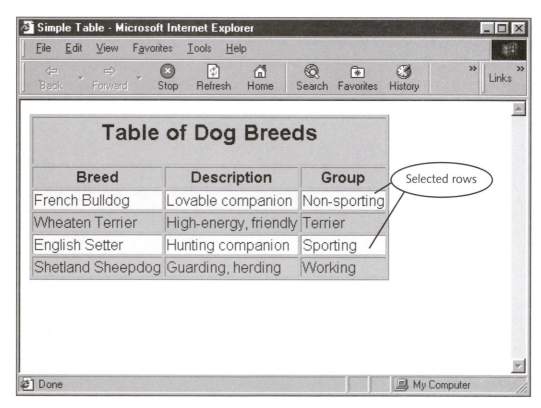

Figure 6-5   Selecting table rows with a class selector

Applying Styles to Table Cells

You can choose to apply styles to individual table cells, using either <TD> or <TH> as the selecting element. As with the <TR> element, if you apply a style to the <TD> element, it is applied across the entire table. To narrow down the selection, use a class selector to apply styles to a specific cell or range of cells. For this example, examine the table code for the first row of the table that contains the COLSPAN cell:

```
<TR><TD COLSPAN="3"><H2 ALIGN="CENTER">Table of Dog Breeds
</H2></TD></TR>
```

Currently, the <H2> element provides a larger font and centers the text "Table of Dog Breeds." You can achieve these same results (and more) by using a style rule for the cell instead. This requires removing the <H2> element so that the cell will contain only plain text. The code now looks like this:

```
<TR><TD COLSPAN="3">Table of Dog Breeds</TD></TR>
```

The style rule for this cell uses a class name "banner." The rule specifies a number of properties for the cell:

```
TD.banner {background-color: #999999;
           color: #ffffff;
           font-size: 2em;
           padding: 20px;
           text-align: center;
           border: solid thin black;
}
```

Apply this style rule to the table cell with the CLASS attribute:

```
<TR><TD COLSPAN="3" CLASS="banner">Table of Dog Breeds</TD>
</TR>
```

Figure 6-6 shows the completed table, followed by the complete page code.

6

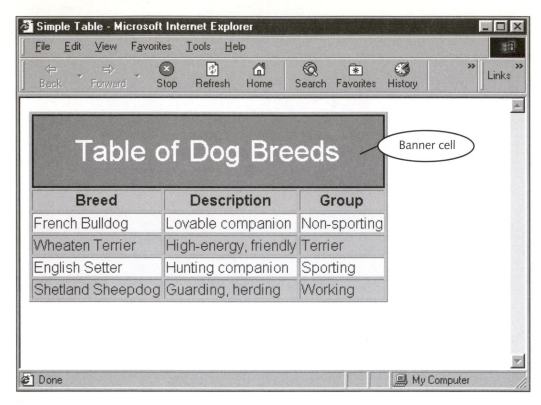

Figure 6-6 Applying styles to a single cell with a class name

```
<HTML>
<HEAD>
<TITLE>Simple Table</TITLE>
<STYLE>
TABLE {
font-family: arial, helvetica;
background-color: #cccccc;
}
TR.highlight {background-color: #ffff00;}
TD.banner {background-color: #999999;
          color: #ffffff;
          font-size: 2em;
          padding: 20px;
          text-align: center;
          border: solid thin black;
          }
</STYLE>
</HEAD>
<BODY>
<TABLE BORDER>
```

```
<TR><TD COLSPAN="3" CLASS="banner">Table of Dog Breeds</TD>
</TR>

<TR><TH>Breed</TH><TH>Description</TH><TH>Group</TH></TR>

<TR class="highlight"><TD>French Bulldog</TD><TD>Lovable
companion</TD><TD>Non-sporting</TD></TR>

<TR><TD>Wheaten Terrier</TD><TD>High-
energy, friendly</TD><TD>Terrier</TD></TR>

<TR class="highlight"><TD>English Setter</TD><TD>Hunting
companion</TD><TD>Sporting</TD></TR>

<TR><TD>Shetland Sheepdog</TD><TD>Guarding, herding</TD>
<TD>Working</TD></TR>
</TABLE>
</BODY>
</HTML>
```

6

BUILDING A PAGE LAYOUT TABLE

Although CSS positioning will eventually replace tables as a page layout tool, the current state of the Web is still dominated by tables that designers use to control the grid layout of a Web page. In the following set of steps, you will see how you can use CSS style rules to enhance and control page layouts with tables. This advanced exercise uses a range of properties that you have worked with in the previous chapters. As you work through the exercise, refer to Figure 6-12 to see the results you will achieve. Save your file and test your work in the browser as you complete each step.

1. Open the file **howl.htm** in your HTML editor, and save it in your work folder as **howl1.htm**.

2. Copy the image files **doghowl.gif** and **pawback.gif** into your work folder.

3. In your browser, open the file **howl1.htm**. When you open the file it looks like Figure 6-7.

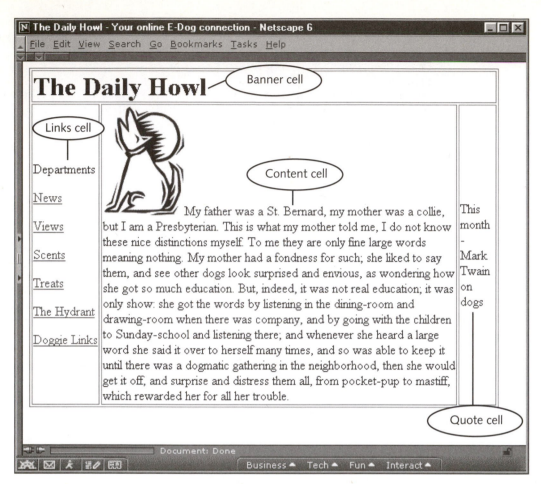

Figure 6-7   The basic document elements

4. Examine the code in the file. As you can see in Figure 6-7, the page contains a basic layout table with sample content. The complete code for the page follows. When you examine the code, notice that the file has an empty <STYLE> element in the head section. This is where you will add the style rules. Also, notice the HTML comments that describe each cell of the table. Finally, notice that the table has the border visible, allowing you to see the structure of the table grid.

```
<HTML>
<HEAD>
<TITLE>The Daily Howl - Your Online
E-Dog Connection</TITLE>
<STYLE TYPE="text/css">

</STYLE>
```

```
  </HEAD>
<BODY>
<TABLE BORDER WIDTH="580">
<TR>
<!-- The Banner Cell -->
<TD COLSPAN="3"><H1>The Daily Howl</H1></TD></TR>
<TR>
<!-- The Links Cell -->
<TD><P>Departments<BR><BR>
<A HREF="news.htm">News</A><BR><BR>
<A HREF="views.htm">Views</A><BR><BR>
<A HREF="scents.htm">Scents</A><BR><BR>
<A HREF="treats.htm">Treats</A><BR><BR>
<A HREF="hydrant.htm">The Hydrant</A><BR><BR>
<A HREF="links.htm">Doggie Links</A></P></TD>
<!-- The Content Cell -->
<TD>
<P><IMG SRC="doghowl.gif">My father was a St. Bernard, my
mother was a collie, but I am a Presbyterian. This is what
my mother told me, I do not know these nice distinctions
myself. To me they are only fine large words meaning
nothing. My mother had a fondness for such; she liked to
say them, and see other dogs look surprised and envious,
as wondering how she got so much education. But, indeed,
it was not real education; it was only show:  she got the
words by listening in the dining-room and drawing-room
when there was company, and by going with the children to
Sunday-school and listening there; and whenever she heard
a large word she said it over to herself many times, and
so was able to keep it until there was a dogmatic gathering
in the neighborhood, then she would get it off, and
surprise and distress them all, from pocket-pup to
mastiff, which rewarded her for all her trouble.</P></TD>
<!-- The Quote Cell -->
<TD>
<P>This<BR>month<BR>-
<BR>Mark<BR>Twain<BR>on<BR>dogs</P></TD></TR>
</TABLE>
</BODY>
</HTML>
```

Specifying Global Settings

Before writing style rules for the table content, set two global style properties.

To set the global style properties:

1. Start by setting the background color for the Web page. Because the finished design uses a white background, you want to force a white background

regardless of the user's browser background color. Write a style rule that uses BODY as the selector and sets the background-color property to white:

```
BODY {background-color: #ffffff;}
```

2. Next, write a rule for the table cells that will vertically align the table contents to the top of the cells. This rule overrides the table's default middle alignment:

```
TD {vertical-align: top;}
```

Styling the Banner Cell

The banner cell contains the name of the Web site. This text needs to be large and have enough surrounding white space to set it off from the rest of the page. To add a distinctive look, the banner cell will contain a background graphic and bottom rule as well. The text in the banner cell is contained within an <H1> element.

To style the banner cell:

1. Write a style rule for the <H1> element that centers the text and increases the size to 2.5 em:

```
H1 {text-align: center;
    font-size: 2.5em;
}
```

2. Now add padding to the <H1> tag to provide active white space that sets the heading off from the rest of the page. Set the padding-top to 30 px and the padding-bottom to 20 px. Finally, add a 1-px black border to the bottom of the <H1> element:

```
H1 {  text-align:center;
font-size:2.5em;
    padding-top: 30px;
    padding-bottom: 20px;
    border-bottom: solid 1px black;
}
```

3. You can now add a background image to the banner table cell. Figure 6-8 shows the source image, pawback.gif.

Figure 6-8   The source background image

This image will look good tiled across the top of the banner cell. To achieve this, write a rule using a class selector that you can apply to the banner

<TD> element. Set the background-repeat to "repeat-x" and specify the background image URL:

```
TD.banner {background-image: url(pawback.gif);
          background-repeat: repeat-x;
}
```

4. Now apply the class to the banner cell in the table code. Figure 6-9 shows the completed banner cell.

```
<!-- The Banner Cell -->
<TD COLSPAN="3" CLASS="banner"><H1>The Daily Howl</H1>
</TD>
```

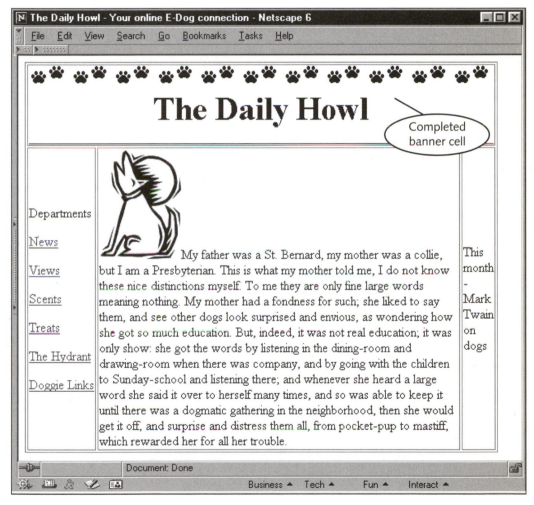

Figure 6-9 The completed banner cell

Styling the Links Cell

The links cell contains <A> elements that link to the other pages in the Web site. To make the links stand out, the content in this cell should be bold and centered. Also, some additional padding around the contents will help set the links off from the rest of the page.

To style the links cell:

1. To group the contents of the cell for styling, add a <DIV> element within the cell and set the CLASS to "links," as shown next:

```
<!-- The Links Cell -->
<TD>
<DIV CLASS="links">
<P>Departments<BR><BR>
<A HREF="news.htm">News</A><BR><BR>
<A HREF="views.htm">Views</A><BR><BR>
<A HREF="scents.htm">Scents</A><BR><BR>
<A HREF="treats.htm">Treats</A><BR><BR>
<A HREF="hydrant.htm">The Hydrant</A><BR><BR>
<A HREF="links.htm">Doggie Links</A><BR><BR></P>
</DIV>
</TD>
```

2. Now write the style rule in the <STYLE> section, using DIV as the selector with a class name of "links". Set the font-weight to bold and text-align to center. Also, set both left and right padding to 20 px:

```
DIV.links {text-align: center;
           font-weight: bold;
           padding-left: 20px;
           padding-right: 20px;
}
```

Figure 6-10 shows the result of this style rule.

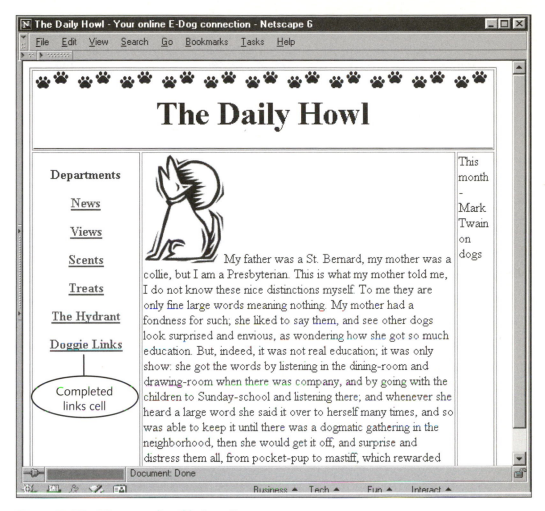

Figure 6-10   The completed links cell

Styling the Content Cell

The content cell contains an image and text. Currently, these are both aligned at the baseline of the image. The text should flow down from the top of the cell and wrap around the image, as shown in Figure 6-12. Also, you will use the first-line pseudo-element (discussed in the "Understanding CSS Selection Techniques" chapter) to set the first line of the text in small caps.

To style the content cell:

1. Write a rule for the IMG selector that sets the float property to left. Use the margin-right property to add 20 px of white space to the right side of the image:

```
IMG {float: left; padding-right: 20px;}
```

2. Write a separate rule for the content paragraph that uses "content" as a class selector. Add the first-line pseudo-class to the selector to choose only the first line of text in the paragraph. Use the font-variant property to display the first line of text in small caps:

```
P.content:first-line {font-variant: small-caps;}
```

3. Now apply the class to the <P> element in the content cell as shown in the following code fragment.

```
<!-- The Content Cell -->
<TD><P CLASS="content"><IMG SRC="doghowl.gif">My father
was a St. Bernard, my mother was…
```

Figure 6-11 shows floating image and first-line element styles.

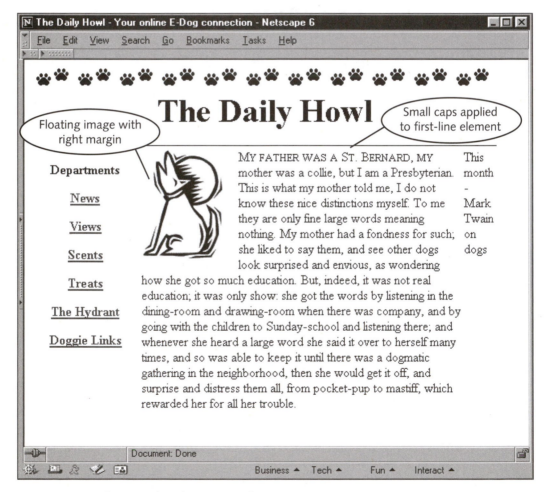

Figure 6-11   The completed content cell

Styling the Quote Cell

The final cell to style is the quote cell. This contains a pull quote from the article or other important text that should attract the reader's attention. This cell currently contains a paragraph element with text as shown next. The <BR> tags isolate each word on its own line within the paragraph.

```
<!-- The Quote Cell -->
<TD><P> This<BR>month<BR>-
<BR>Mark<BR>Twain<BR>on<BR>dogs </P></TD>
```

To style the quote cell:

1. To single out this <P> element, use a selector with a class name of "quote." Set the font-family to arial with a size of 1.75 em. Center the text with the text-align property:

```
P.quote { font-family: arial;
          font-size: 1.75em;
          text-align: center;
}
```

2. To provide some additional white space around the quote text, add 30-px padding on the top side of the paragraph and 20-px padding on the left side.

```
P.quote { font-family: arial;
          font-size: 1.75em;
          text-align: center;
          padding-top: 30px;
          padding-left: 20px;
}
```

3. Now apply the class to the <P> element in the quote cell, as shown in the following code.

```
<!-- The Quote Cell -->
<TD><P CLASS="quote">This<BR>month<BR>-
<BR>Mark<BR>Twain<BR>on<BR>dogs</P></TD></TR>
```

4. Remove the border attribute (highlighted in the following code) from the opening <TABLE> element to turn off the default border.

```
<TABLE WIDTH="580" BORDER>
```

Figure 6-12 shows the completed Web page including the styled quote cell.

6

Figure 6-12   The completed page layout in Netscape 6.0

Testing the Page Layout

Now that you have completed the style rules for the document, it is time to test it in the different browsers that support CSS. To test the finished layout, view it in different browsers and look for any discrepancies. Minor spacing differences can be ignored, but you might have to make adjustments if a property is not supported by one of the browsers. Figure 6–12 shows the Web page in Netscape 6.0. Figures 6–13 and 6–14 show the finished page layout in Internet Explorer 5.5 and Opera 5.0, respectively. As you can see, the page layout displays consistently in all three browsers.

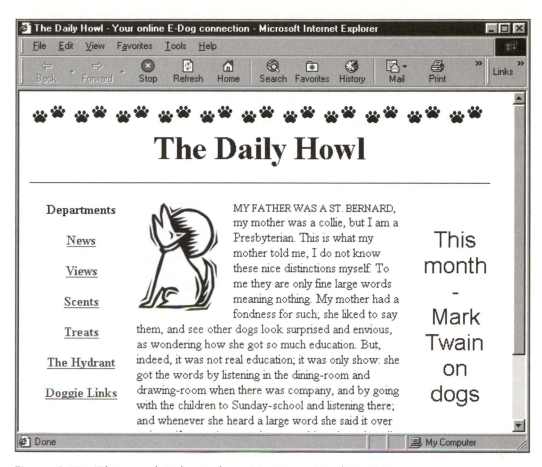

Figure 6-13   The completed page layout in Internet Explorer 5.5

Figure 6-14   The completed page layout in Opera 5.0

UNDERSTANDING THE CSS2 TABLE MODEL

The CSS2 table model expands upon the HTML 4.0 table model. The CSS2 table model is intended for data only, not page layout. CSS2 tables can be expressed as both a visual layout of data and an aural (audio) organization of data. The addition of aural capabilities increases the accessibility of HTML-formatted data to users with sight disabilities and to other applications. The CSS2 table model is not yet commonly supported by browsers, but the concepts are introduced here to give you a look at future capabilities of the style language.

The CSS2 **visual table model** controls the appearance of tables in the browser. You can specify rows and columns of cells to build tables. You can align data both vertically and horizontally, add captions, and set margins around the table. CSS2 supports two table border models that provide complete control over table border appearance. The **separated borders** model lets you control the borders of individual cells. The **collapsed border** model lets you control borders that are continuous across an entire table.

In the CSS2 **aural table model**, you can specify the spoken rendering of a table and determine the order in which data should be spoken. The spoken rendering of document is commonly used by the blind community but also has other applications including spoken-word media (such as audio tapes), industrial or medical services, or any other situation where listening to information is appropriate. The aural style sheet properties let you determine the sequence in which table data is spoken. For example, you can label heading cells to be spoken before data cells. A user with a speech browser would hear a header spoken before the associated data is spoken. You can read more about aural style sheets in Appendix B.

The Visual Table Model

6

The CSS2 table model closely matches the HTML 4.0 table model. The HTML table consists of rows of cells, accompanied by an optional caption and borders if desired. The table model is row dominated, in that you specify rows and cells, not columns. The number of columns in the table is determined by the number of cells in the row. You can also group rows and columns to more easily apply styles and borders.

One of the most interesting aspects of the CSS2 table model is that it provides the ability to assign visual table display properties to any element. This ability is included in CSS to support the Extensible Markup Language (XML), which has no built-in table elements. Defined briefly, XML lets you create elements that match your particular information type, rather than working with a predefined set of elements as in HTML.

Using the display property (see the "Using the Box Properties" chapter), you can set the display type for any element to one of the values listed in Table 6-2.

Table 6-2 CSS2 table display values

Value	Equivalent HTML Element	Description
table	<TABLE>	Specifies that an element defines a block-level table
inline-table	<TABLE>	Specifies that an element defines an inline-level table
table-row	TR	Specifies that an element is a row of cells
table-row-group	TBODY	Specifies that an element groups one or more rows
table-header-group	THEAD	Like table-row-group, but for visual formatting, the row group is always displayed before all other rows and row groups and after any top captions
table-footer-group	TFOOT	Like table-row-group, but for visual formatting, the row group is always displayed after all other rows and row groups and before any bottom captions
table-column	COL	Specifies that an element describes a column of cells
table-column-group	COLGROUP	Specifies that an element groups one or more columns
table-cell	TD TH	Specifies that an element represents a table cell
table-caption	CAPTION	Specifies a caption for the table

The following example demonstrates how you can apply the table display values to XML data. The following code shows some XML-coded information from a spreadsheet. Notice that the element names are particular to this set of data:

```
<SPREADSHEET>
<NAME>Team Phone Numbers</NAME>
<ROW><CELL>Jim</CELL><CELL>555-3486</CELL></ROW>
<ROW><CELL>Steve</CELL><CELL>555-5563</CELL></ROW>
<ROW><CELL>Mary</CELL><CELL>555-3439</CELL></ROW>
</SPREADSHEET>
```

The style sheet for this XML data would look like this:

```
SPREADSHEET {display: table}
NAME {display: table-caption}
ROW {display: table-row}
CELL {display: table-cell}
```

This style sheet lets the XML elements appear as HTML table elements in the browser, enabling the XML-coded data to be presented on the Web without the need of translating the XML information into HTML.

CSS2 Table Properties

CSS2 adds a handful of new properties that are designed for use with tables. Because these properties are not yet well supported, they are described briefly here in Table 6-3.

Table 6-3 CSS2 table properties

Property	Description
table-layout	Controls whether the table has a fixed or flexible layout
caption-side	Determines where the caption will appear
border-collapse	Selects the table's border model, either "separated" or "collapsed"
border-spacing	Specifies the distance that separates adjacent cell borders
empty-cell	In the separated borders model, this property controls the rendering of borders around cells that have no visible content
speak-header	Specifies whether table headers are spoken before every cell or only before a cell when that cell is associated with a different header than the previous cell

CUSTOMIZING LISTS

The list-style properties let you control the visual characteristics of elements that have a display property (see the "Using the Box Properties" chapter) value of "list-item." These properties let you set the appearance of the marker that indicates each item within the list. With CSS, the marker can be a symbol, number, or image. You can also determine the position of the marker next to the list content.

The two common elements that have a default display value of "list-item" are <UL> and <OL>, which generate a bulleted and ordered list, respectively. The following code shows a sample of each type of list:

```
<!-- Bulleted List -->
<H3>Things to do...</H3>
<UL>
<LI>Buy dog food</LI>
<LI>Clean up the house</LI>
<LI>Take a rest</LI>
</UL>
<!-- Ordered List -->
<H3>Places to go...</H3>
<OL>
<LI>Paris</LI>
<LI>Sydney</LI>
<LI>Cairo</LI>
</OL>
```

Figure 6-15 shows the result of this code. Notice that the default markers are a solid bullet, called a "disc," for the <UL> list, and an Arabic numeral, called "decimal," for the <OL> list. Of course, with CSS list-style properties, you can change these marker values.

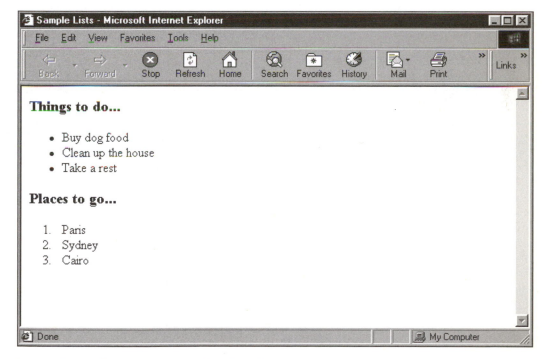

Figure 6-15   The unordered and ordered list elements

Specifying the list-style-type

list-style-type	
Value:	disc | circle | square | decimal | decimal-leading-zero | lower-roman | upper-roman | lower-greek | lower-alpha | lower-latin | upper-alpha | upper-latin | hebrew | armenian | georgian | cjk-ideographic | hiragana | katakana | hira-gana-iroha | katakana-iroha | none
Initial:	disc
Applies to:	elements with 'display: list-item'
Inherited:	yes
Percentages:	N/A

The list-style-type property lets you customize the list marker to a variety of different values. It lets you specify one of three types of markers for a list. You can choose either a symbol, a numbering system, or an alphabetical system. CSS2 allows a wide variety of marker values, some of which are not currently supported. Tables 6-4, 6-5, and 6-6 list the different values and their descriptions.

Table 6-4   Bulleted list values

Value	Description
disc	A filled circle (see Figure 6-16)
circle	A hollow circle (see Figure 6-16)
square	A filled square (see Figure 6-16)

Table 6-5 Numerical list values

Value	Description
decimal	Decimal numbers, beginning with 1; this is the default numbering
decimal-leading-zero	Decimal numbers padded by initial zeros (01, 02, 03…)
lower-roman	Lowercase roman numerals (i, ii, iii…)
upper-roman	Uppercase roman numerals (I, II, III…)
hebrew	Traditional Hebrew numbering
georgian	Traditional Georgian numbering
armenian	Traditional Armenian numbering
cjk-ideographic	Plain ideographic numbers
hiragana	Japanese hiragana language characters
katakana	Japanese katakana language characters
hiragana-iroha	Japanese hiragana-iroha language characters
katakana-iroha	Japanese katakana-iroha language characters

Table 6-6 Alphabetical list values

Value	Description
lower-alpha	Lowercase ASCII letters (a, b, c, … z)
upper-alpha	Uppercase ASCII letters (A, B, C, … Z)
lower-greek	Lowercase classical Greek

The Netscape 6 browser offers the most complete support (at the time of this writing) for the different list-style values. Figure 6-16 shows the different supported list types in Netscape 6.0.

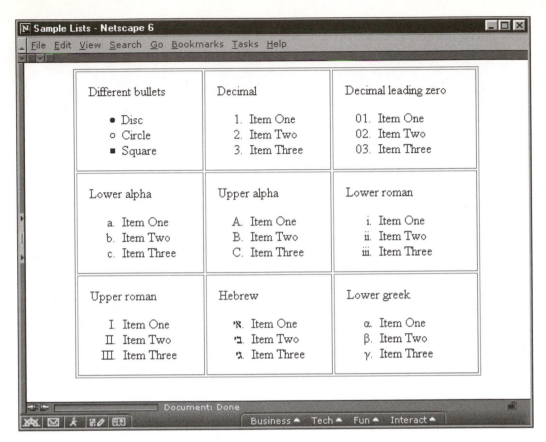

Figure 6-16 Different list types in Netscape 6

To specify a list-style-type, select the list container element, either UL or OL, and specify the value as shown in the following style rules:

```
OL {list-style-type: decimal-leading-zero;}
UL {list-style-type: circle;}
```

There may be times when you want to specify a list-style-type within an individual list. You can do this by using the STYLE attribute within the <UL> or <OL> element, as shown next:

```
<OL STYLE="list-style-type: lower-alpha;">
<LI>Item One</LI>
<LI>Item Two</LI>
<LI>Item Three</LI>
</OL>
```

This style rule affects only this one instance of the list.

Specifying the list-style-image

list-style-image

Value:	\<url\> | none | inherit
Initial:	none
Applies to:	elements with 'display: list-item'
Inherited:	yes
Percentages:	N/A
Media:	visual

The list-style-image property defined below lets you easily attach an image to a list and have it repeated as the marker symbol. It lets you replace the standard symbol with an image of your choice. The following code shows the style rule that attaches an image to a bulleted list:

```
UL {list-style-image: url(pawprint.gif);}
```

Figure 6-17 shows the result of the style rule. The image is repeated whenever a list element is used.

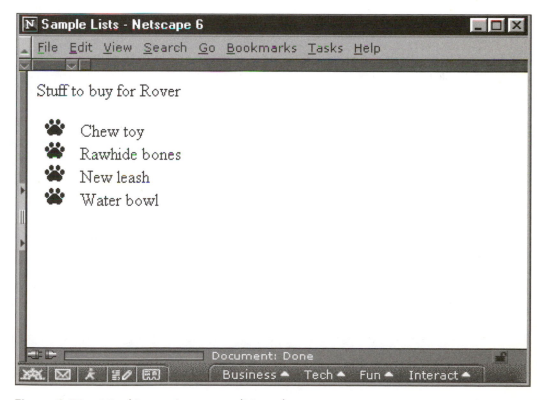

Figure 6-17   Attaching an image as a list marker

Specifying the list-style-position

list-style-position	
Value:	inside | outside | inherit
Initial:	outside
Applies to:	elements with 'display: list-item'
Inherited:	yes
Percentages:	N/A
Media:	visual

The list-style-position property lets you determine the placement of a list marker, either inside or outside of the list-item content box. The default value is outside. Figure 6-18 shows the two types of list position values in Netscape 6, currently the only browser that correctly supports the two values.

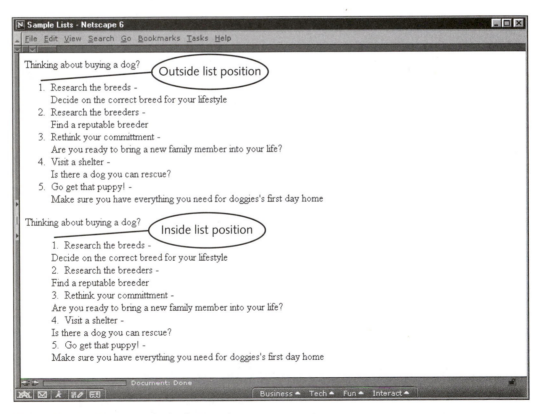

Figure 6-18   Positioning the list marker

This figure shows two <OL> lists. The style rules for this page use a class selector to differentiate between the two:

```
OL.outside {list-style-position: outside;}
OL.inside {list-style-position: inside;}
```

The class is then applied to each <OL> element, as shown in the following code fragment for the first list:

```
<OL class="outside">
```

The class is applied to the second list in the same way:

```
<OL class="inside">
```

Using the list-style Shorthand Property

list-style shorthand property description	
Value:	[<list-style-type> || <list-style-position> || <list-style-image>] | inherit
Initial:	not defined for shorthand properties
Applies to:	elements with 'display: list-item'
Inherited:	yes
Percentages:	N/A
Media:	visual

Like the other shorthand properties, the list-style property lets you write a single rule to specify all of the list-item properties. The list-style shortcut property lets you state the following list-style properties in one concise style rule.

- list-style-type
- list-style-image
- list-style-position

You can specify values in any order. In the following style rule, the list is set to lower alphabetical letters that are inside the list box:

```
OL {list-style: lower-alpha inside;}
```

Applying the List-Style Properties

In the following set of steps, you will learn how to style list-item elements with the list-style properties. As you work through the exercise, refer to Figure 6-20 to see the results you will achieve. Save your file, and test your work in the browser as you complete each step.

To apply the list style properties:

1. Open the file **lists.htm** in your HTML editor, and save it in your work folder as **lists1.htm**.

2. Copy the image file **diamond.gif** into your work folder.

3. In your browser, open the file **lists1.htm**. When you open the file, it looks like Figure 6-19. Notice that the file contains three lists. You will apply a different list-style to each list.

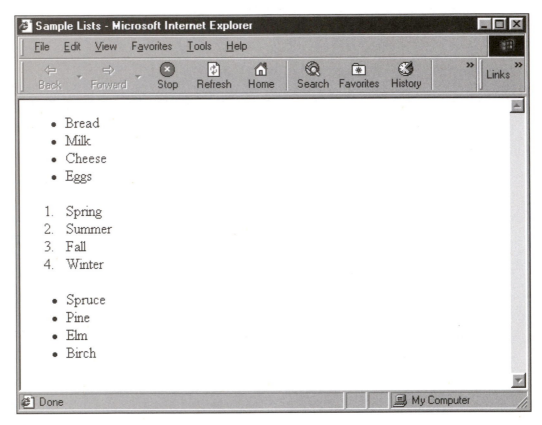

Figure 6-19   The beginning Web page

4. The first list on the page is a bulleted list that currently displays the default disc bullet style. Write a style rule that uses a class selector "circle" to uniquely select the list. Set the list-style-type property to change the bullet style to circle.

```
UL.circle {list-style-type: circle;}
```

5. Now apply the style to the first list by adding the CLASS attribute to the <UL> element.

```
<!-- Bulleted List -->
<UL CLASS="circle">
<LI>Bread</LI>
<LI>Milk</LI>
<LI>Cheese</LI>
<LI>Eggs</LI>
</UL>
```

6. The second list on the page is an ordered list that currently displays the default decimal style. Write a style rule that uses a class selector "alpha" to uniquely select the list. Set the list-style-type property to change the style to upper-alpha.

```
OL.alpha {list-style-type: upper-alpha;}
```

7. Now apply the style to the first list by adding the CLASS attribute to the <OL> element.

```
<!-- Alphabetical List -->
<OL CLASS="alpha">
<LI>Spring</LI>
<LI>Summer</LI>
<LI>Fall</LI>
<LI>Winter</LI>
</OL>
```

8. The third list on the page is an unordered list that currently displays the default bullet style. Write a style rule that uses a class selector "image" to uniquely select the list. Set the list-style-image property to a URL value, using the image file diamond.gif.

```
UL.image {list-style-image: url(diamond.gif);}
```

9. Now apply the style to the first list by adding the CLASS attribute to the <OL> element. Figure 6-20 shows the finished document.

```
<!-- List Image -->
<UL CLASS="image">
<LI>Spruce</LI>
<LI>Pine</LI>
<LI>Elm</LI>
<LI>Birch</LI>
</UL>
```

6

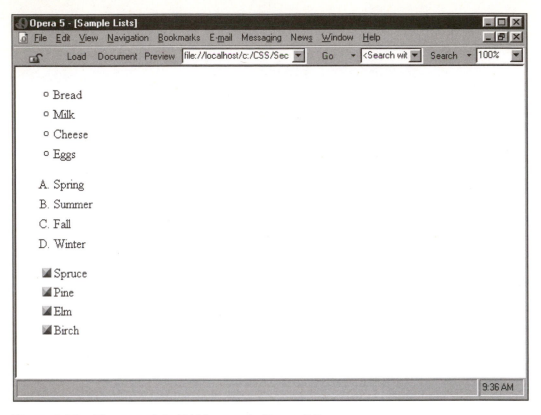

Figure 6-20   The completed Web page in Opera 5.0

CHAPTER SUMMARY

In this chapter, you learned about the table and list-item elements and how to apply CSS style rules to both methods of organizing data. You learned how to apply properties both to the table elements and to content contained within table elements. You saw how CSS style rules can be applied when tables are used to create page layouts. You learned how CSS2 will handle table styles, how the table display properties will allow XML-coded information to display in table formats, and how the aural rendering of table data could be used in future applications. Finally, you examined the list-style properties and learned how to apply them to customize bulleted and ordered lists.

❑ Remember that even though tables were designed for tabular data, they are widely used to build page layout templates and to control the display of information on the Web.

❑ Based on the type of effect you are trying to achieve, it is sometimes better to apply the style rule to the table element. In other instances, applying the style rule to the content within the table cells provides better results.

❑ The CSS2 table model is intended for data only, not page layout. CSS2 will support both a visual and aural rendering of table data.

❑ CSS2 table display values let you set the display type for any element display as a table. This capability is important for displaying XML data in table format.

❑ The list-style properties let you control the visual characteristics of elements that create bulleted and ordered lists. These properties let you set the appearance and positioning of list-item markers.

REVIEW QUESTIONS

1. What was the primary purpose of the HTML table elements?

2. What CSS properties will eventually replace tables as a page layout tool?

3. What are the three commonly used table elements?

4. Which of the table elements contains the table data?

5. What element lets you create table header cells?

6. What are the two built-in characteristics of the table header element?

7. What table element would you use as a selector to affect the entire table?

8. How can you narrow down the selection to a single cell within a table?

9. Write a style rule for a table that sets the vertical alignment in all cells to top.

10. Why would the CSS2 table display values not be used with HTML data?

11. Which two elements are used to create lists in HTML?

12. What are the three types of list styles you can specify?

HANDS-ON PROJECTS

1. Using the Web as a research tool, especially the World Wide Web Consortium site (http://www.w3.org), research the accessibility problems that occur when tables are used as a layout tool. Write a short paper that details the problem and how the CSS2 table model can help solve it.

2. In this project, you will experiment with applying CSS properties to table data.

   a. Open the file plants.htm in your HTML editor, and save it in your work folder as plants1.htm.

   b. In your browser, open the file plants1.htm. When you open the file, it looks like Figure 6-21.

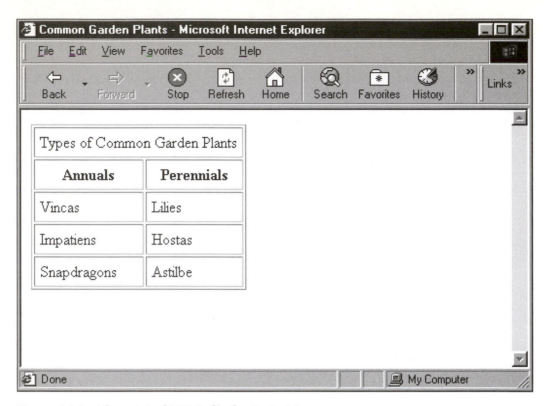

Figure 6-21   The original HTML file for Project 2

c. Examine the code. Notice that there is an existing <STYLE> element in which you can add your style rules. The complete code for the page follows:

```
<HTML>
<HEAD>
<TITLE>Common Garden Plants</TITLE>
<STYLE TYPE="text/css">

</STYLE>
</HEAD>
<BODY>
<TABLE BORDER CELLPADDING=5>
<TR><TD COLSPAN=2>Types of Common Garden Plants</TD></TR>
<TR><TH>Annuals</TH><TH>Perennials</TH></TR>
<TR><TD>Vincas</TD><TD>Lilies</TD></TR>
<TR><TD>Impatiens</TD><TD>Hostas</TD></TR>
<TR><TD>Snapdragons</TD><TD>Astilbe</TD></TR>
</TABLE>
</BODY>
</HTML>
```

d. Use the <TABLE> element as a selector to apply styles to the entire table. Write a style rule that sets the font-family property to monospace.

e. Write a rule for the first row in the table that will create a class named "title." Set the font size to 1.2 em, font style to arial, and add a padding value of 1 em.

f. Apply the title class to the <TD> element in the first row of the table.

g. Write a style rule for the <TH> element row of the table. Set the background color to #000000 (black) and the text color to #FFFFFF (white). Figure 6-22 shows the finished HTML file.

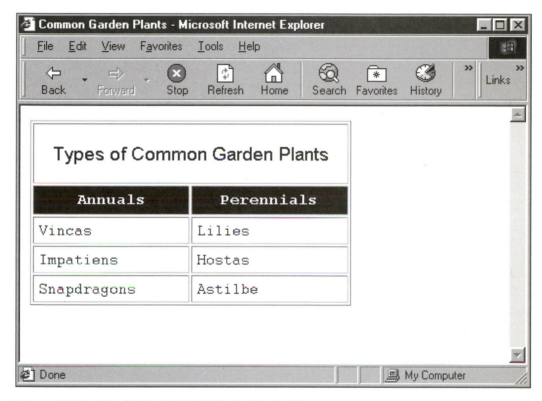

Figure 6-22 The finished HTML file for Project 2

3. In this project, you will experiment with applying CSS properties to lists. This is an open-ended project, so there is no one correct answer.

a. Open the file lists.htm in your HTML editor, and save it in your work folder as lists2.htm.

b. In your browser, open the file lists2.htm. When you open the file, it looks like Figure 6-23.

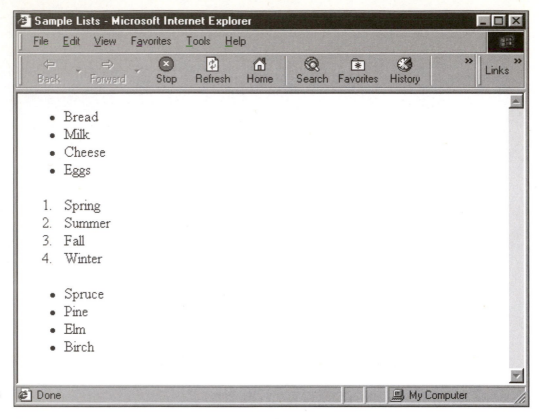

Figure 6-23   The original HTML file for Project 3

    c. Experiment with the different list-style properties you learned about in this chapter. For example, try setting the bulleted list values to the circle or square bullet types.

    d. Set the ordered list to different numbering systems. Test the results using different browsers to determine which browser supports the different list styles.

4. Continue working with the list file list2.htm from Project 3. Experiment with adding different types of bullet images to the lists in the file, using the list-style-image property. You can use your own bullet images, or download some of the sample images provided on the Companion Web site.

5. In this project, you can experiment with different styles applied to a page layout table. This is an open-ended project, so there is no one correct answer.

    a. Open the file howl.htm in your HTML editor, and save it in your work folder as howl2.htm.

    b. Make sure that the image files doghowl.gif and pawback.gif reside in your work folder.

c. In your browser, open the file howl2.htm. When you open the file, it looks like Figure 6–24.

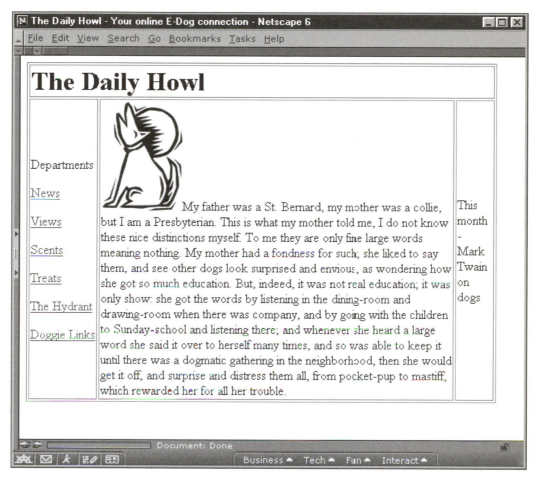

Figure 6-24   The original HTML file for Project 5

d. Experiment with different styles for the different sections of the page.

e. For example, you might want to apply the image pawback.gif as a vertical background within one of the table cells.

f. Try building a list item with the links in the left-hand column. Can you attach an image to the list of links?

g. Experiment with different styles for the banner of the page.

h. Experiment with different styles for the article copy. Try different line-height settings to increase the legibility of the content.

Case Study

You will now have to decide on the page layout templates you will need to create for the different levels of information on your Web site. Because CSS2 positioning is still not widely supported, the page templates will have to be built with tables. The companion Web site contains a number of page templates that you can use as they are or adapt them to your own needs.

Think about the different information levels on your site and which type of page layout can best present that information. Select a few page templates and use them consistently throughout your site. Build style rules for the table contents that you can apply across your entire site, using class names where necessary to select specific types of table cells. Test your work in multiple browsers as you build your designs. Submit sample pages that are populated with test content to demonstrate the page design.

7

USING THE POSITIONING PROPERTIES

When you complete this chapter, you will be able to:

♦ Understand basic positioning concepts

♦ Apply CSS positioning properties

♦ Build a page layout with positioned elements

In a standard HTML document, the default positioning of elements is generally top to bottom and left to right. This basic display scheme frustrated designers who wanted to build more complex layouts, resulting in the use of tables as a page layout tool. The CSS2 positioning properties let you build Web pages without using cumbersome tables to control page layout. With positioning you can choose the exact placement of elements within the browser window. The new generation of browsers offers more robust support for positioning, as you will see in the examples throughout the chapter.

POSITIONING ELEMENTS

The CSS positioning properties give you control over the way element boxes are laid out in a Web page. As you will see, these properties let you specify four different types of positioning. They let you control the positioning of the elements and remove them from the normal flow of elements on the page. The CSS positioning properties let you build pages that have elements positioned at different places in a Web page without using tables as containers, making content more accessible and reserving the use of tables for tabular data (see the "Working with Tables and Lists" chapter).

You also can use the CSS positioning properties with scripts to provide more interactive content to the user. **Scripts** are small pieces of programming that are written with a scripting language such as JavaScript, which was originally designed by Netscape for use in its own browser. JavaScript is now generally supported by all of the major browsers, although Microsoft has its own version, called JScript. When scripting languages are combined with the CSS positioning properties, Web pages can offer more user interaction than simple clicking of hypertext links. Scripts can change the contents of a Web page after it has been displayed in the browser, build interactive forms and games, and simulate animation effects. Although scripts are beyond the scope of this book, you should know how the CSS positioning properties can be used by scripting languages to manipulate an element's placement on a Web page.

Understanding the Normal Flow of Elements

By default, the browser normally displays elements on the page one after the other, depending on whether the elements are block-level or inline elements. Some elements float to the left or right of other elements on the page, as you saw in the "Using the Box Properties" chapter. Element position can be affected by margin or padding properties, but generally the browser lays out element boxes from top to bottom and left to right until all elements that comprise the Web page have been displayed.

In the normal flow for block-level elements, boxes are laid out vertically one after another, beginning at the top of the containing block. Each box's left edge touches the left edge of the containing element unless they are floated or the layout model is right to left, as in a right-aligned language such as Hebrew. The space between boxes is determined by the margin settings. The normal flow determines the sequence of element display that you are familiar with in standard HTML. For an example of the normal flow, examine the following HTML code fragment and the resulting normal flow diagram in Figure 7-1.

```
<BODY>
<H1>The document heading</H1>
<P>A paragraph of some text</P>
<P>Another paragraph of text</P>
</BODY>
```

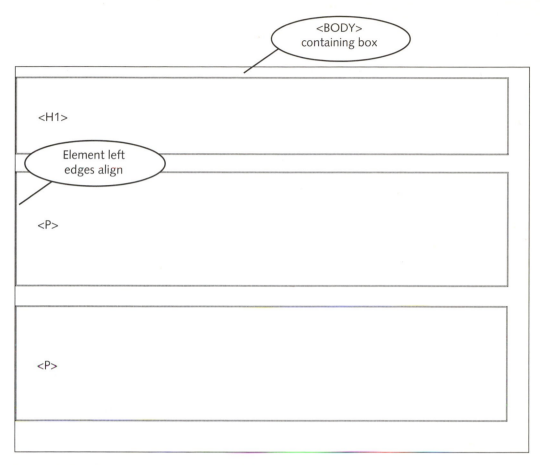

Figure 7-1   Block-level element normal flow

<BODY> is the containing element for the content section of the Web page. The elements within <BODY> display exactly in the order they appear in the code from top to bottom—in this example, an <H1> element followed by two <P> elements. Elements do not appear next to each other unless they are floated (see the "Using the Box Properties" chapter) or have a display type of "inline."

In the normal flow for inline elements, boxes are laid out horizontally, beginning at the top of the containing block. The inline boxes comprise the lines of text within, for example, a paragraph element. The browser flows the text into the inline boxes, wrapping the text to the next line box as determined by the constraints of the containing box or the browser window size.

Specifying Box Position Type

position property description	
Value:	static | relative | absolute | fixed
Initial:	static
Applies to:	all elements, excluding generated content
Inherited:	no
Percentages:	N/A

The position property lets you specify the type of positioning for an element if it will be something other than the default positioning type, which is static. Table 7-1 lists the different positioning values and their meanings.

Table 7-1   Position property value descriptions

Value	Description
static	This is the default value. The element box is a normal box, laid out according to the normal document flow.
absolute	The box's position is specified with the position offset properties, described later in this section. These properties specify offsets with respect to the box's containing box. Absolutely positioned boxes are removed from the normal flow. They have no impact on the layout of other elements on the page.
fixed	The box's position is calculated according to the "absolute" model, but in addition, the box is fixed with respect to the browser window. When the user scrolls the document, fixed elements do not move, but appear in the same position.
relative	The element box position is calculated relative to its normal position in the document flow.

The following style rule uses the position property to set a <DIV> element's position type to absolute.

```
DIV {position: absolute;}
```

Specifying Box Position Offsets

box offset properties: top, right, bottom, left	
Value:	<length> | <percentage> | auto
Initial:	auto
Applies to:	positioned elements
Inherited:	no
Percentages:	refer to width of containing block

The box offset properties let you specify the exact positioning values for any element that has a position property set to absolute, fixed, or relative.

The offset properties determine the position of an element based on its containing box. The values refer to the distance from the edges of the containing block. For example, the following HTML code and style rule create an absolutely positioned <DIV> element that is offset in its containing box by 130 px from the left edge and 100 px from the top edge.

```
<HTML>
<HEAD>
<TITLE>Absolute Positioning</TITLE>
<STYLE TYPE="text/css">
DIV {position: absolute; left: 130px; top: 100px;
background-color: #cccccc;}
</STYLE>
</HEAD>
<BODY>
<DIV>This is an absolutely positioned division element.
</DIV>
</BODY>
</HTML>
```

7

The containing box in this example is the <BODY> element. The division is offset 130 px from the left side of the containing block and 100 px from the top side. Additionally, a background color has been specified to make the division easier to see in the browser. The result of this code is shown in Figure 7-2.

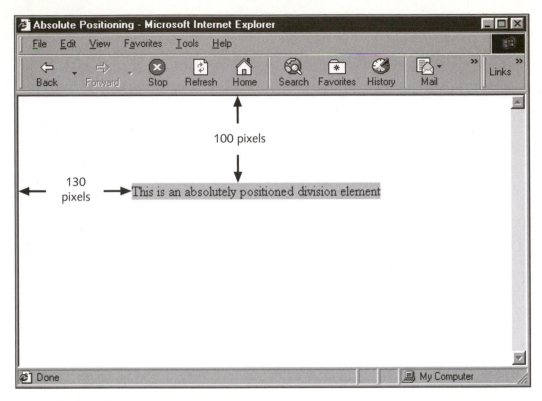

Figure 7-2 Offset box positioning

 Pixels are the most convenient measurement unit when you are specifying absolute or fixed offset values. To avoid guessing screen measurements, use a shareware tool like Screen Ruler, from *http://www.microfox.com/*, to easily measure pixels on your computer monitor.

In Figure 7-2, the width of the <DIV> element is determined by the content it contains. You can use the width property, described in the "Using the Box Properties" chapter, to specify a width for the positioned division. You can also use the height property if the height of the element needs to be controlled. The following style rule shows the addition of the width property to further define the appearance of the element.

```
DIV {position: absolute; left: 130px; top: 100px;
background-color: #cccccc; width: 100px;}
```

Figure 7-3 shows the result of adding the width property to the style rule.

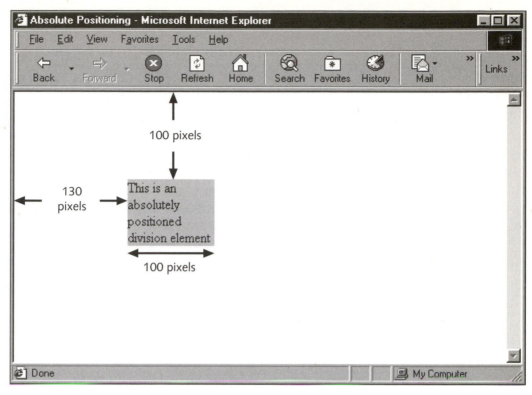

Figure 7-3   Specifying element width

Absolute Positioning

When you specify absolute positioning, an element's position is explicitly stated with respect to its containing box, as you saw in Figure 7-2. An absolutely positioned element is removed from the normal document flow and has no impact on other elements, but it does establish a new containing box for child elements. The child elements of an absolutely positioned element can follow the normal flow or have positioning types of their own. Absolute elements also can overlap the contents of another box, depending on their z-index property (described later in the chapter).

The following HTML code and style rules create two nested <DIV> elements. The outside <DIV> element is positioned within its containing <BODY> element. The inside <DIV> element is positioned within its containing outside <DIV>.

```
<HTML>
<HEAD>
<TITLE>Absolute Positioning</TITLE>
<STYLE TYPE="text/css">
DIV.outside {position: absolute; left: 130px; top: 100px;
background-color: #cccccc; width: 200px; height: 200px;}
```

```
DIV.inside {position: absolute; top: 150px; left: 150px;
width: 50px; height: 50px; border: solid thin black;}
</STYLE>
</HEAD>
<BODY>
<DIV class="outside">Outside
<DIV class="inside">Inside</DIV>
</DIV>
</BODY>
</HTML>
```

Figure 7-4 shows the result of this code.

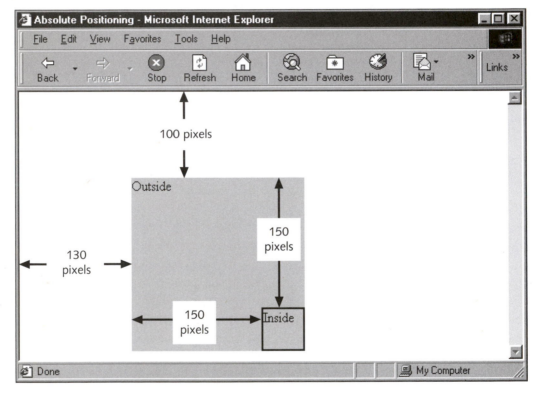

Figure 7-4 Nested positioned elements

Fixed Positioning

Fixed positioning is a subcategory of absolute positioning, with the only difference being that the containing box for a fixed element is always the browser window. Fixed elements stay in the same place at all times, regardless of how the user scrolls the document. Fixing an element lets you create a frame-type layout, where a content element can be scrolled independently of an adjoining navigation element, as shown in Figure 7-5.

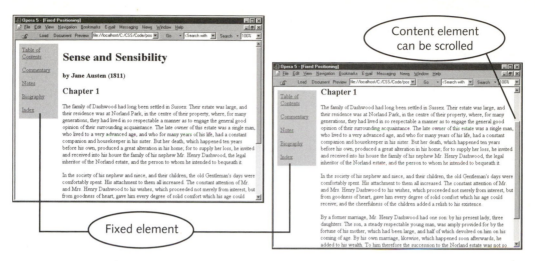

Figure 7-5   Fixed positioning

The following code shows the style rules for both elements in Figure 7-5.

```
DIV.fixed {position: fixed;
    left: 10px;
    top: 10px;
    background-color: #cccccc;
    width: 100px;
    height: 200px;
    padding-top: .5em;
    padding-left: .5em;
}
DIV.content {position: absolute; left: 130px;}
```

Notice that the fixed element has a specific width and height that sets the size of the element in the browser window. The left and top offset properties specify the fixed position of the element. The content element, which contains the page content, has no specific width or height properties, allowing the element size to be flexible based on the browser window size. The left offset property positions the element so it will not overlap the fixed element.

As you can see from the previous example, the ability to fix an element is a powerful design feature that will be very useful when it is fully supported. At the time of this writing, however, the fixed value is currently supported only by the Opera 5.0 browser.

Relative Positioning

The relative position value is intended for use with scripting languages to animate and move elements within the browser window. Specifying a relative position moves an element from its default position in the normal flow. The offset properties let you adjust the position of the element. Relative elements do not affect the position of other elements on the page, which in some instances could cause elements to overlap.

By itself, there is no strong reason to use the relative position value on a static Web page. Scripting languages can use the relative value, along with the dynamic properties (described in Appendix D), to build simple animations and to provide a more interactive environment where a user action, such as clicking, could cause elements to appear or change order.

Specifying Visibility

visibility property description	
Value:	visible | hidden | inherit
Initial:	inherit
Applies to:	all elements
Inherited:	no
Percentages:	N/A

The visibility element specifies whether an element is displayed in the browser. Setting an element's visibility to hidden is different from setting the display property to none, because elements that are set to hidden still take up space in the normal flow. Elements that have their display property set to none are removed from the normal flow. The visibility property will normally be used with scripts to add or remove elements based on user interactions.

Specifying Stacking Level

z-index property description	
Value:	auto | <integer> | inherit
Initial:	auto
Applies to:	positioned elements
Inherited:	no
Percentages:	N/A

The z-index property lets you specify an element's stacking level. In CSS2, each element can be positioned horizontally (the x-axis), vertically (the y-axis), and from front to back as the user faces the computer screen (the z-axis). The **stacking level** is the ordering of elements on the z-axis.

The z-axis can be important if element boxes overlap or if boxes are moved using a script. With scripting, the stacking level can be changed for an element as the user interacts, allowing content to change layers based on user input.

You can use an integer, either positive or negative, to specify the stacking level. Levels are always based on the root element, usually <BODY>, which has a stacking level of 0. Therefore, positive numbers stack in front of <BODY>, while negative numbers stack behind. Figure 7-6 shows a conceptual illustration of the stacking levels.

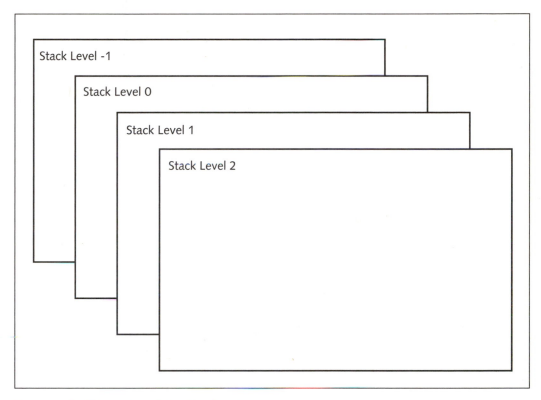

Figure 7-6   The order of stacking levels

Because every element can be a container of other elements, each element establishes its own stacking level context. Therefore, an element that is at stack level 1 sets its own stacking context, starting with level 0, for any contained elements.

The following code shows style rules for four <DIV> elements, each with a different stacking level.

```
DIV.behind {position: absolute;
     top: 10px;
     left: 10px;
     z-index: -1;
     width: 100px;
     height: 200px;
     border: solid thin black;
     background: #ffffff;
}
```

```
DIV {position: absolute;
     top: 40px;
     left: 40px;
     width: 400px;
     height: 200px;
     border: solid thin black;
     background: #ffffff;
}
DIV.level1 {position: absolute;
     top: 80px;
     left: 80px;
     z-index: 1;
     width: 100px;
     height: 200px;
     border: solid thin black;
     background: #ffffff;}

DIV.level2 {
     position: absolute;
     top: 120px;
     left: 120px;
     z-index: 2;
     width: 100px;
     height: 200px;
     border: solid thin black;
     background: #ffffff;}
```

These style rules set the stacking levels for the four <DIV> elements shown in Figure 7-7.

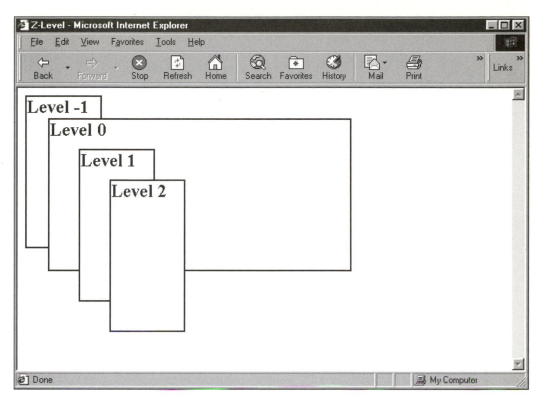

Figure 7-7   Stacking levels in the browser

BUILDING A PAGE LAYOUT WITH POSITIONED ELEMENTS

In the following set of steps, you will see how you can use the CSS positioning and off-set properties to build a page layout without the use of any tables. This set of steps uses the same page content that you worked with when you built a table-based layout in the "Working with Tables and Lists" chapter. The source file for these steps, daily.htm, contains four <DIV> elements that are already completely styled with font effects, background images, and so on. You will position the styled elements to complete the page design. As you work through the steps, refer to Figure 7-12 to see the results you will achieve. Save your file and test your work in the browser as you complete each step.

You can add borders to each element, making it easier to see the dimensions of the page objects as you develop this page layout. Add the border property for each element:

`border: solid thin black;`

You can remove the border property from each element when you have completed the layout.

To position the styled elements to complete the page design:

1. Open the file **daily.htm** in your HTML editor, and save it in your work folder as **daily1.htm**.

2. In your browser, open the file **daily1.htm**. It should look like the file illustrated in Figure 7-8. The four <DIV> elements are laid out according to the normal flow; that is, they are laid out in the order in which they appear in the code.

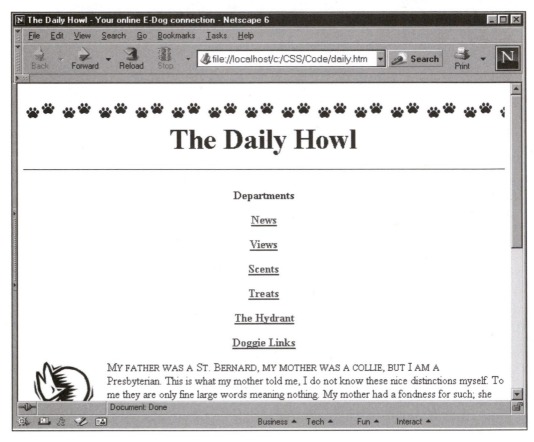

Figure 7-8 The beginning Web page

3. Examine the code in the file. The style section contains comments that explain the style rules. The <BODY> section of the document contains the following <DIV> elements:

- banner element
- links element
- content element
- quote element

The complete code for the page follows.

```html
<HTML>
<HEAD>
<TITLE>The Daily Howl - Your online E-
Dog connection</TITLE>
<STYLE TYPE="text/css">

/* Sets page background to white */
BODY {background-color: #ffffff;}

/* Styles the H1 within the banner element */
H1 {text-align: center;
    font-size: 2.5em;
    padding-top: 30px;
    padding-bottom: 20px;
    border-bottom: solid 1px black;
}

/* The banner element */
DIV.banner {background-image: url(pawback.gif);
        background-repeat: repeat-x;
}

/* The links element */
DIV.links {text-align: center;
        font-weight: bold;
        padding-left: 20px;
        padding-right: 20px;
}

/* Floats the image in the content division */
IMG {float: left; margin-right: 20px;}

/* Styles the content element paragraph first line */
P.article:first-line {font-variant: small-caps;}

/* The content element */
DIV.content {}

/* The quote element */
DIV.quote {font-family: arial;
        font-size: 1.75em;
        text-align: center;
        padding-top: 30px;
        padding-left: 20px;
}
</STYLE>
</HEAD>
<BODY>
```

```
<!-- The Banner Element -->
<DIV CLASS="banner"><H1>The Daily Howl</H1></DIV>

<!-- The Links Element -->
<DIV CLASS="links">
<P>Departments</P>
<P><A HREF="news.htm">News</A></P>
<P><A HREF="views.htm">Views</A></P>
<P><A HREF="scents.htm">Scents</A></P>
<P><A HREF="treats.htm">Treats</A></P>
<P><A HREF="hydrant.htm">The Hydrant</A></P>
<P><A HREF="links.htm">Doggie Links</A></P>
</DIV>

<!-- The Content Element -->
<DIV class="content"><P class="article"><IMG SRC="doghowl.
gif">My father was a St. Bernard, my mother was a collie,
but I am a Presbyterian.  This is what my mother told me, I
do not know these nice distinctions myself.  To me they
are only fine large words meaning nothing.  My mother had
a fondness for such; she liked to say them, and see other
dogs look surprised and envious, as wondering how she got
so much education.  But, indeed, it was not real education;
it was only show:  she got the words by listening in the
dining-room and drawing-room when there was company, and by
going with the children to Sunday-school and listening
there; and whenever she heard a large word she said it over
to herself many times, and so was able to keep it until
there was a dogmatic gathering in the neighborhood, then
she would get it off, and surprise and distress them all,
from pocket-pup to mastiff, which rewarded her for all her
trouble.</P></DIV>

<!-- The Quote Element -->
<DIV CLASS="quote">This<BR>month<BR>-
<BR>Mark<BR>Twain<BR>on<BR>dogs</DIV>
</BODY>
</HTML>
```

Positioning the Banner Element

The banner element is the first object in the page layout. The normal flow of the document controls the position of this element, so no explicit positioning is necessary. However, because no tables contain the element, you must specify a width and height for the element. You will also specify a margin setting to offset the banner from the edge of the browser window.

To position the banner element:

1. Find the rule for the banner element in the document's <STYLE> section. Specify a width of 595 px and a height of 100 px by adding the following highlighted code.

```
/* The banner element */
DIV.banner {background-image: url(pawback.gif);
        background-repeat: repeat-x;
        width: 595px;
        height: 100px;
}
```

2. Set the margin for the banner element to 10 px, as in the following high-lighted code. Figure 7-9 shows the completed banner element.

```
/* The banner element */
DIV.banner {background-image: url(pawback.gif);
        background-repeat: repeat-x;
        width: 595px;
        height: 100px;
        margin: 10px;
}
```

7

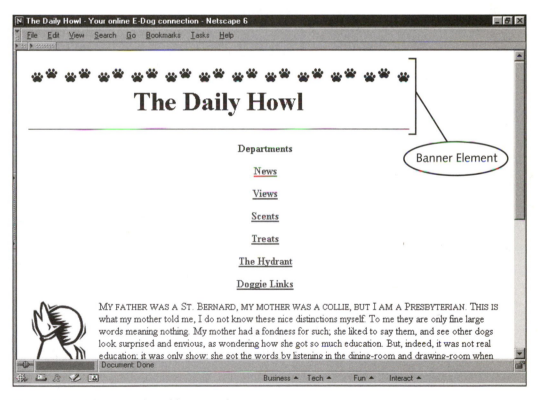

Figure 7-9 The completed banner element

Positioning the Links Element

The links element fills the left column of the lower half section of the layout (see Figure 7-12). You will need to specify width and height properties as you did with the banner element. Although this element would align to the left side of the page in the normal flow, you will specify absolute positioning and offset properties to make sure that this element is placed exactly where you want it to appear on the page.

To position the links element:

1. Find the rule for the links element in the document's <STYLE> section. Specify a width of 150 px and a height of 300 px by adding the following highlighted code.

```
/* The links element */
DIV.links {text-align: center;
     font-weight: bold;
     padding-left: 20px;
     padding-right: 20px;
     width: 150px;
     height: 300px;
}
```

2. Set the link element's position property to absolute, and offset it from the top of the page by 130 px by adding the following highlighted code.

```
/* The links element */
DIV.links {text-align: center;
     font-weight: bold;
     padding-left: 20px;
     padding-right: 20px;
     width: 150px;
     height: 300px;
     position: absolute;
     top: 130px;
}
```

Figure 7-10 shows the completed links element. Notice that the content element has moved and now appears behind the links element. This occurs because you have removed the links element from the normal flow by specifying absolute positioning. The content element is still following the normal flow and moves into place as if the links element was not there. As you continue through these steps, you will adjust the content element to correct this behavior.

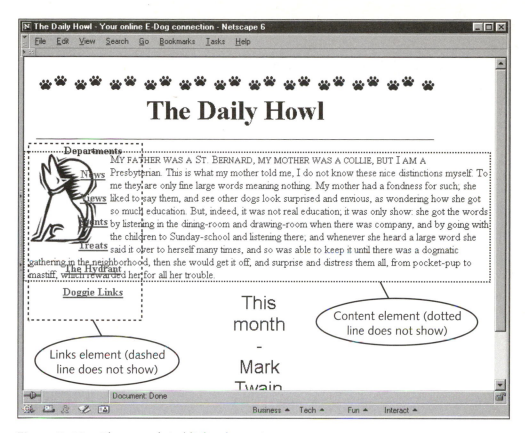

Figure 7-10   The completed links element

Positioning the Content Element

The content <DIV> element fills the middle of the browser window. Currently, the style rule for this element contains no style properties. You will set this element's width and height, and position it in the middle of the page with the offset properties.

To position the <DIV> element:

1. Find the rule for the content element in the document's <STYLE> section. Specify a width of 320 px and a height of 300 px by adding the code highlighted below.

```
/* The content element */
DIV.content {width: 320px;
    height: 300px;
}
```

2. Set the content element's position property to absolute. Offset it from the top of the page by 130 px and from the left side of the page by 180 px by adding the following highlighted code.

```
/* The content element */
DIV.content {width: 320px;
    height: 300px;
    position: absolute;
    left: 180px;
    top: 130px;
}
```

Figure 7-11 shows the completed content element. Notice that the quote element has moved and now appears behind the content element. As with the previous links element, the content element is now removed from the normal flow because of absolute positioning. The next set of steps will move the quote element into its correct position.

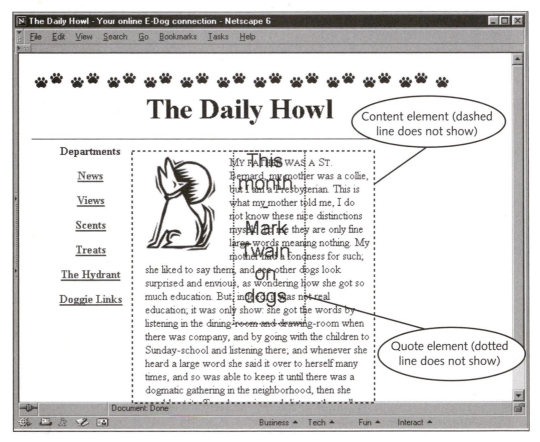

Figure 7-11 The completed content element

Positioning the Quote Element

The quote <DIV> element fills the lower-right half of the browser window. As with the other page elements, you will specify the element's width, height, and position.

To position the quote element:

1. Find the rule for the quote element in the document's <STYLE> section. Specify a width of 100 px and a height of 300 px by adding the code highlighted below.

```
/* The quote element */
DIV.quote {font-family: arial;
    font-size: 1.75em;
    text-align: center;
    width: 100px;
    height: 300px;
}
```

2. Set the quote element's position property to absolute. Offset the element's position from the top of the page by 130 px to align it with the other elements on the page. Also, add an offset from the left side of the page of 540 px by adding the following code.

```
/* The quote element */
DIV.quote {font-family: arial;
    font-size: 1.75em;
    text-align: center;
    width: 100px;
    height: 300px;
    position: absolute;
    left: 540px;
    top: 130px;
}
```

Figure 7-12 shows the completed Web page with the positioned quote element.

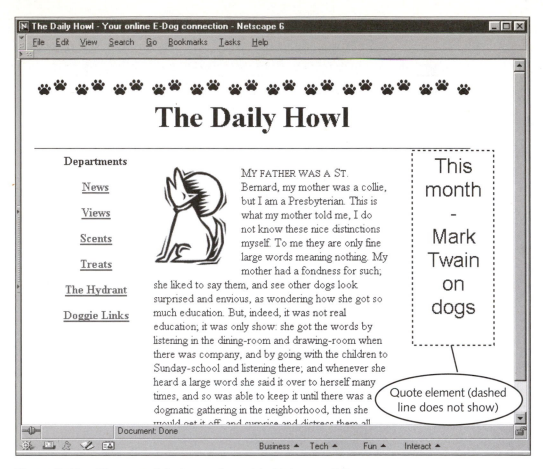

Figure 7-12   The completed page layout in Netscape 6.0

Testing the Page Layout

Now that you have completed the style rules for the document, it is time to test it in the different browsers that support CSS. To test the finished layout, view it in different browsers and look for any discrepancies. Figure 7-10 shows the Web page in Netscape 6.0. Figures 7-13 and 7-14 show the finished page layout in Internet Explorer 5.5 and Opera 5.0, respectively. As you can see, the page layout displays consistently in all three browsers. The only noticeable difference is that Internet Explorer 5.5 does not support the font-variant property that changes the first line of the paragraph to small caps.

Figure 7-13   The completed page layout in Internet Explorer 5.5

Figure 7-14   The completed page layout in Opera 5.0

CHAPTER SUMMARY

In this chapter, you learned about the positioning properties and how to apply them to Web page design. You learned about the normal flow of elements in the document and how the positioning properties let you remove elements from the normal flow. You examined the positioning properties and saw how the different positioning values affected an element's behavior. You also learned how to position elements using offsets for horizontal and vertical positioning and stacking levels for z-axis overlapping. Finally, you applied what you learned by building a complete page layout using the positioning properties.

❑ Remember that the CSS positioning properties are also intended for use with programming scripts that can build interaction and animation into Web pages.

❑ The normal flow dictates the way in which elements normally display in the browser window.

❐ When you remove an element from the normal flow, you may see unexpected behavior from other elements that are following the normal flow.

❐ Pixels are the most convenient measuring unit for offset values.

❐ Use the width and height properties to specify element sizes.

❐ Each containing box sets its own context for positioning. For example, an absolutely positioned box can contain elements that follow the normal flow.

❐ Fixed positioning "pastes" the element to one position, regardless of how the user scrolls.

❐ Relative positioning, stacking levels, and visibility are normally used with scripting languages to create dynamic effects.

REVIEW QUESTIONS

1. What is the normal flow for block-level elements?
2. What are the four types of positioning?
3. What determines space between boxes in the normal flow?
4. What is the default horizontal positioning for block-level elements?
5. What is the default positioning type?
6. How is the position for an absolute element determined?
7. What is the containing element for the content section of a Web page?
8. In the normal flow, which property lets you position elements next to each other?
9. What is the difference between absolute and fixed positioning?
10. What standard HTML layout device can you create using fixed positioning?
11. What is relative positioning used for?
12. What does the z-index property determine?
13. What is the most convenient measurement value when you are specifying absolute or fixed offset values?
14. What determines the default width of a positioned element?

HANDS-ON PROJECTS

1. Explain why using CSS positioning is preferable to using tables to control page layout.
2. Download the shareware version of Screen Ruler from the Web at *http://microfox.com*. Install the software on your computer, and learn to use it to measure pixel distances in your page layouts.

3. In this exercise, you will experiment with absolute positioning.

  a. Open the file position.htm in your HTML editor, and save it in your work folder as position1.htm.

  b. In your browser, open the file position1.htm. When you open the file, it looks like Figure 7-15.

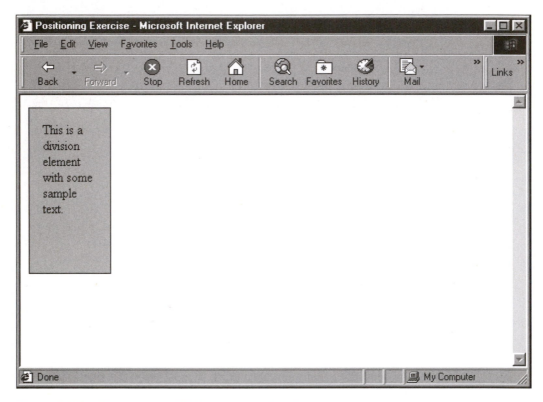

Figure 7-15   The original HTML file for Project 3

  c. Examine the code. Notice that there is an existing style section with a style rule for the <DIV> element that sets the basic characteristics you see in Figure 7-14. The style section code for the document follows:

```
<STYLE TYPE="text/css">
DIV {background-color: #cccccc;
     width: 100px;
     height: 200px;
     padding: 1em;
     border: solid 1px;
     }
</STYLE>
```

  d. Add a position property to the style rule, and set the value to "absolute."

e. Add a left property to the style rule, and experiment with different measurement values to offset the <DIV> element from the left side of the browser window.

f. Add a top property to the style rule, and experiment with different measurement values to offset the <DIV> element from the top of the browser window.

4. In this exercise, you will experiment with relative positioning.

a. Open the file relative.htm in your HTML editor, and save it in your work folder as relative1.htm.

b. In your browser, open the file relative1.htm. When you open the file, it looks like Figure 7-16.

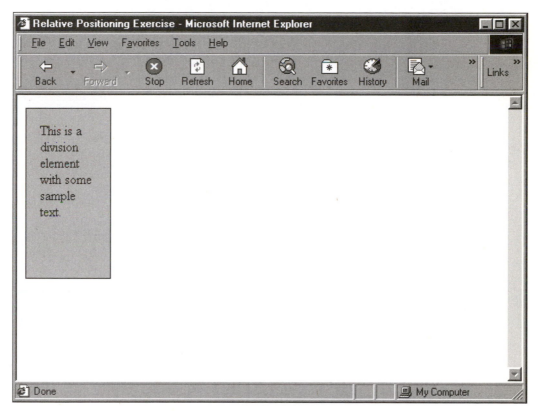

Figure 7-16   The original HTML file for Project 4

c. Add a position property to the style rule, and set the value to "relative."

d. Add a left property to the style rule, and experiment with different percentage measurement values to offset the <DIV> element from the left side of the browser window.

e. Resize your browser to test the relative positioning. Notice that the <DIV> element moves to accommodate the different browser sizes.

f. Add a top property to the style rule, and experiment with different relative measurement values to offset the <DIV> element from the top of the browser window.

g. Resize your browser to test the relative positioning. Notice that the <DIV> element moves to accommodate the different browser sizes.

5. Create an HTML document that has three <DIV> elements. Build a three-column layout with absolute positioning where each <DIV> fills one-third of the browser window at 800 × 600 resolution.

6. Choose a page from your project Web site that uses tables to control the page layout, and rebuild it using positioning. You will have to remove the table elements entirely from the page and rebuild each cell's content as a unique element that can be selected and positioned on the page. Refer to the "Daily Howl" example in this chapter and the previous one. Submit two sample pages—one controlled with tables and the other controlled with positioning properties.

CASE STUDY

You will not use positioning properties in your project Web site because many of your users will not have the latest browsers that support positioning. Now that your page templates are complete and your style rules are built, it is time to populate your site with content and to start usability testing. Choose a test set of users, and have them test your site. Let users navigate the site without your help. Design a feedback form, and ask your users consistent questions about the site. For example:

❑ Did you find the information you needed?

❑ Was it easy or difficult to find information?

❑ Did you find the content easy to read?

❑ Is the Web site visually attractive?

Add other questions of your own that will help you understand the user's view of your site. Based on user input, you may decide to implement final changes to the site before submitting it as your final project.

DESIGNING WITH CASCADING STYLE SHEETS

When you complete this chapter, you will be able to:

♦ Apply the skills you learned throughout this book by building three different types of complete Web pages using CSS

♦ Build a style sheet for online software documentation that users can view with any browser

♦ Design a promotional Web page using a table to create a two-column layout and using classes to create styles for the different sections of the document

♦ Design a home page for a Web site using a variety of CSS properties, including positioning properties

In this chapter, you will get a chance to apply a wide variety of CSS properties by building three complete Web pages. The first project is a style sheet for technical documentation that can be used as online help. This project uses basic CSS techniques, such as applying styles to headings, paragraphs, and numbered lists, and changing the link colors. The second project is a promotional Web page for a fictional conference that can be posted on the Web or e-mailed as an HTML attachment. In this project, you use more advanced CSS skills, such as setting the page background and page banner, and styling elements such as column headings and footer paragraphs. The final project makes extensive use of the CSS positioning properties to build a main page for a fictional company's Web site. In the final project, you synthesize all that you have learned about CSS to produce a professional-quality Web page.

BUILDING A TECHNICAL DOCUMENTATION STYLE SHEET

In the following set of steps, you will use CSS properties to build a style sheet for software documentation. Instead of the traditional paper manual, many software products now come with HTML-based online help that users can view with any browser. These online manuals can be delivered to the user along with the software on a CD-ROM or posted on a public Web site. The latter option allows the product documentation to be easily updated when changes occur in the software.

This example has a few basic requirements that must be followed during the development of the style rules:

- The documentation pages must already be marked up with standard HTML elements.

- The new style rules must apply to the existing documentation with a minimum of changes.

- No new elements can be added.

The source file for this exercise, software.htm, contains the basic page layout, as shown in Figure 8-1. As you work through the exercise, refer to Figure 8-6 to see the results you will achieve. Save your file and test your work in the browser as you complete each step.

To start working on the file:

1. Open the file **software.htm** in your HTML editor, and save it in your work folder as **software1.htm**.

2. In your browser, open the file **software1.htm**. When you open the file, it looks like Figure 8-1. The file contains standard HTML elements.

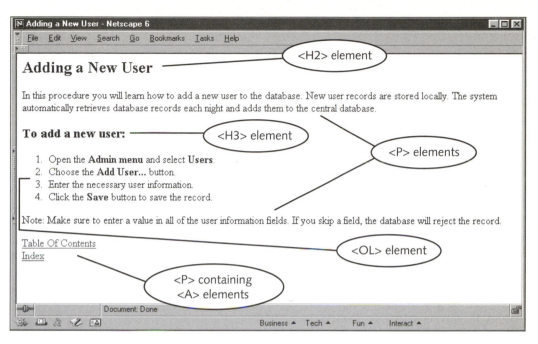

Figure 8-1   The beginning technical documentation Web page

3. Examine the code in the file. Notice the empty <STYLE> element in the <HEAD> section where you will add the style rules. The complete code for the page follows.

```
<HTML>
<HEAD>
<TITLE>Adding a New User</TITLE>
<STYLE TYPE="text/css">
</STYLE>
</HEAD>
<BODY>
<H2>Adding a New User</H2>
<P>In this procedure you will learn how to add a new user
to the database. New user records are stored locally. The
system automatically retrieves database records each
night and adds them to the central database.</P>
<H3>To add a new user:</H3>
<OL>
<LI>Open the <B>Admin menu</B> and select
<B>Users</B>.</LI>
<LI>Choose the <B>Add User...</B> button.</LI>
<LI>Enter the necessary user information. </LI>
<LI>Click the <B>Save</B> button to save the record.</LI>
</OL>
<P>
```

```
Note: Make sure to enter a value in all of the user
information fields. If you skip a field, the database
will reject the record.
</P>
<P>
<A HREF="toc.htm">Table Of Contents</A>
<BR>
<A HREF="index.htm">Index</A>
</P>
</BODY>
</HTML>
```

Styling the <H2> Element

The <H2> element contains the main heading text for the page. To make the heading more distinctive, you will specify a sans-serif font and add margins and a bottom rule.

To style the <H2> element:

1. Write a style rule for the <H2> element that sets the font family to a sans-serif font. Use font substitution to specify both Arial and Helvetica, and then use the generic font family (sans-serif) in case neither style is available on the user's computer.

   ```
   H2 {font-family: arial, helvetica, sans-serif;}
   ```

2. Set the left and right margins for the H2 element to 20 px.

   ```
   H2 {font-family: arial, helvetica, sans-serif;
       margin-left: 20px;
       margin-right: 20px;}
   ```

3. Add a solid 1-px bottom border to the element. Set the border off from the bottom of the <H2> text by adding a padding-bottom value of .25 em.

   ```
   H2 {font-family: arial, helvetica, sans-serif;
       margin-left: 20px;
       margin-right: 20px;
       border-bottom: solid 1px;
       padding-bottom: .25em;}
   ```

Figure 8-2 shows the result of the <H2> style rule.

Figure 8-2   The styled <H2> element

Styling the Standard Paragraph

The <P> paragraph elements are standard throughout the documentation. The note paragraph will have a special class, as you will see later, but all paragraphs share 20-px left and right margins.

To style the <P> elements:

1. Add a rule for the <P> elements that specifies margin-left and margin-right of 20 px.

    ```
    P {margin-left: 20px; margin-right: 20px;}
    ```

2. View the page in the browser. As Figure 8-3 shows, the paragraphs on the page now have a left margin and a right margin that align them with the <H2> element.

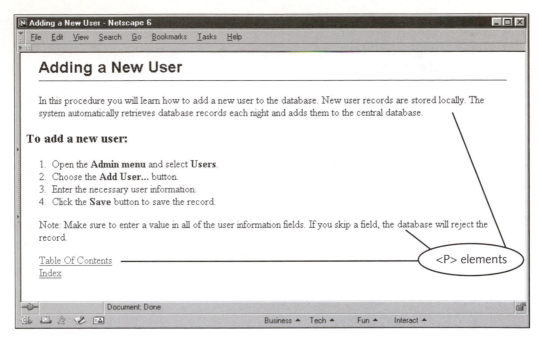

Figure 8-3 The standard paragraph style

Styling the <H3> Element

The <H3> heading is the title for the procedural steps. To match the <H2> heading style you created previously, you will write a style rule that indents the heading and changes the font family.

To style the <H3> element:

1. Write a style rule for the <H3> element that sets the font family to a sans-serif font. Use font substitution to specify both Arial and Helvetica, and then use the generic font family (sans-serif) in case neither style is available on the user's computer.

   ```
   H3 {font-family: arial, helvetica, sans-serif;}
   ```

2. Set the left and right margins for the H3 element to 20 px.

   ```
   H3 {font-family: arial, helvetica, sans-serif;
       margin-left: 20px;
       margin-right: 20px;}
   ```

3. View the page in the browser. Figure 8-4 shows the result of the new <H3> style rule.

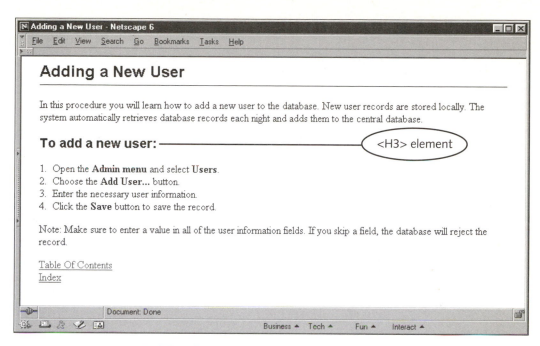

Figure 8-4   The styled <H3> element

Styling the Numbered List

The <OL> element contains the <LI> (list item) elements that comprise the numbered procedure. Within each <LI> are descendant <B> elements that emphasize the menu items users choose to perform the procedure. You will write a style rule that uses descendant selection (see the "Understanding CSS Selection Techniques" chapter) to style the <B> elements with a bold weight and sans-serif font family. You will also indent the entire list to adjust for the new margins you have created for the other page elements.

To style the <B> elements within the <LI> elements:

1. Write a style rule that uses descendant selection to select <B> elements within <LI> elements. Set the font family to a sans-serif font. Use font substitution to specify both Arial and Helvetica, and then use the generic font family (sans-serif) in the event that neither style is available on the user's computer.

   ```
   LI B {font-family: arial, helvetica, sans-serif;}
   ```

2. The <B> elements in the sans-serif font are too large for the default Times Roman <LI> text. Set the font size to .85 em to bring the size slightly below the default font size.

   ```
   LI B {font-family: arial, helvetica, sans-serif;
         font-size: .85em;
         }
   ```

3. Now write a separate style rule that uses descendant selection to select the <LI> elements within the <OL> containing box. This rule specifies a left margin of 20 px that will indent the numbered list.

```
OL LI {margin-left: 20px;}
```

4. View the page in the browser. Figure 8-5 shows the completed list element.

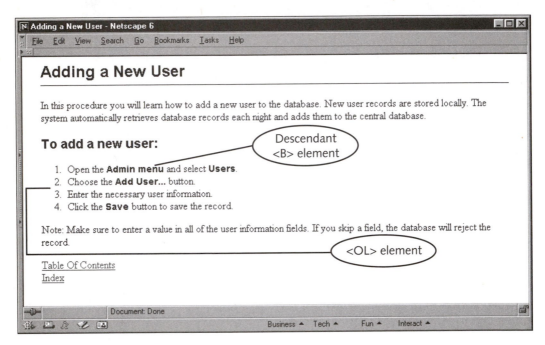

Figure 8-5   The styled list element

Styling the Note Paragraph

The note paragraph needs a special style to set it off from the regular paragraphs on the page. To select this paragraph as a special type, you will use a class selector and apply it to the note paragraph with the CLASS attribute (see the "Understanding the CSS Selection Techniques" chapter). The style rule for the note paragraph will use a background color and border to emphasize the note for the user.

To style the note class:

1. Write a style rule that uses "note" as the class selector. Restrict the use of the "note" class to <P> elements only. Set the background color of the element to hexadecimal value #CCCCCC.

```
P.note {background-color: #CCCCCC;}
```

2. Add a 1-px solid border to the rule. The border will default to the black text color, so no color value is necessary.

```
P.note {background-color: #CCCCCC;
        border: solid 1px;}
```

3. Finally, add 1 em of padding to offset the border from the text.

```
P.note {background-color: #CCCCCC;
        border: solid 1px;
        padding:  1em;}
```

4. Apply the "note" class to the note paragraph by adding the CLASS attribute to the correct <P> element, as shown in the following code fragment:

```
<P class="note">
Note: Make sure to enter a value in all of the user
information fields. If you skip a field, the database
will reject the record.
</P>
```

5. View the file in the browser. Figure 8-6 shows the completed "note" paragraph.

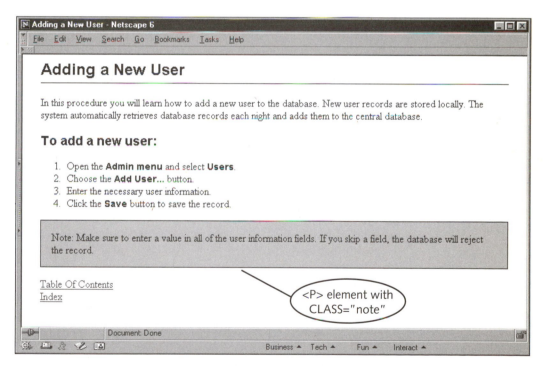

Figure 8-6 The styled note paragraph

Changing the Link Colors

Online documentation, such as the document you are working on for this set of steps, often has different link color conventions from standard Web pages. The links at the bottom of the page currently default to the standard blue for unvisited links and purple for visited links. For this exercise, you will use the link pseudo-classes (see the "Understanding CSS Selection Techniques" chapter) to change the link colors to green for new links and red for visited links.

To change the link colors:

1. Write a rule that uses the link pseudo-class to change the color of the new link to #006600, as shown in the following code.

   ```
   :link {color: #006600;}
   ```

2. Write a rule that uses the visited pseudo-class to change the color of the visited link to hex #FF0000, as shown in the following code.

   ```
   :visited {color: #FF0000;}
   ```

3. View your changes in the browser. The two links at the bottom of the page should now appear green.

You have completed the design of the page. The complete page code follows.

```
<HTML>
<HEAD>
<TITLE>Adding a New User</TITLE>
<STYLE TYPE="text/css">
H2 {font-family: arial, helvetica, sans-serif;
    margin-left: 20px;
    margin-right: 20px;
    border-bottom: solid 1px;
    padding-bottom: .25em;
}
P {margin-left: 20px;
    margin-right: 20px;

}
H3 {font-family: arial, helvetica, sans-serif;
    margin-left: 20px;
    margin-right: 20px;
}
LI B {font-family: arial, helvetica, sans-serif;
    font-size: .85em;
}
OL LI {margin-left: 20px;}
P.note {background-color: #CCCCCC;
    border: solid 1px;
    padding: 1em;
```

```
}
:link {color: #006600;}
:visited {color: #FF00FF;}
</STYLE>
</HEAD>
<BODY>
<H2>Adding a New User</H2>
<P>In this procedure you will learn how to add a new user
to the database. New user records are stored locally. The
system automatically retrieves database records each night
and adds them to the central database.</P>
<H3>To add a new user:</H3>
<OL>
<LI>Open the <B>Admin menu</B> and select <B>Users</B>.</L
I>
<LI>Choose the <B>Add User...</B> button.</LI>
<LI>Enter the necessary user information.</LI>
<LI>Click the <B>Save</B> button to save the record.</LI>
</OL>
<P class="note">
Note: Make sure to enter a value in all of the user infor-
mation fields. If you skip a field, the database will reje
ct the record.
</P>
<P>
<A HREF="toc.htm">Table Of Contents</A>
<BR>
<A HREF="index.htm">Index</A>
</P>
</BODY>
</HTML>
```

BUILDING A PROMOTIONAL LAYOUT

In the following set of steps, you will use CSS properties to design a promotional Web page for a fictional conference. This page could be posted on a Web site or e-mailed to potential conference attendees as an HTML attachment. This Web page uses a table to create a two-column layout. You will create styles for the different sections of the document using classes (See the "Understanding the Selection Techniques" chapter) that you will apply to the existing document elements.

The source file for this exercise, conference.htm, contains the basic page layout, as shown in Figure 8-7. As you work through the exercise, refer to Figure 8-14 to see the results you will achieve. Save your file and test your work in the browser as you complete each step.

To start working on the file:

1. Open the file **conference.htm** in your HTML editor, and save it in your work folder as **conference1.htm**.

2. In your browser, open the file **conference1.htm**. When you open the file, it looks like Figure 8-7. The file contains standard HTML elements and a table that has the border showing. When you complete the design, you will hide the table border.

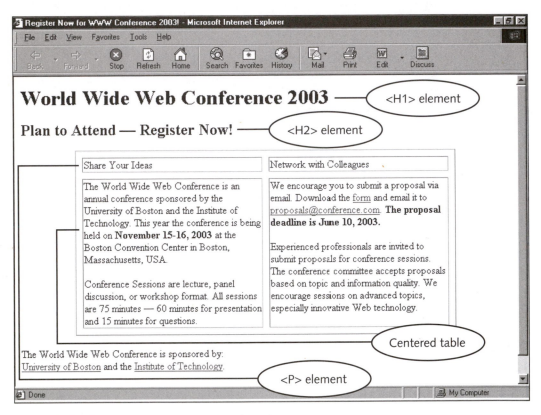

Figure 8-7   The beginning promotional Web page

3. Examine the code in the file. Notice the empty <STYLE> element in the <HEAD> section where you will add the style rules. Also note the HTML comments that indicate the different document elements. The complete code for the page follows.

```
<HTML>
<HEAD>
<TITLE>Register Now for WWW Conference 2003!</TITLE>
<STYLE TYPE="text/css">
</STYLE>
```

```
</HEAD>
<BODY>
<!--Banner -->
<H1>World Wide Web Conference 2003</H1>
<!-- Subheading -->
<H2>Plan to Attend &#0151; Register Now!</H2>
<!-- 2-Column Content Table -->
<DIV ALIGN="CENTER">
<TABLE WIDTH=580  BORDER CELLSPACING="10">
<TR>
<TD WIDTH="50%">
<P>Share Your Ideas</P>
</TD>
<TD WIDTH="50%">
<P>Network with Colleagues</P>
</TD>
</TR>
<TR VALIGN="TOP">
<TD>
<P>The World Wide Web Conference is an annual
conference sponsored by the University of Boston and the
Institute of Technology. This year the conference is
being held on <B>November 15-16, 2003</B> at the Boston
Convention Center in Boston, Massachusetts, USA.</P>
<P>Conference Sessions are lecture, panel discussion, or
workshop format. All sessions are 75 minutes &#0151; 60
minutes for presentation and 15 minutes for questions.</P>
</TD>
<TD>
<P>We encourage you to submit a proposal via email.
Download the <A HREF="proposal.doc">form</A> and email
it to <A HREF="MAILTO:">proposals@conference.com</A>.
<B>The proposal deadline is June 10, 2003.</B></P>
<P>Experienced professionals are invited to submit
proposals for conference sessions. The conference
committee accepts proposals based on topic and
information quality.  We encourage sessions on advanced
topics, especially innovative Web technology.</P>
</TD>
</TR>
</TABLE>
</DIV>
<!-- Sponsors -->
<P>The World Wide Web Conference is sponsored by:<BR>
<A href="index.htm">University of Boston</A> and the
<A HREF="index.htm">Institute of Technology</A>.</P>
<!-- Footer -->
```

```
<P>For more information contact the conference office at
555-555-1234 or email <A HREF="MAILTO: info@conference.com">
</A>.</P>
</BODY>
</HTML>
```

Specifying the Page Background

The finished page design contains a background image that repeats across the top of the page (see the "Using the Color and Background Properties" chapter). You will also want to specify a page background color to ensure that the page displays consistently across different browsers.

To style the page background:

1. Write a style rule using the <BODY> element as the selector. Specify a white background color, using the hexadecimal value #FFFFFF.

   ```
   body {background-color: #FFFFFF;}
   ```

2. Copy the image **wwwtri.jpg** into your work folder.

3. Write a style rule that specifies wwwtri.jpg as the background image. Set the background-repeat property to tile the image across the x-axis of the page, as shown in the following style rule:

   ```
   body {background-color: #FFFFFF;
         background-image: url(wwwtri.jpg);
         background-repeat: repeat-x;}
   ```

4. View the page in the browser. Figure 8-8 shows the result. Notice that the <H1> heading is illegible in its current position. You will adjust the <H1> element in the next section.

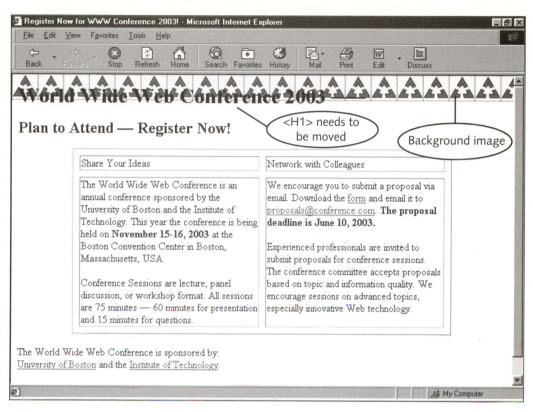

Figure 8-8   The background image

Styling the Page Banner

The <H1> element contains the banner text for the page. You will center the text, change the size and color, and add a top margin to move the element beneath the background graphic. You will apply the style to the <H1> element with a class selector.

To style the page banner:

1. Write a style rule for the <H1> element that uses a class selector "banner." Use the text-align property to center the text on the page.

```
.banner {text-align: center;}
```

2. Set the font size to 2.5 em. Specify a green text color that matches as closely as possible the green in the background image, using a hexadecimal value of #336600, as shown in the following style rule:

```
.banner {text-align: center;
        font-size: 2.5em;
        color: #336600;
}
```

3. Specify a top margin of 50 px to offset the <H1> element from the top of the page.

```
.banner {text-align: center;
    font-size: 2.5em;
    color: #336600;
    margin-top: 50px;
}
```

4. Apply the class to the <H1> element by adding the CLASS attribute and setting the value to "banner," as shown in the following code:

```
<!--Banner -->
<H1 CLASS="banner">World Wide Web Conference 2003</H1>
```

5. View the page in the browser. Figure 8-9 shows the result. Notice that the <H1> heading no longer conflicts with the background image.

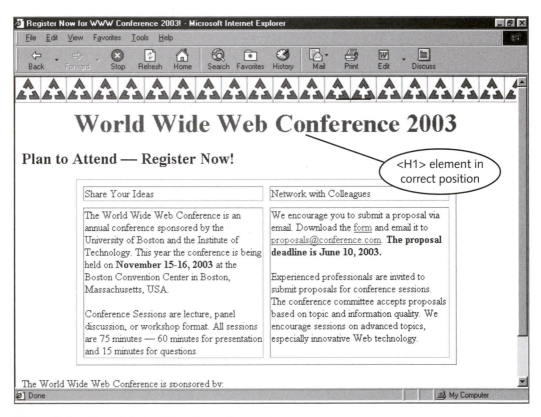

Figure 8-9 The styled <H1> element page banner

Styling the Page Subheading

The <H2> element contains the subheading text for the page. You will change the font-family, center the text, create a text reverse, and add padding and margins (see the "Using the Box Properties" chapter) to the element. You will apply the style to the <H2> element with a class selector.

To style the page subheading:

1. Write a style rule for the <H2> element that uses a class selector "subheading." Set the font family to a sans-serif font. Use font substitution to specify both Arial and Helvetica, and then use the generic font family (sans-serif) in the event that neither style is available on the user's computer.

   ```
   .subheading {font-family: arial, helvetica, sans-serif;}
   ```

2. Use the text-align property to center the text on the page.

   ```
   .subheading {font-family: arial, helvetica, sans-serif;
               text-align: center;}
   ```

3. Create the text reverse. Set the background color to deep red, using hexadecimal value #CC0000. Set the text color to white, using the hexadecimal value #FFFFFF.

   ```
   .subheading {font-family: arial, helvetica, sans-serif;
               text-align: center;
               background-color: #CC0000;
               color: #FFFFFF;}
   ```

4. Set the left and right margins to align the subheading with the columns of text. Use a value of 80 px for both margins.

   ```
   .subheading {font-family: arial, helvetica, sans-serif;
               text-align: center;
               background-color: #CC0000;
               color: #FFFFFF;
               margin-left: 80px;
               margin-right: 80px;
               }
   ```

5. Set the top and bottom padding values to .5 em to increase the background color area around the text.

   ```
   .subheading {font-family: arial, helvetica, sans-serif;
               text-align: center;
               background-color: #CC0000;
               color: #FFFFFF;
               margin-left: 80px;
               margin-right: 80px;
               padding-top: .5em;
               padding-bottom: .5em;
               }
   ```

8

6. Apply the class to the <H2> element by adding the CLASS attribute and setting the value to "subheading," as shown in the following code:

```
<!-- Subheading -->
<H2 CLASS="subheading">Plan to Attend &#0151; Register
Now!</H2>
```

7. View the page in the browser. Figure 8-10 shows the result.

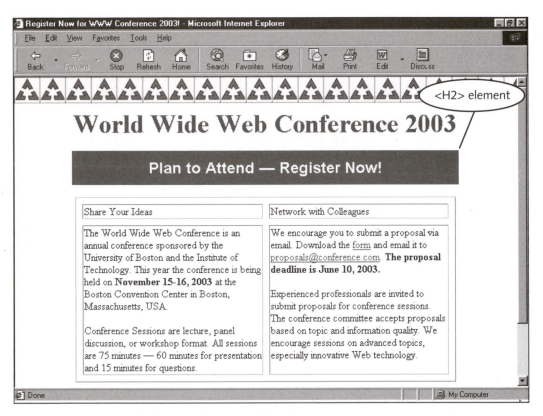

Figure 8-10   The styled <H2> element subheading

Styling the Column Headings

The first row of the table contains <P> elements that are the column headings for the two columns of table content. You will change the font family, adjust the font weight and size, center the text, and add a colored border to the element. You will apply the style to the <P> element with a class selector.

To style the column headings:

1. Write a style rule that uses a class selector "columnheading." Set the font family to a sans-serif font. Use font substitution to specify both Arial and

Helvetica, and then use the generic font family (sans-serif) in the event that neither style is available on the user's computer.

```
.columnheading {font-family: arial, helvetica,
sans-serif;}
```

2. Use the text-align property to center the text on the page.

```
.columnheading {font-family: arial, helvetica,
sans-serif;
                text-align: center;
                }
```

3. Set the font weight to bold and the font size to 1.25 em.

```
.columnheading {font-family: arial, helvetica,
sans-serif;
                text-align: center;
                font-weight: bold;
                font-size: 1.25em;
                }
```

4. Use the border shortcut property (see the "Using the Box Properties" chapter) to create a border around the column heading. Set the border style to solid, the border weight to 2 px, and the border color to the dark red you used in the subheading text reverse, hexadecimal value #CC0000. Add a padding value of 1 em to offset the border from the text.

```
.columnheading {font-family: arial, helvetica,
sans-serif;
                text-align: center;
                font-weight: bold;
                font-size: 1.25em;
                border: solid 2px #CC0000;
                padding: 1em;
                }
```

5. Apply the class to the <P> elements in the first table row by adding the CLASS attribute and setting the value to "columnheading," as shown in the following code:

```
<!-- 2-Column Content Table -->
<DIV ALIGN="CENTER">
<TABLE WIDTH=590  BORDER CELLSPACING="10">
<TR>
<TD WIDTH="50%">
<P CLASS="columnheading">Share Your Ideas</P>
</TD>
<TD WIDTH="50%">
<P CLASS="columnheading">Network with Colleagues</P>
</TD>
</TR>
```

8

6. View the page in the browser. Figure 8–11 shows the result.

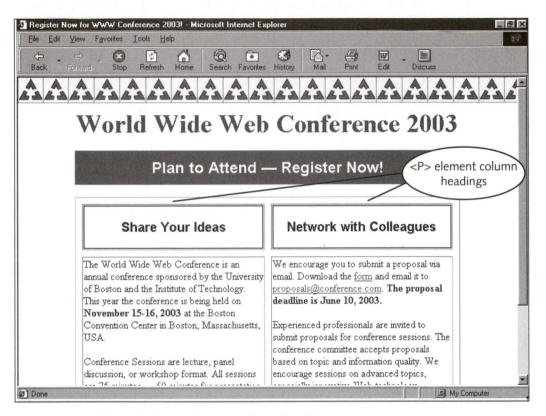

Figure 8-11   The styled <P> element column headings

Styling the Copy Paragraphs

The second row of the table contains <P> elements that are the standard copy of the Web page. You will change the font family and color and adjust the line height to make the text more legible. As in the previous page elements, you will apply the style to the <P> element with a class selector.

To style the copy paragraphs:

1. Write a style rule that uses a class selector "copy." Set the font family to the sans-serif font substitution values that you used for the subheading and column heading elements.

   ```
   .copy {font-family: arial, helvetica, sans-serif;}
   ```

2. Specify the same dark red hexadecimal value you used in the column headings.

   ```
   .copy {font-family: arial, helvetica, sans-serif;
          color: #CC0000;}
   ```

3. Specify a line height value (see the "Using the Font and Text Properties" chapter) to increase the legibility of the text by adding more white space between the lines of text. This example uses a value of 1.5 em, but you can experiment with different settings until you find one you feel is the best choice.

```
.copy {font-family: arial, helvetica, sans-serif;
       color: #CC0000;
       line-height: 1.5em;}
```

4. Apply the "copy" class to the <P> elements contained within the second row of the table. The following code fragment shows only one of the <P> elements. You will have to apply the class to all four <P> elements within the table to achieve the correct results. You can refer to the complete page code at the end of this exercise if you need help.

```
<P CLASS="copy">The World Wide Web Conference is an
annual conference sponsored by the University of Boston
and the Institute of Technology. This year the
conference is being held on <B>November 15-16, 2003
</B> at the Boston Convention Center in Boston,
Massachusetts, USA.</P>
```

5. View the page in the browser. Figure 8-12 shows the result.

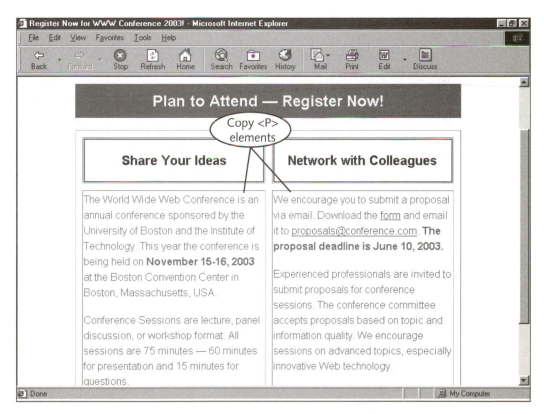

Figure 8-12   The styled <P> copy elements

Styling the Footer Paragraphs

The bottom of the page contains two <P> elements that must be selected with different classes because they have slightly different style requirements. Because these two classes have almost exactly the same property values, you will write both style rules at the same time.

To style the footer paragraphs:

1. Write two style rules—one that uses the class selector "sponsors" for the <P> element that contains the sponsor information and one that uses a class "footer" for the <P> element that is at the bottom of the page. Set the font family to the sans-serif font substitution values that you used for the subheading and column heading elements.

   ```
   .sponsors {font-family: arial, helvetica, sans-serif;}

   .footer {font-family: arial, helvetica, sans-serif;}
   ```

2. Set the font size to .75 em for both classes.

   ```
   .sponsors {font-family: arial, helvetica, sans-serif;
           font-size: .75em;
           }

   .footer {font-family: arial, helvetica, sans-serif;
           font-size: .75em;
           }
   ```

3. Set the line height to 1.2 em and the text alignment to center for both classes. This completes the styling of the "sponsors" class.

   ```
   .sponsors {font-family: arial, helvetica, sans-serif;
           font-size: .75em;
           line-height: 1.2em;
           text-align: center;
           }

   .footer {font-family: arial, helvetica, sans-serif;
           font-size: .75em;
           line-height: 1.2em;
           text-align: center;
           }
   ```

4. Add bottom border and padding values to the "footer" class only. Set the bottom border style to solid, the weight to 2 px, and the color to #CC0000. Add a padding value of 1 em to offset the border from the bottom of the text.

   ```
   .footer {font-family: arial, helvetica, sans-serif;
           font-size: .75em;
           line-height: 1.2em;
           text-align: center;
   ```

```
border-bottom: solid 2px #CC0000;
padding-bottom: 1em;
}
```

5. Apply the "sponsors" and "footer" classes to the appropriate <P> elements within the file, as shown in the following code:

```
<!-- Sponsors -->
<P CLASS="sponsors">The World Wide Web Conference is
sponsored by:<BR> <A href="index.htm">University of
Boston</A> and the <A HREF="index.htm">Institute of
Technology</A>.</P>


<!-- Footer -->
<P CLASS="footer">For more information contact the
conference office at 555-555-1234 or email <A HREF=
"MAILTO:">info@conference.com</A>.</P>
```

6. View your changes in the browser. Figure 8-13 shows the results.

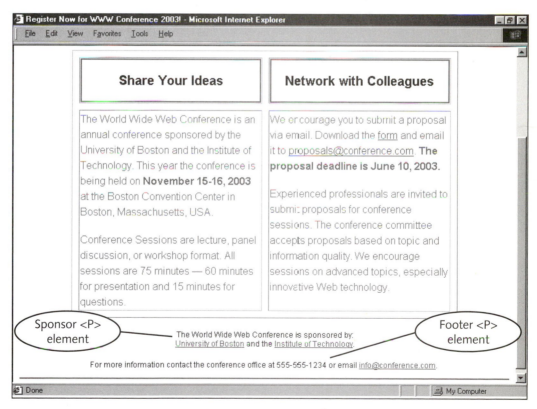

Figure 8-13   The sponsors and footer <P> elements

7. To complete the design, remove the BORDER attribute from the opening <TABLE> tag to hide the table border.

```
<TABLE WIDTH=590 BORDER CELLSPACING="10">
```

The opening <TABLE> element now looks like the following:

```
<TABLE WIDTH=590 CELLSPACING="10">
```

8. View your changes in the browser. Figure 8-14 shows the finished page design.

Figure 8-14   The finished page design

You have completed the design of the page. The complete page code follows.

```
<HTML>
<HEAD>
<TITLE>Register Now for WWW Conference 2003!</TITLE>
<STYLE TYPE="text/css">
body { background-color: #FFFFFF;
      background-image: url(wwwtri.jpg);
      background-repeat: repeat-x;
      }
.banner {text-align:center;
      font-size: 2.5em;
      color: #336600;
      margin-top: 50px;
      }
.subheading {font-family: arial, helvetica, sans-serif;
            text-align: center;
            background-color: #CC0000;
            color: #FFFFFF;
            margin-left: 80px;
            margin-right: 80px;
            padding-top: .5em;
            padding-bottom: .5em;
            }
.columnhead    {font-family: arial, helvetica, sans-serif;
            text-align: center;
            font-weight: bold;
            font-size: 1.25em;
            border: solid 2px #CC0000;
            padding: 1em;
            }
.copy       {font-family: arial, helvetica, sans-serif;
            color: #CC0000;
            line-height: 1.5em;
            }
.sponsors {font-family: arial, helvetica, sans-serif;
            font-size: .75em;
            line-height: 1.2em;
            text-align: center;}
.footer {font-family: arial, helvetica, sans-serif;
            font-size: .75em;
            line-height: 1.2em;
            text-align: center;
            border-bottom: solid 2px #CC0000;
            padding-bottom: 1em;
            }
</STYLE>
</HEAD>
<BODY>
```

8

```
<!--Banner -->
<H1 CLASS="banner">World Wide Web Conference 2003</H1>

<!-- Subheading -->
<H2 CLASS="subheading">Plan to Attend &#0151; Register Now
!</H2>

<!-- 2-Column Content Table -->
<DIV ALIGN="CENTER">
<TABLE WIDTH=590 border CELLSPACING="10">
<TR>
<TD WIDTH="50%">
<P CLASS="columnheading">Share Your Ideas</P>
</TD>
<TD WIDTH="50%">
<P CLASS="columnheading">Network with Colleagues</P>
</TD>
</TR>
<TR VALIGN="TOP">
<TD>
<P CLASS="copy">The World Wide Web Conference is an annual
conference sponsored by the University of Boston and the I
nstitute of Technology. This year the conference is being
held on <B>November 15-16, 2003</B> at the Boston
Convention Center in Boston, Massachusetts, USA.</P>
<P CLASS="copy">Conference Sessions are lecture, panel
discussion, or workshop format. All sessions are 75
minutes &#0151; 60 minutes for presentation and 15
minutes for questions.</P>
</TD>
<TD>
<P CLASS="copy">We encourage you to submit a proposal via
email. Download the <A HREF="proposal.doc">form</A> and
email it to <A HREF="MAILTO:">proposals@conference.com
</A>.  <B>The proposal deadline is June 10, 2003.</B></P>
<P CLASS="copy">Experienced professionals are invited to
submit proposals for conference sessions. The conference
committee accepts proposals based on topic and informa-
tion quality.  We encourage sessions on advanced topics,
especially innovative Web technology.</P>
</TD>
</TR>
</TABLE>
</DIV>

<!-- Sponsors -->
<P CLASS="sponsors">The World Wide Web Conference is
sponsored by:<BR> <A href="index.htm">University of Boston
</A> and the <A HREF="index.htm">Institute of Technology
</A>.</P>
```

```
<!-- Footer -->
<P CLASS="footer">For more information contact the
conference office at 555-555-1234 or email
<A HREF="MAILTO:">info@conference.com</A>.</P>
</BODY>
</HTML>
```

BUILDING A WEB SITE MAIN PAGE

In the following set of steps, you will use CSS properties to design a main Web page (commonly called a home page) for a fictional company. This page will be the first page visitors see when they come to the company's Web site. The page should be attractive, easy to read, and quick to load. You will use a variety of CSS properties, including positioning properties (see the "Using the Positioning Properties" chapter) to build the page. Remember to save your file and view your work in the browser after you complete each step.

Figure 8-15 shows the results you will achieve and the different <DIV> class names you will use when creating the page.

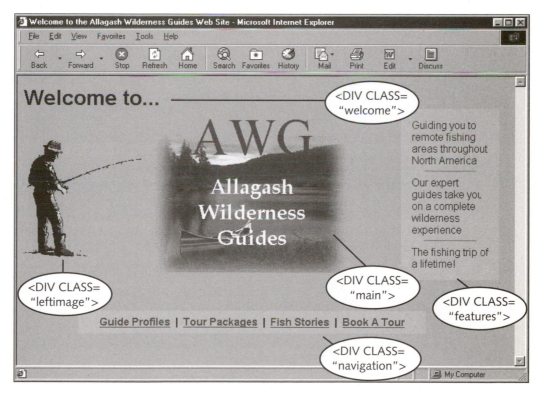

Figure 8-15   The finished home page design

Keep the following important points in mind as you work with this design:

- This is a fixed design for the most commonly used screen resolution, 800 × 600. The current browsers do not support relative positioning.

- This design will display properly only in the latest browsers, especially Internet Explorer 5.5 and Netscape 6.0. Opera 5.0 has trouble displaying the design. Newer browsers released after this book is published will probably display the design correctly, but remember to always test your work.

- Older browsers will not display this design properly.

To start working on the file:

1. Open the file **allagash.htm** in your HTML editor, and save it in your work folder as **allagash1.htm**.

2. Copy the image files, **canoe.jpg** and **fishguy.gif**, into your work folder.

3. Examine the code in the file. The file contains only the standard HTML elements, including an empty <STYLE> element in the <HEAD> section where you will add the style rules. You will add the content for each division as you build the page. The complete code for the page follows.

```
<HTML>
<HEAD>
<TITLE>Welcome to the  Allagash Wilderness Guides Web
Site</TITLE>
<STYLE TYPE="text/css">

</STYLE>
</HEAD>
<BODY>

</BODY>
</HTML>
```

4. Add a style rule that sets the background color for the page. The hexadecimal value is #99CC99. Use <BODY> as the selector to apply the background color to the entire page.

```
body {background-color: #99CC99;}
```

Building the "welcome" Division

The "welcome" division (see Figure 8-15) is positioned in the normal flow (see the "Using the Positioning Properties" chapter). The style rules use basic font properties.

To build the "welcome" division:

1. In the <BODY> section of the document, add a comment and the <DIV> element with text, as shown in the following code:

```
<BODY>
<!-- The welcome division -->
<DIV>
Welcome to...
</DIV>
</BODY>
```

2. Write a style rule that uses "welcome" as the class selector. Set the font family to a sans-serif font. Use font substitution to specify both Arial and Helvetica, and then use the generic font family (sans-serif) in the event that neither style is available on the user's computer.

```
.welcome {font-family: arial, helvetica, sans-serif;}
```

3. Set the font size to 2 em and the font weight to bold.

```
.welcome {font-family: arial, helvetica, sans-serif;
          font-size: 2em;
          font-weight: bold;
          }
```

4. Apply the style rule to the division using the CLASS attribute. Set the attribute value to "welcome," as shown in the following code.

```
<!-- The welcome division -->
<DIV CLASS="welcome">
Welcome to...
</DIV>
```

5. View your work in the browser. Figure 8-16 shows the results.

8

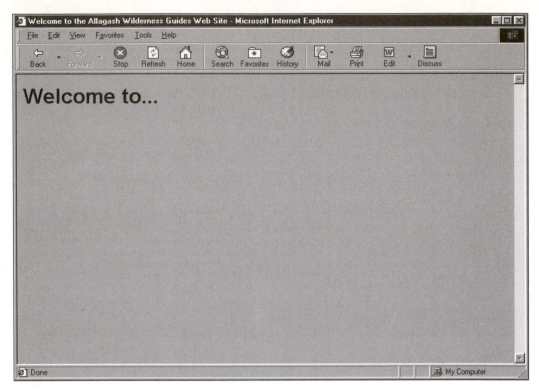

Figure 8-16   The finished "welcome" division

Building the "leftimage" Division

The "leftimage" division (see Figure 8-15) contains the fisherman image named fishguy.gif. The image is positioned on the left side of the Web page.

To build the "leftimage" division:

1. In the <BODY> section of the document, add a comment and the <IMG> element with WIDTH, HEIGHT and ALT attributes, as shown in the following code.

```
<BODY>
<!-- The welcome division -->
<DIV CLASS="welcome">
Welcome to...
</DIV>
<!-- The fisherman image -->
<IMG SRC="fishguy.gif" WIDTH="180" HEIGHT="178" ALT="A
satisfied fisherman">
</BODY>
```

2. Write a style rule with "leftimage" as the class selector. Specify absolute positioning. Set the top offset value to 100 px and the left offset position to 10 px. You do not have to specify a width and height for the division because those variables are defined within the <IMG> element.

```
.leftimage {position: absolute;
           top: 100px;
           left:10px;
           }
```

3. Add the border shortcut property to the style rule. Set the border style to solid and the border weight to 1 px. You will use the border to test the positioning of the element.

```
.leftimage {position: absolute;
           top: 100px;
           left:10px;
           border: solid 1px;}
```

4. Apply the style rule to the division using the CLASS attribute. Set the attribute value to "leftimage," as shown in the following code.

```
<!-- The fisherman image -->
<IMG SRC="fishguy.gif" CLASS="leftimage" WIDTH="180"
HEIGHT="178" ALT="A satisfied fisherman">
```

5. View the results in the browser. You can use Screen Ruler (available from *www.microfox.com/*) to measure the placement on the screen, as shown in Figure 8-17. You can continue to use Screen Ruler to check the positioning of the remaining page elements as you work through the rest of this exercise.

6. Delete the border property from the "leftimage" style rule to remove the border. The style rule now looks like the following:

```
.leftimage {position: absolute;
           top: 100px;
           left: 10px;
           }
```

8

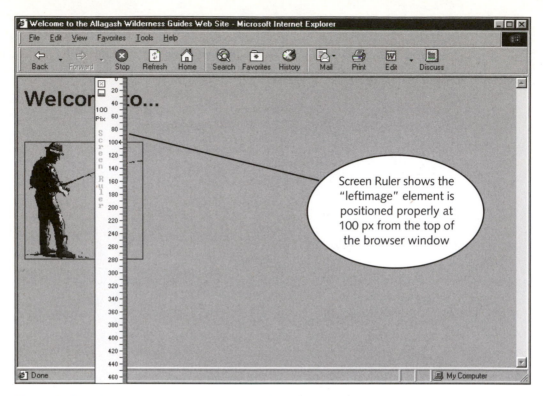

Figure 8-17   Measuring the placement of the finished "leftimage" division

Building the "main" Division

The "main" division (see Figure 8-15) contains a background image as well as two child <DIV> elements. Figure 8-18 shows the "main"<DIV> as well as the two child <DIV> elements and their class names. The element borders are displayed so you can see the structure of the elements.

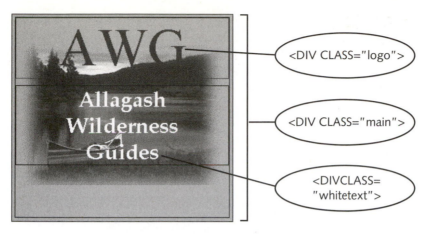

Figure 8-18   The "main" division and its child divisions

8

To build the "main" division:

1. In the <BODY> section of the document, add a comment and an empty <DIV> element with a CLASS attribute set to "main," as show in the following code:

```
<BODY>
<!-- The welcome division -->
<DIV CLASS="welcome">
Welcome to...
</DIV>
<!-- The fisherman image -->
<IMG SRC="fishguy.gif" CLASS="leftimage" WIDTH="180"
HEIGHT="178" ALT="A satisfied fisherman">
<!-- The main division -->
<DIV CLASS="main">

</DIV>
</BODY>
```

2. Write a style rule using "main" as a class selector. Set the position to absolute. Set the top offset to 50 px and the left offset to 200 px.

```
.main {position: absolute;
        top: 50px;
        left: 200px;
        }
```

3. Set the width of the division to 320 px and the height to 300 px, as shown in the following code:

```
.main {position: absolute;
        top: 50px;
        left: 200px;
        width: 320px;
        height: 300px;
        }
```

4. Add the background image **canoe.jpg** to the division element using the background-image property (see the "Using the Color and Background Properties" chapter).

```
.main {position: absolute;
        top: 50px;
        left: 200px;
        width: 320px;
        height: 300px;
        background-image: url(canoe.jpg);
        }
```

5. Set the properties for the background image. Use the background-repeat property to specify that the image does not repeat and the background-position property to center the image.

```
.main {position: absolute;
        top: 50px;
        left: 200px;
        width: 320px;
        height: 300px;
        background-image: url(canoe.jpg);
        background-repeat: no-repeat;
        background-position: center;
        }
```

6. View your changes in the browser. Figure 8-19 shows the finished "main" division with the border displaying so you can see the size of the element.

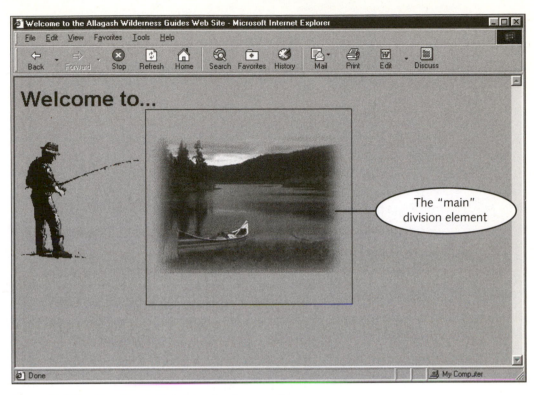

Figure 8-19   The "main" division background image

Building the "logo" Child Division

The "logo" division is contained with the "main" division, as shown in Figure 8-18. It contains the acronym for the fictional company.

To build the "logo" division:

1. In the <DIV CLASS="main"> division of the document, add a comment, the child <DIV> element, and the text "AWG" as shown in the following code.

```
<BODY>
<!-- The welcome division -->
<DIV CLASS="welcome">
Welcome to...
</DIV>
<!-- The fisherman image -->
<IMG SRC="fishguy.gif" CLASS="leftimage" WIDTH="180" HEIG
HT="178" ALT="A satisfied fisherman">
<!-- The main division -->
```

```
<DIV CLASS="main">
    <!-- The logo division -->
    <DIV>
    AWG
    </DIV>
</DIV>
</BODY>
```

2. Write a style rule with the class selector "logo." Set the font size to 5 em and the color of the text to hexadecimal value #663333.

```
.logo {font-size: 5em;
       color: #663333;
       }
```

3. Use the text-align property to align the logo text to the center of the element.

```
.logo {font-size: 5em;
       color: #663333;
       text-align: center;
       }
```

4. Apply the style rule to the division using the CLASS attribute. Set the attribute value to "logo," as shown in the following code.

```
<!-- The main division -->
<DIV CLASS="main">
    <!-- The logo division -->
    <DIV CLASS="logo">
    AWG
    </DIV>
</DIV>
```

5. View your changes in the browser. Figure 8-20 shows the results of adding the new division.

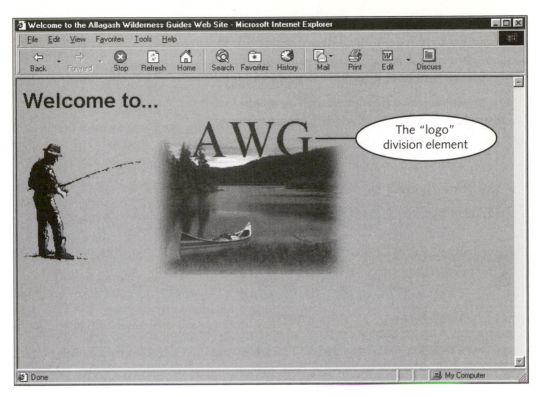

Figure 8-20   The "logo" child division

Building the "whitetext" Child Division

The "whitetext" division is also contained within the "main" division. It contains the name of the fictional company. The text is white to make it legible against the background image contained in the parent division.

To build the "whitetext" division:

1. In the <DIV CLASS="main"> division of the document, add a comment, the child <DIV> element, and the text, as shown in the following code:

```
<BODY>
<!-- The welcome division -->
<DIV CLASS="welcome">
Welcome to...
</DIV>
<!-- The fisherman image -->
<IMG SRC="fishguy.gif" CLASS="leftimage" WIDTH="180" HEIG
HT="178" ALT="A satisfied fisherman">
<!-- The main division -->
```

```
<DIV CLASS="main">
     <!-- The logo division -->
     <DIV CLASS="logo">
     AWG
     </DIV>
     <!--The whitetext division -->
     <DIV>
     Allagash<BR>
     Wilderness<BR>
     Guides
     </DIV>
</DIV>
</BODY>
```

2. Write a style rule using the class selector "whitetext." Set the font size to 2 em, the font weight to bold, and the color to white using hexadecimal value #FFFFFF.

```
.whitetext {font-size: 2em;
            font-weight: bold;
            color: #FFFFFF;
            }
```

3. Set the text alignment to center, and add a top margin of 10 px to offset the white text from the logo above.

```
.whitetext {font-size: 2em;
            font-weight: bold;
            color: #FFFFFF;
            text-align: center;
            margin-top: 10px;
            }
```

4. Apply the style rule to the division using the CLASS attribute. Set the attribute value to "whitetext," as shown in the following code.

```
<!-- The main division-->
<DIV CLASS="main">
     <!-- The logo division -->
     <DIV CLASS="logo">
     AWG
     </DIV>
     <DIV CLASS="whitetext">
     Allagash<BR>
     Wilderness<BR>
     Guides
     </DIV>
</DIV>
```

5. View your changes in the browser. Figure 8-21 shows the results of adding the new division.

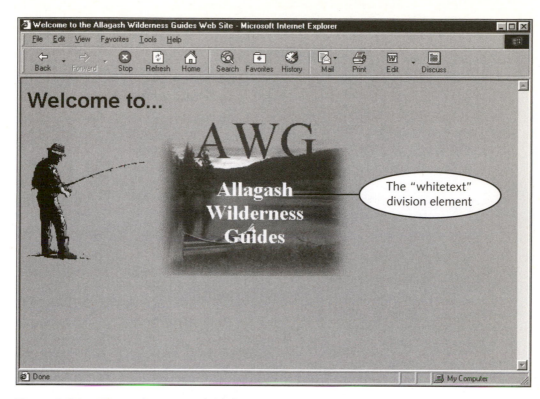

Figure 8-21   The "whitetext" child division

Building the "features" Division

The "features" division (see Figure 8-15) contains three short sentences of promotional text separated by simple <HR> (horizontal rule) elements. It is positioned on the right side of the Web page.

To build the "features" division:

1. In the <BODY> section of the document, add a comment and the <DIV> element with text, as shown in the following code. Notice that the CLASS attribute is included and set to the value "features."

```
<BODY>
<!-- The welcome division -->
<DIV CLASS="welcome">
Welcome to...
</DIV>
<!-- The fisherman image -->
<IMG SRC="fishguy.gif" CLASS="leftimage" WIDTH="180"
HEIGHT="178" ALT="A satisfied fisherman">
<!-- The main element -->
```

```
<DIV CLASS="main">
    <!-- The logo division -->
    <DIV CLASS="logo">
    AWG
    </DIV>
    <!--The whitetext division -->
    <DIV>
    Allagash<BR>
    Wilderness<BR>
    Guides
    </DIV>
</DIV>
<!-- The features division -->
<DIV CLASS="features">
Guiding you to remote fishing areas throughout<BR>
North America
<HR WIDTH="80">
Our expert guides take you on
a complete wilderness experience
<HR WIDTH="80">
The fishing trip of a lifetime!
</DIV>
</BODY>
```

2. Write a style rule that uses a class selector "features." Set the position to absolute. Set the top offset to 50 px and the left offset to 590 px.

```
.features {position: absolute;
          top: 50px;
          left: 590px;
          }
```

3. Set the width of the division to 150 px and the height to 250 px, as shown in the following code:

```
.features {position: absolute;
          top: 50px;
          left: 590px;
          width: 150px;
          height: 250px;
          }
```

4. Set a light tan background color for the division, using hexadecimal value #CCCC99.

```
.features {position: absolute;
          top: 50px;
          left: 590px;
          width: 150px;
          height: 250px;
          background-color: #CCCC99;
          }
```

5. View your changes in the browser. Figure 8-22 shows the results. You can see that the text still remains to be styled. Also notice that the <HR> elements are horizontally centered within the division. This is their default alignment, so no style property is necessary.

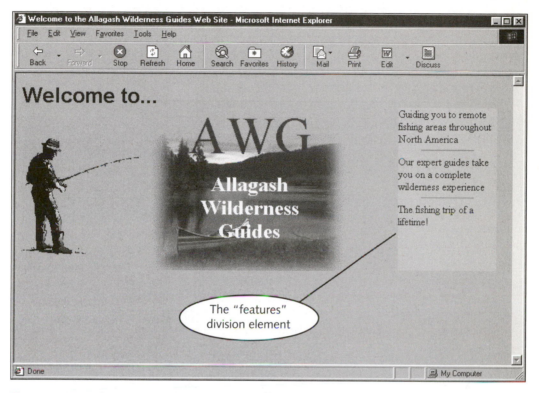

Figure 8-22   The partially styled "features" division

6. Specify the font family for the division. Set the font family to a sans-serif font. Use font substitution to specify both Arial and Helvetica, and then use the generic font family (sans-serif) in the event that neither style is available on the user's computer.

```
.features {position: absolute;
        top: 50px;
        left: 590px;
        width: 150px;
        height: 250px;
        background-color: #CCCC99;
        font-family: arial, helvetica, sans-serif;
        }
```

7. Finally, add 1 em of padding to the division to increase the background color space around the text.

```
.features {position: absolute;
          top: 50px;
          left: 590px;
          width: 150px;
          height: 250px;
          background-color: #CCCC99;
          font-family: arial, helvetica, sans-serif;
          padding: 1em;}
```

8. View your changes in the browser. Figure 8-23 shows the finished "features" division.

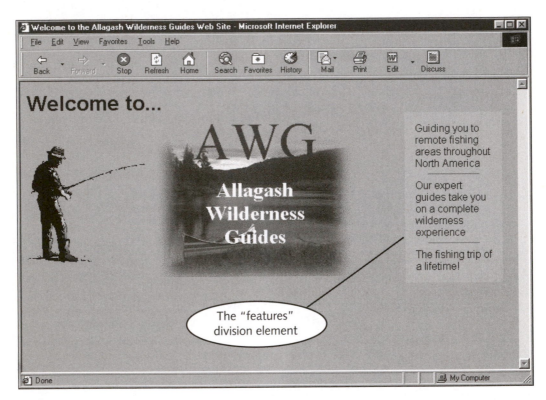

Figure 8-23   The finished "features" division

Building the "navigation" Division

The "navigation" division (see Figure 8-15) contains the hypertext links to the other pages within the Web site. This division is located at the center bottom of the Web page. After you build and style this division, you will change the hypertext link colors to match the colors of the Web site, instead of using the standard blue and purple link colors.

To build the "navigation" division:

1. In the <BODY> section of the document, add a comment, the <DIV> element, and the hyperlinked text contained within. Notice that the CLASS attribute is included and set to a value of "navigation." Additionally, notice that nonbreaking space character entities ( ) are included to provide extra space between the linked text.

```
<BODY>
<!-- The welcome division -->
<DIV CLASS="welcome">
Welcome to...
</DIV>
<!-- The fisherman image -->
<IMG SRC="fishguy.gif" CLASS="leftimage" WIDTH="180" HEIG
HT="178" ALT="A satisfied fisherman">
<!-- The main division -->
<DIV CLASS="main">
     <!-- The logo division -->
     <DIV CLASS="logo">
     AWG
     </DIV>
     <!--The whitetext division -->
     <DIV>
     Allagash<BR>
     Wilderness<BR>
     Guides
     </DIV>
</DIV>
<!-- The features division -->
<DIV CLASS="features">
Guiding you to remote fishing areas throughout<BR>
North America
<HR WIDTH="80">
Our expert guides take you on
a complete wilderness experience
<HR WIDTH="80">
The fishing trip of a lifetime!
</DIV>
<!-- The navigation division -->
<DIV CLASS="navigation">
<P><A HREF="guides.htm">Guide Profiles</A>  |  
<A HREF="tours.htm">Tour Packages</A>  |  <A
HREF="stories.htm">Fish Stories</A>  |  <A
HREF="book.htm">Book A Tour</A></P>
</DIV>
</BODY>
```

8

2. Write a style rule that uses a class selector set to "navigation." Set the position to absolute. Set the top offset to 350 px and the left offset to 95 px. You will not set a width and height for this element; instead you will let the content determine the width and height.

```
.navigation {position: absolute;
        top: 360px;
        left: 95px;
        }
```

3. Set the font family to sans-serif, using the same font substitution values as you have used throughout this exercise. Also, set the font weight to bold.

```
.navigation {position: absolute;
            top: 360px;
            left: 95px;
            font-family: arial, helvetica, sans-serif;
            font-weight: bold;
            }
```

4. Set the background color to match the "features" division, using the hexadecimal code #CCCC99. Set the text alignment to center.

```
.navigation {position: absolute;
            top: 360px;
            left: 95px;
            font-family: arial, helvetica, sans-serif;
            font-weight: bold;
            background-color: #CCCC99;
            text-align: center;
            }
```

5. Specify padding values for the element to provide additional space for the background color around the content. Set the top and bottom padding to .5 em, and the left and right padding values to 2 em.

```
.navigation {position: absolute;
            top: 360px;
            left: 95px;
            font-family: arial, helvetica, sans-serif;
            font-weight: bold;
            background-color: #CCCC99;
            text-align: center;
            padding-top: .5em;
            padding-bottom: .5em;
            padding-left: 2em;
            padding-right: 2em;
            }
```

6. Write two separate style rules that specify the color of new links and visited links. To match the layout colors, you will specify brown for new links, hexadecimal #663333, and the background light green for visited links, hexadecimal #99CC99. Use the :link and :vlink pseudo-class selectors for these rules, as shown.

```
:link {color: #663333;}
:visited {color: #99CC99;}
```

7. View your final changes in the browser. Figure 8-24 shows the finished page design.

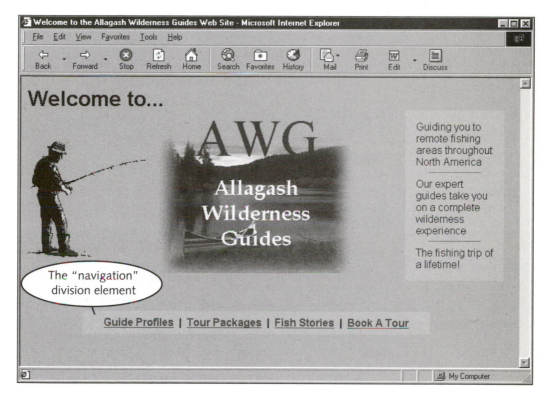

Figure 8-24   The finished "navigation" division and page design

The complete code for the page follows.

```
<HTML>
<HEAD>
<TITLE>Welcome to the Allagash Wilderness Guides Web Site<
/TITLE>

<STYLE TYPE="text/css">
body {background-color: #99CC99;}
```

```
.welcome {font-family: arial, helvetica, sans-serif;
         font-size: 2em;
         font-weight: bold;
         }


.leftimage {position: absolute;
         top: 100px;
         left: 10px;
         }

.main {position: absolute;
         top: 50px;
         left: 200px;
         width: 320px;
         height: 300px;
         background-image: url(canoe.jpg);
         background-repeat: no-repeat;
         background-position: center;
         }

.logo {font-size: 5em;
     color: #663333;
     text-align: center;
     }

.whitetext {font-size: 2em;
         font-weight: bold;
         color: #FFFFFF;
         text-align: center;
         margin-top: 10px;
         }

.features {position: absolute;
         top: 50px;
         left: 590px;
         width: 150px;
         height: 250px;
         background-color: #CCCC99;
         font-family: arial, helvetica, sans-serif;
         padding: 1em;
         }

.navigation {position: absolute;
         top: 360px;
         left: 95px;
         font-family: arial, helvetica, sans-serif;
         font-weight: bold;
         background-color: #CCCC99;
```

```
              text-align: center;
              padding-top: .5em;
              padding-bottom: .5em;
              padding-left: 2em;
              padding-right: 2em;
              }

:link {color: #663333;}
:visited {color: #99CC99:}
</STYLE>
</HEAD>
<BODY>

<!-- The welcome division -->
<DIV CLASS="welcome">
Welcome to...
</DIV>

<!-- The fisherman image -->
<IMG SRC="fishguy.gif" CLASS="leftimage" WIDTH="180"
HEIGHT="178" ALT="A satisfied fisherman">

<!-- The main division-->
<DIV CLASS="main">

      <!-- The logo division -->
      <DIV CLASS="logo">
      AWG
      </DIV>
      <!--The whitetext division-->
      <DIV CLASS="whitetext">
      Allagash<BR>
      Wilderness<BR>
      Guides
      </DIV>
</DIV>

<!-- The features division -->
<DIV class="features">
Guiding you to remote fishing areas throughout<BR>North
America
<HR WIDTH="80">
Our expert guides take you on
a complete wilderness experience
<HR WIDTH="80">
The fishing trip of a lifetime!
</DIV>
```

8

```
<!-- The navigation division -->
<DIV CLASS="navigation" ALIGN="CENTER">
<P><A HREF="guides.htm">Guide Profiles</A>  |  
<A HREF="tours.htm">Tour Packages</A>  |  <A HRE
F="stories.htm">Fish Stories</A>  |  <A HREF=
"book.htm">Book A Tour</A></P>
</DIV>
</BODY>
</HTML>
```

CHAPTER SUMMARY

In this chapter, you had the opportunity to use your CSS skills to build a variety of complete Web pages. You saw that CSS lets you build anything from simple pages that have standard HTML markup to more complex pages that rely on customized divisions and CSS positioning.

❏ You can use CSS properties to build a style sheet for online software documentation that users can view with any browser. If you post an online manual on a public Web site, the product documentation styles can be easily updated when changes occur in the software.

❏ You can use CSS properties to build any type of Web page, including the promotional page example you worked on in this chapter. With CSS, you can build pages that contain rich stylistic components without resorting to graphics that increase download time.

❏ When the CSS positioning properties become widely supported, you will be able to build designed pages with less code than current web pages contain because you will not have to use tables to build page structure. You will only need to use table elements when you want to build data tables, for which the table elements were originally intended.

REVIEW QUESTIONS

1. In the technical documentation style sheet example, what would be the most efficient method of sharing the style rules across multiple HTML files?

2. What is the benefit of applying CSS rules to standard HTML markup?

3. What properties can you use to make standard heading elements, such as <H1> or <H2>, more distinctive?

4. In the technical documentation example, what is the benefit of using descendant selection to style the <B> elements that reside within the ordered list?

5. Why is it a good practice to state a background color for a Web page even when you are choosing white as the color?

6. What is the benefit of adding a line height setting to your standard content paragraphs, as you did in the promotional page exercise?

7. When specifying a font family, what is the benefit of using a font substitution value?

8. Why would you specify absolute rather than relative positioning when building a page layout?

9. What is the benefit of using the em as a measurement value, especially for fonts?

10. What is the benefit of working with visible element or table borders when you are designing a Web page?

8

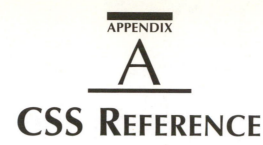

A

CSS REFERENCE

This appendix includes the most commonly used CSS property descriptions, sorted both alphabetically and by category. Appendix B contains additional property descriptions for newer CSS technologies, such as aural style sheets and paged media. For more detailed information, visit the World Wide Web Consortium Web site at *www.w3.org*.

ALPHABETICAL CSS PROPERTY NOTATION REFERENCE

Table A-1   CSS property notations

Notation	Definition
<>	Words between angle brackets specify a type of value. For example, **<color>** enters a color value such as red.
|	A single vertical bar between values means one or the other must occur. For example, **scroll | fixed** means choose scroll or fixed.
||	Two vertical bars separating values means one or the other or both values can occur. For example, **<border-width> || <border-style> || <color>** means any or all of the three values can occur.
[ ]	Square brackets group parts of the property value together. For example, **none | [underline || overline || line-through || blink]** means the value is either none or one of the values within the square brackets.

ALPHABETICAL CSS PROPERTY REFERENCE

Table A-2   CSS properties

Property	Values	Default	Applies to
Background (Shorthand property)	<background-color> II <background-image> II <background-repeat> II <background-attachment> II <background-position>	No default for shorthand properties	All elements
Background-attachment	scroll I fixed	Scroll	All elements
Background-color	color name or hexadecimal value I transparent	Transparent	All elements
Background-image	<url> I none	None	All elements
Background-position	[<percentage> I <length>]{1,2} I [top I center I bottom] II [left I center I right]	0% 0%	Block-level and replaced elements
Background-repeat	repeat I repeat-x I repeat-y I no-repeat	Repeat	All elements
Border (Shorthand property)	<border-width> II <border-style> II <color>	No default for shorthand properties	All elements
Border-bottom	<border-bottom-width> II <border-style> II <color>	No default for shorthand properties	All elements
Border-bottom-color	<color>	The value of the 'color' property	All elements
Border-bottom-style	none I dotted I dashed I solid I double I groove I ridge I inset I outset	None	All elements
Border-bottom-width	thin I medium I thick I <length>	'Medium'	All elements
Border-color	<color>	The value of the 'color' property	All elements
Border-left (Shorthand property)	<border-left-width> II <border-style> II <color>	No default for shorthand properties	All elements
Border-left-color	<color>	The value of the 'color' property	All elements
Border-left-style	none I dotted I dashed I solid I double I groove I ridge I inset I outset	None	All elements
Border-left-width	thin I medium I thick I <length>	'Medium'	All elements

Table A-2   CSS properties (continued)

Property	Values	Default	Applies to
Border-right (Shorthand property)	\<border-right-width\> || \<border-style\> || \<color\>	No default for shorthand properties	All elements
Border-right-color	\<color\>	The value of the 'color' property	All elements
Border-right-style	none | dotted | dashed | solid | double | groove | ridge | inset | outset	None	All elements
Border-right-width	thin | medium | thick | \<length\>	'Medium'	All elements
Border-style	none | dotted | dashed | solid | double | groove | ridge | inset | outset	None	All elements
Border-top (Shorthand property)	\<border-top-width\> || \<border-style\> || \<color\>	No default for shorthand properties	All elements
Border-top-color	\<color\>	The value of the color' property	All elements
Border-top-style	none | dotted | dashed | solid | double | groove | ridge | inset | outset	None	All elements
Border-top-width	thin | medium | thick | \<length\>	'Medium'	All elements
Border-width (Shorthand property)	[thin | medium | thick | \<length\>]	No default for shorthand properties	All elements
Bottom	\<length\> | \<percentage\> | auto	Auto	Positioned elements
Clear	none | left | right | both	None	All elements
Color	\<color\>	Browser specific	All elements
Display	inline | block | list-item | run-in | compact | marker | table | inline-table | table-row-group | table-header-group | table-footer-group | table-row | table-column-group | table-column | table-cell | table-caption | none	Inline	All elements
Float	left | right | none	None	All elements
Font (Shorthand property)	[\<font-style\> || \<font-variant\> || \<font-weight\>] \<font-size\> [/ \<line-height\>] \<font-family\>	No default for shorthand properties	All elements
Font-family	Font family name (such as Times) or generic family name (such as sans-serif)	Browser specific	All elements

Table A-2   CSS properties (continued)

Property	Values	Default	Applies to
Font-size	<absolute-size> I <relative-size> I <length> I <percentage>	Medium	All elements
Font-stretch	normal I wider I narrower I ultra-condensed I extra-condensed I condensed I semi-condensed I semi-expanded I expanded I extra-expanded I ultra-expanded	Normal	All elements
Font-style	normal I italic I oblique	Normal	All elements
Font-variant	normal I small-caps	Normal	All elements
Font-weight	normal I bold I bolder I lighter I 100 I 200 I 300 I 400 I 500 I 600 I 700 I 800 I 900	Normal	All elements
Height	<length> I <percentage> I auto	Auto	Block-level and replaced elements; also all elements except inline elements
Left	<length> I <percentage> I auto	Auto	Positioned elements
Letter-spacing	normal I <length>	Normal	All elements
Line-height	normal I <number> I <length> I <percentage>	Normal	All elements
List-style (Shorthand property)	<keyword> II <position> II <url>	No default for shorthand properties	Elements with 'display' value 'list-item'
List-style-image	<url> I none	None	Elements with 'display' value 'list-item'
List-style-position	inside I outside	Outside	Elements with 'display' value 'list-item'
List-style-type	disc I circle I square I decimal I lower-roman I upper-roman I lower-alpha I upper-alpha I none	Disc	Elements with 'display' value 'list-item'
Margin (Shorthand property)	[<length> I <percentage> I auto]	No default for shorthand properties	All elements
Margin-bottom	<length> I <percentage> I auto	0	All elements
Margin-left	<length> I <percentage> I auto	0	All elements
Margin-right	<length> I <percentage> I auto	0	All elements
Margin-top	<length> I <percentage> I auto	0	All elements

Table A-2   CSS properties (continued)

Property	Values	Default	Applies to
Padding	<length>	<percentage>	0	All elements
Padding-bottom	<length>	<percentage>	0	All elements
Padding-left	<length>	<percentage>	0	All elements
Padding-right	<length>	<percentage>	0	All elements
Padding-top	<length>	<percentage>	0	All elements
Position	static	relative	absolute	fixed	Static	All elements except generated content
Right	<length>	<percentage>	auto	Auto	Positioned elements
Text-align	left	right	center	justify	Depends on browser and language direction	Block-level elements
Text-decoration	none	[underline		overline		line-through		blink]	None	All elements
Text-indent	<length>	<percentage>	0	Block-level elements
Text-shadow	none	[<color>		<length> <length> <length>? ,]* [<color>		<length> <length> <length>?]	None	All elements
Text-transform	capitalize	uppercase	lowercase	none	None	All elements
Top	<length>	<percentage>	auto	Auto	Positioned elements
Vertical-align	baseline	sub	super	top	text-top	middle	bottom	text-bottom	<percentage>	Baseline	Inline elements
White-space	normal	pre	nowrap	Normal	Block-level elements
Width	<length>	<percentage>	auto	Auto	Block-level and replaced elements; also all elements except inline elements
Word-spacing	normal	<length>	Normal	All elements
Z-index	auto	integer	Auto	Positioned elements

CSS Properties by Category

Table A-3   Font and text properties

Property	Values	Default	Applies to
Color	<color>	Browser specific	All elements
Font (Shorthand property)	[<font-style> || <font-variant> || <font-weight>] <font-size> [/ <line-height>] <font-family>	No default for shorthand properties	All elements
Font-family	Font family name (such as Times) or generic family name (such as sans-serif)	Browser specific	All elements
Font-size	<absolute-size>	<relative-size>	<length>	<percentage>	Medium	All elements
Font-style	normal	italic	oblique	Normal	All elements
Font-stretch	normal	wider	narrower	ultra-condensed	extra-condensed	condensed	semi-condensed	semi-expanded	expanded	extra-expanded	ultra-expanded	Normal	All elements
Font-variant	normal	small-caps	Normal	All elements
Font-weight	normal	bold	bolder	lighter	100	200	300	400	500	600	700	800	900	Normal	All elements
Letter-spacing	normal	<length>	Normal	All elements
Line-height	normal	<number>	<length>	<percentage>	Normal	All elements
Text-align	left	right	center	justify	Depends on browser and language direction	Block-level elements
Text-decoration	none	[underline		overline		line-through		blink]	None	All elements
Text-indent	<length>	<percentage>	0	Block-level elements
Text-shadow	none	[<color>		<length> <length> <length>? ,]* [<color>		<length> <length> <length>?]	None	All elements
Text-transform	capitalize	uppercase	lowercase	none	None	All elements
Vertical-align	baseline	sub	super	top	text-top	middle	bottom	text-bottom	<percentage>	Baseline	Inline elements
Word-spacing	normal	<length>	Normal	All elements

Table A-4   Box properties

Property	Values	Default	Applies to
Margin (Shorthand property)	[<length> | <percentage> | auto]	No default for shorthand properties	All elements
Margin-bottom	<length> | <percentage> | auto	0	All elements
Margin-left	<length> | <percentage> | auto	0	All elements
Margin-right	<length> | <percentage> | auto	0	All elements
Margin-top	<length> | <percentage> | auto	0	All elements
Padding	<length> | <percentage>	0	All elements
Padding-bottom	<length> | <percentage>	0	All elements
Padding-left	<length> | <percentage>	0	All elements
Padding-right	<length> | <percentage>	0	All elements
Padding-top	<length> | <percentage>	0	All elements
Border (Shorthand property)	<border-width> || <border-style> || <color>	No default for shorthand properties	All elements
Border-bottom	<border-bottom-width> || <border-style> || <color>	No default for shorthand properties	All elements
Border-bottom-color	<color>	The value of the 'color' property	All elements
Border-bottom-style	none | dotted | dashed | solid | double | groove | ridge | inset | outset	None	All elements
Border-bottom-width	thin | medium | thick | <length>	'Medium'	All elements
Border-color	<color>	The value of the 'color' property	All elements
Border-left (Shorthand property)	<border-left-width> || <border-style> || <color>	No default for shorthand properties	All elements
Border-left-color	<color>	The value of the 'color' property	All elements
Border-left-style	none | dotted | dashed | solid | double | groove | ridge | inset | outset	None	All elements
Border-left-width	thin | medium | thick | <length>	'Medium'	All elements
Border-right (Shorthand property)	<border-right-width> || <border-style> || <color>	No default for shorthand properties	All elements
Border-right-color	<color>	The value of the 'color' property	All elements

Table A-4   Box properties (continued)

Property	Values	Default	Applies to
Border-right-style	none I dotted I dashed I solid I double I groove I ridge I inset I outset	None	All elements
Border-right-width	thin I medium I thick I <length>	'Medium'	All elements
Border-style	none I dotted I dashed I solid I double I groove I ridge I inset I outset	None	All elements
Border-top (Shorthand property)	<border-top-width> II <border-style> II <color>	No default for shorthand properties	All elements
Border-top-color	<color>	The value of the 'color' property	All elements
Border-top-style	none I dotted I dashed I solid I double I groove I ridge I inset I outset	None	All elements
Border-top-width	thin I medium I thick I <length>	'Medium'	All elements
Border-width (Shorthand property)	[thin I medium I thick I <length>]	No default for shorthand properties	All elements
Clear	none I left I right I both	None	All elements
Float	left I right I none	None	All elements
Height	<length> I <percentage> I auto	Auto	Block-level and replaced elements
Width	<length> I <percentage> I auto	Auto	Block-level and replaced elements

Table A-5   Background properties

Property	Values	Default	Applies to
Background (Shorthand property)	<background-color> II <background-image> II <background-repeat> II <background-attachment> II <background-position>	No default for shorthand properties	All elements
Background-attachment	scroll I fixed	Scroll	All elements
Background-color	color name or hexadecimal value I transparent	Transparent	All elements
Background-image	<url> I none	None	All elements
Background-position	[<percentage> I <length>]{1,2} I [top I center I bottom] II [left I center I right]	0% 0%	Block-level and replaced elements
Background-repeat	repeat I repeat-x I repeat-y I no-repeat	Repeat	All elements

Table A-6   Visual properties

Property	Values	Default	Applies to
Position	static | relative | absolute | fixed	Static	All elements except generated content
Z-index	auto | integer	Auto	Positioned elements
Top	<length> | <percentage> | auto	Auto	Positioned elements
Right	<length> | <percentage> | auto	Auto	Positioned elements
Bottom	<length> | <percentage> | auto	Auto	Positioned elements
Left	<length> | <percentage> | auto	Auto	Positioned elements
Height	<length> | <percentage> | auto	Auto	All elements except inline elements
Width	<length> | <percentage> | auto	Auto	All elements except inline elements

Table A-7   Classification properties

Property	Values	Default	Applies to
Display	inline | block | list-item | run-in | compact | marker | table | inline-table | table-row-group | table-header-group | table-footer-group | table-row | table-column-group | table-column | table-cell | table-caption | none	Inline	All elements
List-style (Shorthand property)	<keyword> || <position> || <url>	No default for shorthand properties	Elements with 'display' value 'list-item'
List-style-image	<url> | none	None	Elements with 'display' value 'list-item'
List-style-position	inside | outside	Outside	Elements with 'display' value 'list-item'

Table A-7   Classification properties (continued)

Property	Values	Default	Applies to
List-style-type	disc I circle I square I decimal I lower-roman I upper-roman I lower-alpha I upper-alpha I none	Disc	Elements with 'display' value 'list-item'
White-space	normal I pre I nowrap	Normal	Block-level elements

CSS MEASUREMENT UNITS

Table A-8   CSS measurement units

Unit	Code Abbreviation	Description
Centimeter	cm	Standard metric centimeter
Em	em	The width of the capital M in the current font, usually the same as the font size
Ex	ex	The height of the letter x in the current font
Inch	in	Standard U.S. inch
Millimeter	mm	Standard metric millimeter
Relative	For example: 150%	Sets a font size relative to the base font size. 150% equals one-and-one-half the base font size.
Pica	pc	Standard publishing unit equal to 12 points
Pixel	px	The size of a pixel on the current display
Point	pt	Standard publishing unit, there are 72 points in an inch

ISO 369 TWO-LETTER LANGUAGE CODES

Table A-9   ISO 369 language codes

Code	Language
AA	Afar
AB	Abkhazian
AF	Afrikaans
AM	Amharic
AR	Arabic
AS	Assamese
AY	Aymara
AZ	Azerbaijani

Table A-9   ISO 369 language codes (continued)

Code	Language
BA	Bashkir
BE	Byelorussian
BG	Bulgarian
BH	Bihari
BI	Bislama
BN	Bengali Bangla
BO	Tibetan
BR	Breton
CA	Catalan
CO	Corsican
CS	Czech
CY	Welsh
DA	Danish
DE	German
DZ	Bhutani
EL	Greek
EN	English American
EO	Esperanto
ES	Spanish
ET	Estonian
EU	Basque
FA	Persian
FI	Finnish
FJ	Fiji
FO	Faeroese
FR	French
FY	Frisian
GA	Irish
GD	Gaelic Scots Gaelic
GL	Galician
GN	Guarani
GU	Gujarati
HA	Hausa
HI	Hindi
HR	Croatian
HU	Hungarian

Table A-9 ISO 369 language codes (continued)

Code	Language
HY	Armenian
IA	Interlingua
IE	Interlingue
IK	Inupiak
IN	Indonesian
IS	Icelandic
IT	Italian
IW	Hebrew
JA	Japanese
JI	Yiddish
JW	Javanese
KA	Georgian
KK	Kazakh
KL	Greenlandic
KM	Cambodian
KN	Kannada
KO	Korean
KS	Kashmiri
KU	Kurdish
KY	Kirghiz
LA	Latin
LN	Lingala
LO	Laothian
LT	Lithuanian
LV	Latvian Lettish
MG	Malagasy
MI	Maori
MK	Macedonian
ML	Malayalam
MN	Mongolian
MO	Moldavian
MR	Marathi
MS	Malay
MT	Maltese
MY	Burmese
NA	Nauru

A

Table A-9   ISO 369 language codes (continued)

Code	Language
NE	Nepali
NL	Dutch
NO	Norwegian
OC	Occitan
OM	Oromo Afan
OR	Oriya
PA	Punjabi
PL	Polish
PS	Pashto Pushto
PT	Portuguese
QU	Quechua
RM	Rhaeto-Romance
RN	Kirundi
RO	Romanian
RU	Russian
RW	Kinyarwanda
SA	Sanskrit
SD	Sindhi
SG	Sangro
SH	Serbo-Croatian
SI	Singhalese
SK	Slovak
SL	Slovenian
SM	Samoan
SN	Shona
SO	Somali
SQ	Albanian
SR	Serbian
SS	Siswati
ST	Sesotho
SU	Sudanese
SV	Swedish
SW	Swahili
TA	Tamil
TE	Tegulu
TG	Tajik

Table A-9   ISO 369 language codes (continued)

Code	Language
TH	Thai
TI	Tigrinya
TK	Turkmen
TL	Tagalog
TN	Setswana
TO	Tonga
TR	Turkish
TS	Tsonga
TT	Tatar
TW	Twi
UK	Ukrainian
UR	Urdu
UZ	Uzbek
VI	Vietnamese
VO	Volapuk
WO	Wolof
XH	Xhosa
YO	Yoruba
ZH	Chinese
ZU	Zulu

B

CSS2 PROPERTIES NOT CURRENTLY SUPPORTED BY MAJOR BROWSERS

This appendix includes descriptions of the new, less-supported CSS2 features, including media types, aural style sheets, generated content, and paged media properties. Portions of this appendix are taken verbatim from the Cascading Style Sheets, level 2 CSS2 Specification, document # REC-CSS2-19980512 available for public download at the World Wide Web Consortium site *www.w3.org*.

CSS MEDIA TYPES

One of the most important features of style sheets is that they specify how a document is to be presented on different media: on the screen, on paper, with a speech synthesizer, or with a Braille device.

Certain CSS properties are only designed for certain media (such as the 'cue-before' property for aural user agents). On occasion, however, style sheets for different media types may share a property but require different values for that property. For example, the 'font-size' property is useful both for screen and print media. However, the two media are different enough to require different values for the common property; a document will typically need a larger font on a computer screen than on paper. For these reasons, it is necessary to express that a style sheet—or a section of a style sheet—applies to certain media types.

The @media Rule

An @media rule specifies the target media types of a set of rules. The @media keyword allows style sheet rules for various media in the same style sheet. The following style sheet selects "print" as the media type:

```
@media print {BODY { font-size: 10pt }}
```

The following style sheet selects "screen" as the media type:

```
@media screen {BODY { font-size: 12pt }}
```

The following style sheet selects multiple media types separated by a semicolon (;).

```
@media screen, print {BODY { line-height: 1.2 }}
```

Recognized Media Types

A CSS media type names a set of CSS properties. A user agent that claims to support a media type by name must implement all of the properties that apply to that media type.

Table B-1   CCS media type descriptions

Media Type	Description
All	Suitable for all devices
Aural	For speech synthesizers
Braille	For Braille tactile feedback devices
Embossed	For paged Braille printers
Handheld	For handheld devices (typically small screen, monochrome, limited bandwidth)
Print	For paged, opaque material and for documents viewed on screen in print preview mode
Projection	For projected presentations, for example projectors or print to transparencies
Screen	Primarily for color computer screens
Tty	For media using a fixed-pitch character grid, such as teletypes, terminals, or portable devices with limited display capabilities
Tv	For television-type devices (low resolution, color, limited-scrollability screens, sound available

AURAL STYLE SHEETS

The aural rendering of a document, already commonly used by the sight-and print-impaired communities, combines speech synthesis and "auditory icons." Often such aural presentation occurs by converting the document to plain text and feeding this to a screen reader—software or hardware that simply reads all the characters on the screen. This results in less effective presentation than would be the case if the document structure were retained. Style sheet properties for aural presentation may be used together with visual properties (mixed media) or as an aural alternative to visual presentation.

Besides the obvious accessibility advantages, there are other large markets for listening to information, including in-car use, industrial and medical documentation systems (intranets), home entertainment, and help to users learning to read or who have difficulty reading.

When using aural properties, the canvas consists of a three-dimensional physical space (sound surrounds) and a temporal space (one may specify sounds before, during, and after other sounds). The CSS properties also allow authors to vary the quality of synthesized speech (voice type, frequency, inflection, etc.).

Volume Property

The volume property lets you adjust the dynamic range of an audio rendering to a comfortable level.

---
volume property description

Value: \<number> | \<percentage> | silent | x-soft | soft | medium | loud | x-loud | inherit

Initial: medium

Applies to: all elements

Inherited: yes

Percentages: refer to inherited value

Speak Property

The speak property determines whether text will be rendered aurally.

---
speak property description

Value: normal | none | spell-out | inherit

Initial: normal

Applies to: all elements

Inherited: yes

Percentages: N/A

Pause Properties

The pause properties specify a pause to be observed before or after speaking an element's content.

pause, pause-before, pause-after property description

Value: <time> | <percentage> | inherit

Initial: depends on user agent

Applies to: all elements

Inherited: no

Percentages: the inverse of the value of the 'speech-rate' property.

Cue Properties

A sound or auditory icon can be played before or after an element with the cue properties.

cue, cue-before, cue-after property description

Value: <uri> | none | inherit

Initial: none

Applies to: all elements

Inherited: no

Percentages: N/A

Play-during Property

Similar to the cue properties, the play-during property specifies a sound to be played in the background while an element's content is spoken.

play-during property description

Value: <uri> mix? repeat? | auto | none | inherit

Initial: auto

Applies to: all elements

Inherited: no

Percentages: N/A

Spatial Properties

Spatial audio is an important stylistic property for aural presentation. It provides a natural way to tell several voices apart, as in real life (people rarely all stand in the same spot in a room). Stereo speakers produce a lateral sound stage. Binaural headphones or the increasingly popular five-speaker home theater setups can generate full surround sound, and multi-speaker setups can create a true three-dimensional sound stage. VRML 2.0 also includes spatial audio, which implies that in time consumer-priced spatial audio hardware will become more widely available.

Azimuth Property

The azimuth property can be used to provide the illusion of a sound stage. The precise means used to achieve this effect and the number of speakers used to do so are user agent-dependent; this property merely identifies the desired result.

---

azimuth property description

Value: <angle> | [[left-side | far-left | left | center-left | center | center-right | right | far-right | right-side] || behind] | leftwards | rightwards | inherit

Initial: center

Applies to: all elements

Inherited: yes

Percentages: N/A

Elevation Property

The elevation can be used to provide the illusion of a sound stage. The precise means used to achieve this effect and the number of speakers used to do so are user agent-dependent; this property merely identifies the desired result.

---

elevation property description

Value: <angle> | below | level | above | higher | lower | inherit

Initial: level

Applies to: all elements

Inherited: yes

Percentages: N/A

Voice Characteristics Properties

The voice characteristics properties control the nuances of spoken language. These properties include the following:

- speech-rate
- voice-family

- pitch
- pitch-range
- stress
- richness
- speak-punctuation
- speak-numeral
- speak-header

Speech-rate Property

This property controls the rate of speech in words-per-minute.

---

speech-rate property description

Value: <number> | x-slow | slow | medium | fast | x-fast | faster |
slower | inherit
Initial: medium
Applies to: all elements
Inherited: yes
Percentages: N/A

Voice-family Property

This property specifies a comma-separated, prioritized list of voice family names (compare with 'font-family'). Possible values are "male," female," and "child."

---

voice-family property description

Value: [[<specific-voice> | <generic-voice>],]* [<specific-voice> |
<generic-voice>]
Initial: depends on user agent
Applies to: all elements
Inherited: yes
Percentages: N/A

B

Pitch Property

This property specifies average frequency of the speaking voice, allowing for a range of varying inflection and pitch; these variations convey additional meaning and emphasis.

> **pitch property description**
>
> Value: <frequency> | x-low | low | medium | high | x-high | inherit
> Initial: medium
> Applies to: all elements
> Inherited: yes
> Percentages: N/A

Pitch-range Property

This property specifies the allowed range of variation in frequency of the speaking voice.

> **pitch-range property description**
>
> Value: <number> | inherit
> Initial: 50
> Applies to: all elements
> Inherited: yes
> Percentages: N/A

Stress Property

This property specifies the height of "local peaks" in the intonation contour of a voice. For example, English is a stressed language, and different parts of a sentence are assigned primary, secondary, or tertiary stress. The value of 'stress' controls the amount of inflection that results from these stress markers.

> **stress property description**
>
> Value: <number> | inherit
> Initial: 50
> Applies to: all elements
> Inherited: yes
> Percentages: N/A

Richness Property

This property specifies the richness, or brightness, of the speaking voice.

richness property description
Value: <number>	inherit
Initial: 50
Applies to: all elements
Inherited: yes
Percentages: N/A

Speak-punctuation Property

This property specifies whether punctuation marks are spoken literally.

speak-punctuation property description
Value: once	always	inherit
Initial: once
Applies to: elements that have table header information
Inherited: yes
Percentages: N/A

Speak-numeral Property

This property specifies whether numerals are spoken as individual digits or continuously. The numbers "237" can be spoken as either "two three seven" or "two hundred thirty seven."

speak-numeral property description
Value: once	always	inherit
Initial: once
Applies to: elements that have table header information
Inherited: yes
Percentages: N/A

Speak-header Property

When a table is spoken by a speech generator, the relation between the data cells and the header cells must be expressed in a different way than by horizontal and vertical alignment. Some speech browsers may allow a user to move around in the 2-dimensional space, thus giving them the opportunity to map out the spatially represented relations. When that is not possible, the style sheet must specify at which points the headers are spoken.

speak-header property description
Value: once | always
Initial: once
Applies to: elements that have table header information
Inherited: yes
Percentages: N/A

AUTOMATIC COUNTERS AND NUMBERING

Automatic numbering in CSS2 is controlled with two properties, "counter-increment" and "counter-reset." The counters defined by these properties are used with the "content" property.

Counter-increment Property

The 'counter-increment' property accepts one or more names of counters (identifiers), each one optionally followed by an integer. The integer indicates by how much the counter is incremented for every occurrence of the element. The default increment is 1. Zero and negative integers are allowed.

counter-increment property description
Value: [<identifier> <integer>?]+ | none | inherit
Initial: none
Applies to: all elements
Inherited: no
Percentages: N/A

Counter-reset Property

The 'counter-reset' property also contains a list of one or more names of counters, each one optionally followed by an integer. The integer gives the value that the counter is set to on each occurrence of the element. The default is 0.

---

counter-reset property description

Value: [<identifier> <integer>?]+ | none | inherit

Initial: none

Applies to: all elements

Inherited: no

Percentages: N/A

The Content Property

This property is used with the :before and :after pseudo-elements (see the "Understanding CSS Selection Techniques" chapter) to generate content in a document.

---

content property description

Value: [<string> | <uri> | <counter> | attr(X) | open-quote |
close-quote | no-open-quote | no-close-quote]+ | inherit

Initial: empty string

Applies to: :before and :after pseudo-elements

Inherited: no

Percentages: N/A

PAGED MEDIA

Paged media includes printed paper, transparencies, and pages that are displayed on computer screens (such as in Adobe Portable Document Format). Paged media differs from continuous media, such as a Web page that has no finite borders. In paged media, the content of the document is split into one or more discrete pages. To handle page breaks, CSS2 extends the visual formatting model as follows:

- The page box extends the box model (see the "Using the Box Properties" chapter) to allow authors to specify the size of a page, its margins, and other characteristics.

■ The page model extends the visual formatting model (see the "Using the Positioning Properties" chapter) to account for page breaks. The CSS2 page model specifies how a document is formatted within a rectangular area—the page box—that has a finite width and height.

The @page Keyword

The @page keyword lets you build page style rules. An @page rule consists of the keyword "@page", a page selector (followed with no intervening space by an optional page pseudo-class), and a block of property declarations. A sample @page rule follows:

```
@page { size 8.5in 11in; margin: 2cm }
```

:left, :right and :first Pseudo-Classes

When printing double-sided documents, the page boxes on left and right pages should be different. This can be expressed through two CSS pseudo-classes (see the "Understanding CSS Selection Techniques" chapter) that can be defined in the page rule. The user agent will classify all paged document pages as either left or right. Style rules for these pages can be applied using the :left and :right pseudo-class selectors as shown in the following style rules:

```
@page :left {margin-left: 4cm;
      margin-right: 3cm;
      }
@page :right {margin-left: 3cm;

      margin-right: 4cm;
}
```

Size Property

The size property specifies the specifies the size and orientation of a page box.

```
size property description
Value:   <length>{1,2} | auto | portrait | landscape |
Initial:  auto
Applies to:  the page context
Inherited:  N/A
Percentages:  N/A
```

Marks (Crop Marks) Property

The marks property lets you specify whether cross marks or crop marks are rendered just outside the page box edge. Crop marks indicate where the page should be cut. Cross marks (also known as register marks or registration marks) are used to align sheets.

---

marks property description

Value: [crop || cross] | none | inherit

Initial: none

Applies to: page context

Inherited: N/A

Percentages: N/A

Page-break Properties

The page break properties determine whether a page break occurs before, after, or within an element.

---

page-break-before property description

Value: auto | always | avoid | left | right | inherit

Initial: auto

Applies to: block-level elements

Inherited: no

Percentages: N/A

---

page-break-after property description

Value: auto | always | avoid | left | right | inherit

Initial: auto

Applies to: block-level elements

Inherited: no

Percentages: N/A

---

page-break-inside property description

Value: auto | always | avoid | left | right | inherit

Initial: auto

Applies to: block-level elements

Inherited: no

Percentages: N/A

Page Property

The page lets you name a page and then apply styles to based on page name.

---

page property description

Value: <identifier> | auto

Initial: auto

Applies to: block-level elements

Inherited: yes

Percentages: N/A

For example, the following example will put all tables on a right-hand side landscape page (named "rotated"):

```
@page rotated {size: landscape}
TABLE {page: rotated; page-break-before: right}
```

Orphan Property

The 'orphans' property specifies the minimum number of lines of a paragraph that must be left at the bottom of a page.

---

orphan property description

Value: <integer>

Initial: 2

Applies to: block-level elements

Inherited: yes

Percentages: N/A

Widow Property

The 'widows' property specifies the minimum number of lines of a paragraph that must be left at the top of a page.

widow property description

Value: <integer> | inherit

Initial: 2

Applies to: block-level elements

Inherited: yes

Percentages: N/A

Glossary

!important — This keyword lets the user override the author's style setting for a particular element.

@import — This keyword lets you import style rules from other style sheets.

@media — This keyword lets you specify rules for different media in the same style sheet.

Aural table model — In CSS2, this model controls the spoken rendering of a table and lets you determine the order in which table headers and data should be spoken by a text-to-speech device.

Box model — The rules that control the display characteristics of the rectangular boxes that contain content on a Web page.

Cascade — Style sheets originate from three sources: the author, the user, and the browser. The cascading feature of CSS lets these multiple style sheets and style rules interact in the same document.

Collapsed border model — One of the two border models in CSS2. This model lets you control borders that are continuous across an entire table. (See *Separated border model.*)

Containing box — The containing rectangle, or parent element, of any child element. The absolute containing element is the window area of the browser. All other elements are displayed within this containing box, which equates to the <BODY> element of an HTML document. Within <BODY>, elements such as <DIV> or <P> are parents, or containing boxes, for their child elements.

Core attributes — These are the four attributes that can be used with any element. They include ID, TITLE, STYLE, and CLASS.

Cascading Style Sheets (CSS) — A style language, created by the W3C, that allows complete specifications of style for HTML documents. CSS allows HTML authors to use over 50 properties that affect the display of Web pages. CSS style information is contained either within an HTML document or in external documents called style sheets.

Cascading Style Sheets, first edition (CSS1) — The first edition of the Cascading Style Sheets specification from the World Wide Web Consortium, released in 1996.

Cascading Style Sheets, second edition (CSS2) — The second edition of the Cascading Style Sheets specification from the World Wide Web Consortium, released in 1998.

Cursive — Cursive is a generic value for the font-family property. Cursive fonts are designed to resemble handwriting. Most browsers do not support this font family.

Declaration — The declaration portion of a style rule consists of a property name and value. The browser applies the declaration to the selected element.

Em — The em is a printing measurement, commonly used to express horizontal length. In CSS the em can be used for both horizontal and vertical measurement. As a rule of thumb, browsers equate the value of the em to the size of the current font.

Extensible Markup Language (XML) — A meta-language that allows you to create your own elements that meet your information needs, which significantly distinguishes it from the pre-defined elements of HTML. XML provides a format for describing structured data that can be shared by multiple applications across multiple platforms.

External Style Sheets — Separate text files that contain one or more style rules. These usually have a .css extension as in "styles.css". HTML files are linked to the external style sheet with a <LINK> element that specifies the relative location of the style sheet file.

Fantasy — Fantasy is a generic value for the font-family property. Fantasy fonts are primarily decorative. Most browsers do not support this font family.

Font — A typeface in a particular size, such as Times Roman 24 point.

Foreground color — Specified by the color property, this is the color of the text content and the default border color.

Hexadecimal number — A base-16 numbering system that uses the numbers 0-9 and then the letters A-F. Hexadecimal numbers are used to express RGB color values in HTML.

Hypertext Markup Language (HTML) — The markup language that defines the structure and display properties of a Web page. The HTML code is interpreted by the browser to create the displayed results. HTML is an application of SGML. (See *Standard Generalized Markup Language.*)

Internal style sheets — One or more style rules (see *Style rule*) contained within the <STYLE> element in the <HEAD> section of an HTML document. The style rules in an internal style sheet apply only to the document in which they are contained.

Kerning — The printer's term for the adjusting of white space between letters. You can set the kerning using the letter-spacing property.

Leading — The printer's term for the adjusting of white space between lines of text. You can set the leading using the line-height property.

Media types — CSS2 lets you specify how the elements of a document appear in different media types other than the Web. CSS2 supports a variety of different media such as "print," "handheld, " and "Braille." (See *@media.*)

Monospace — Monospace is a generic value for the font-family property. Monospace fonts are fixed width fonts. Every letter has the same horizontal width. Monospace is commonly used to mimic typewritten text or programming code.

Pica — A printing measurement unit, equal to 12 points. Picas are a valid measurement unit in CSS, abbreviated as "pc."

Pixels — The basic display unit of a computer monitor. The number of pixels on the monitor is the screen resolution chosen by the user. Pixels are a valid measurement unit in CSS, abbreviated as "px."

Property — A quality or characteristic stated in a style rule, such as color, font-size, or margin. The property is a part of the style rule declaration. (See *Declaration.*)

Pseudo-classes — Pseudo-classes let you select elements based on characteristics other than their element name.

Pseudo-elements — Pseudo-elements let you change other aspects of a document that are not classified by elements, such as applying style rules to the first letter or first line of a paragraph.

Resolution — The measure of how many pixels fit on a screen. The standard display resolutions are 640 × 480, 800 × 600, and 1024 × 768. The resolution can be changed by the user. (See *Pixels.*)

Reverse — A common printing effect where the background color, which is normally white, and the text color, which is usually black, are reversed.

RGB color space — The three basic colors of red, green, and blue that computers use to display color.

Sans-serif — Sans-serif is a generic value for the font-family property. Sans-serif fonts have no serifs. They are block letters. The most common sans-serif fonts are Helvetica and Arial.

Scripts — Small pieces of programming code that are written with a scripting language such as JavaScript.

Selector — The part of a style rule that determines which HTML element to match. Style rules are applied to any element in the document that matches the selector.

Separated border model — One of the two border models in CSS2. This model lets you control the borders of individual cells. (See *Collapsed border model*.)

Serif — Serif is a generic value for the CSS font-family property. Serif is the traditional printing letter form, with strokes (or serifs) that finish off the top and bottom of the letter. The most common serif fonts on the Web are Times and Times Roman.

Stacking level — The ordering of elements on the z-axis. In CSS2, each element can be positioned horizontally (the x-axis), vertically, the (y-axis), and from front to back as the user faces the computer screen (the z-axis). The CSS z-index property lets you specify the stacking level of an element.

Standard Generalized Markup Language (SGML) — A standard system for specifying document structure using markup tags. SGML is a meta-language, not a language itself, but a method for specifying a language. HTML is an application of SGML.

Style rule — The basic unit of expression in CSS. A style rule is composed of two parts: a selector (see *Selector*) and a declaration (see *Declaration*). The style rule expresses the style information for an element.

Style sheet — A set of style rules that describes a document's display characteristics. There are two types of style sheets: internal (see *Internal style sheets*) and external (see *External style sheets*).

Typeface — The name of type family, such as Times Roman or Futura Condensed.

User agent — The client software that lets the user view the contents of a Web page. The most common user agent is the browser.

Value — The precise specification of a property in a style rule, based on the allowable values for the property. (See *Declaration*.)

Visual formatting model — Describes how a browser processes the document elements for visual display in the browser window.

Visual table model — In CSS2 this model controls the appearance of tables in the browser. The CSS2 table model builds on the HTML 4.0 table model.

World Wide Web Consortium (W3C) — Founded in 1994 at the Massachusetts Institute of Technology to standardize HTML. The W3C, led by Tim Berners-Lee, sets standards for HTML and provides an open, non-proprietary forum for industry and academic representatives to add to the evolution of this new medium.

Index

327